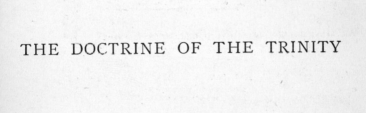

THE DOCTRINE OF THE TRINITY

MACMILLAN AND CO., Limited
LONDON · BOMBAY · CALCUTTA
MELBOURNE

THE MACMILLAN COMPANY
NEW YORK · BOSTON · CHICAGO
ATLANTA · SAN FRANCISCO

THE MACMILLAN CO. OF CANADA, Ltd.
TORONTO

THE DOCTRINE

OF

THE TRINITY

APOLOGETICALLY CONSIDERED

BY

J. R. ILLINGWORTH, M.A., D.D.

Amor alicujus amantis est, et amore
aliquid amatur. Ecce tria sunt, amans, et
quod amatur, et amor.—AUG. *De Trinitate*.

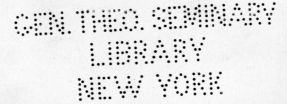
MACMILLAN AND CO., LIMITED
ST. MARTIN'S STREET, LONDON

1907

PREFACE

THERE are signs that the doctrine of the Trinity is again likely to become the battle-ground that it has so often been before in Christian history; —the battle-ground on which the contention for the faith will have, for the time, to be carried on. And though I have several times dealt incidentally with this doctrine in connection with other topics, I now venture to return to the subject, with a view to discussing some of the popular difficulties that are connected with it in the present day. In so doing I have endeavoured to avoid any detailed treatment of points on which I have already enlarged elsewhere, except when criticisms had to be noticed. But the necessary recurrence of certain main lines of argument, I hope, may be rather advantageous than otherwise, as tending to the additional emphasis of principles that, in my judgment, cannot be too often or too widely emphasised.

CONTENTS

CHAPTER I

EVOLUTION PRESUPPOSES GOD

The term "evolution" is sometimes used of religion as if it superseded the necessity for revelation . . . Pages 1-4

But evolution is merely a method 5

And does not seriously affect the fundamental problems of knowledge or being 6-7

It presupposes "a ground reality that is stable and transcends the flux of change" 8-10

Some even maintain "that in the phenomenal system nothing is really evolved, but an idea is successively manifested by phenomena that have their continuity and meaning in the power that produces them" 11-14

"Evolution" therefore does not supersede "revelation" . 15

But given revelation, in what sense does its content admit of subsequent evolution or development . . . 16-17

This is a question with which spiritual experience has as much to do as historic criticism, and on which, therefore, the ancient may still help the modern mind . . . 18-20

CHAPTER II

THE SUBJECTIVE ELEMENT IN CRITICISM

The Incarnation is the only means by which the doctrine of the Trinity could be revealed . . . 21-22

vii

And our belief in the Incarnation depends mainly on its adaptation to man's nature and need.   But this does not supersede the necessity for criticising its evidence   .   Page 23

All such criticism involves hypotheses, but these should not be unduly subjective   24-25

Instances of this fault—

(1) O. Hoffman   26

(2) Loisy   27-30

Such criticism involves an impossible separation of the New Testament from its historic context, the Christian Church   31-32

For the New Testament in this respect cannot be treated like any other book   33-35

Accordingly critics must differ in their conclusions, according as they possess the Christian presuppositions or not   .   36-38

For the Christian critic starts with the belief that the Incarnation is a fact of history, though of history interpreted by faith ; which the unchristian critic denies   .   .   37-41

Destructive ingenuity is not the measure of critical capacity   .   41-42

CHAPTER III

THE TRINITY IN THE NEW TESTAMENT

Paul's epistles are our earliest evidence for Christian doctrine   43-44

And they show that the distinction and divinity of Father, Son, and Spirit must have been taught within the first decade of Christian history   45-46

The Johannine authorship of the Fourth Gospel is now maintained by a great number of its English critics   .   .   47-51

And St. John attributes the teaching in question to Christ Himself   52

Then there is the baptismal formula in St. Matthew .   53

We have therefore sufficient ground for believing that the existence of the Trinity was taught by Christ Himself   .   54-55

The effect of the resurrection upon the disciples was evidently stupendous, and may well have enabled them to apprehend this teaching in a way that was not possible before   .   56-59

The opposite opinion involves a most arbitrary treatment of the New Testament   60

And its improbability is well enforced by Paley   .   .   61-62

Recapitulation   63-64

CONTENTS

CHAPTER IV

THE TRINITY IN PATRISTIC TRADITION

Patristic tradition claimed to transmit the apostolic eye-witness   Page 65

     E.g. Irenæus 66

         Clement of Alexandria . . . 67

         Origen 67-68

         Athanasius 68-69

This tradition precludes the possibility of any radical modification of primitive Christianity by the infiltration of alien
elements 70

Parallelisms in different religions are too readily assumed to
be causally connected 71-73

Thus the Christian Trinity is said to be borrowed from earlier
sources 74

But the critical re-establishment of the early date of the New
Testament leaves no room for this . . . 75-77

And the Patristic tradition attributes the doctrine to Christ Himself—

     E.g. Clement of Rome 78

         Ignatius 78

         Origen 79-80

This was the tradition of a great society . . . 81

It is clear and authoritative, and confirms the obvious evidence
of the New Testament, that the essence of the doctrine was
taught by Christ Himself 82-83

CHAPTER V

DOCTRINAL DEVELOPMENT IN THE NEW TESTAMENT

The sense of guidance by the Holy Spirit was an essential
characteristic of the early Church . . . 84

But this guidance acted through fallible human agents . 85

We have seen reason to believe that the essence of the doctrine
of the Trinity was taught by Christ Himself . . 86

But St. Paul and St. John clothed it in new phraseology, and
to that extent developed it 87

This phraseology, it is sometimes objected, involves obsolete
    modes of thought, and cannot therefore now be retained Pages 87-88
But the terms in question were *ipso facto* taken out of their old
    contexts and invested with a new Christian meaning   .   88-91
And the Church believed, and still believes this to be due to
    the guidance of the Spirit   92-95
While those who regard the development in question as
    erroneous necessarily deny this   96
The result of this guidance was, in the judgment of the Christian
    Church, interpretation but not innovation   .   .   97-98
Compare the language of Athanasius on the Council of Nicæa ;
    as guarding an heirloom, and not introducing a novelty .   99-100
Recapitulation   100-101

CHAPTER VI

DOCTRINAL DEVELOPMENT IN THE FATHERS

The Christian Fathers affirm our knowledge of God's existence,
    but disclaim any knowledge of His nature   .   .   102
        E.g. Clement of Alexandria   .   .   .   103
            Origen   104
            Athanasius   105
            Basil and the two Gregories   .   .   .   106
            Hilary, Augustine   107
            John of Damascus   108
And this is not due to intellectual Agnosticism so much as
    to religious awe   109
They decline, therefore, to speculate on the divine nature, and
    appeal to Scripture and apostolic tradition   .   .   110
First, in their doctrine of the Son—
        E.g. Origen   111-113
            Athanasius   114-116
Secondly, in their doctrine of the Spirit—
        E.g. Gregory Nazianzen   117
            Hilary   118-119
            Nicetas   119
These quotations are typical of the whole patristic attitude .   120
And they show a development of interpretative expression,
    but no new articles of belief   121

While the new terms employed commit us to no obsolete
    modes of thought . . . . . Page 122
The fathers regard Christianity as the issue of Jewish religion
    and not of Greek philosophy 123
And the Christian Church had too intense an individuality in its
    early days to be seriously modified by any unchristian
    environment 124-125

CHAPTER VII

OMNIA EXEUNT IN MYSTERIUM

The object of dogmatic definition was transmission, and not
    explanation 126-128
Hence its largely negative character, its refusal to allow the
    explanation of mysteries 128
Whence it is still valid for us 129
The Christian doctrine is not derived from any of the alien
    sources that have been suggested . . . 130
Nor is its mystery any objection 131
For natural theology is quite as much involved in mystery . 132-133
And so is physical science 134-135
While in some degree the doctrine of the Trinity actually
    assists our thought 136
By helping us to conceive God's metaphysically absolute being 137-138
And morally absolute holiness 139-141
Without which there would be no adequate basis for human
    morality 142-143
In a word, the doctrine gives more meaning to Divine Personality 144

CHAPTER VIII

PRACTICAL POWER OF THE DOCTRINE

The doctrine of the Trinity has been intensely practical in its
    effect 145
It lineally succeeded to the highest previous conception of
    God, *i.e.* the Jewish 146

And involved a clearer conception of divine holiness and human
 duty . . . . Page 147
This was due not to its abstract expression by councils, but to
 its concrete presentation by Christ . . . 148
Thus it gave men—
   1. A fuller conception of the Divine Fatherhood . 149-152
   2. A sense of closer communion with God, through—
     (a) The Incarnation 153-155
     (b) The Atonement 155-156
     Which sprang from the love of the Father,
      as well as the Son . . . 156-158
     (c) The sacraments, which have been an im-
      mense power in the world . . 158-160
   3. A nobler sense of inspiration in the individual . 161-162
    In Scripture and the Church . . . 163
Hence the doctrine has historically proved to be the most
 practical of powers 164-166

CHAPTER IX

ITS WORTH A PRESUMPTION OF ITS TRUTH

We have implied that the practical value of the doctrine creates
 a presumption of its truth. Is this legitimate ? . . 167
The distinction between judgments of value and judgments of
 truth came from Kant through Lotze to Ritschl . . 168
But must not be exaggerated 169
For all judgments are ultimately personal—i.e. proceed from
 our whole personality 170
And none more so than religious judgments . . . 170-172
But a person is a rational inhabitant of a rational world . 173
As well as a spiritual inhabitant of a spiritual world . . 174
And his reason demands the unification of the two ; and that
 what has spiritual value shall also be rationally true . 175
E.g. If the world is rationally ordered the value of God to
 our spiritual life is a presumption of His existence . 175-177
Hence there is a presumption that the doctrine which under-
 lies the only religion that rationally satisfies our moral and
 spiritual aspirations must be true . . . 178-179

CONTENTS

It is objected that other religions are equally satisfactory to their adherents, *e.g.* Buddhism and Mahometanism . . Page 180

But Buddhism rests on belief in the irrationality of the world 181-183

And Mahometanism ignores the rights of human personality, as such 184-186

Both alike therefore fail to satisfy the demands of reason, and are therefore only relative, while Christianity remains the absolute religion 187

CHAPTER X

INTELLECTUAL BEARINGS OF THE DOCTRINE

Though primarily practical the doctrine of the Trinity has also a speculative value 188

Since it assists our conception of absolute personality . . 189

Whose limitation by created being is only a voluntary self-limitation 190

While self-limitation, as we know it, is the condition of self-affirmation 191-192

We conceive of God as transcendent of His creation . . 193-194

But also as immanent in it 194-195

To isolate the former thought leads to Deism and Agnosticism 195

To isolate the latter leads to Pantheism . . . 196

But the doctrine of the Trinity unites them . . . 197-201

And leads us to regard the Divine Immanence as culminating in the Incarnation 202-203

This leads us to the Alexandrian or Scotist view of the Incarnation, as independent of human sin . . . 204-205

And the Incarnation so regarded is seen to be no mere stage in human evolution, but the divine completion of man's creation 206

Which illuminates our intellects, precisely because it is a fresh *datum* for thought, and no mere speculative deduction of our own 207-208

CHAPTER XI

REVELATION THE CONTINUANCE OF CREATION

A revelation through historic events is nowadays often repre-
sented as less spiritual, and therefore less probable than a
revelation purely in the mind of man   .   .   . Page 209
But is this true or philosophical?   210
Since all spiritual life is mediated by material means .   . 211-212
Hence a revelation would presumably include both, and spread
from a historic person   213
But a divine interference in history is resented as contrary to
the rest of our experience   214
Yet each stage in creation is an innovation on past experience 215
And the Incarnation is a new stage in creation introducing
"a new creature"   216-218
The teleological question "Why man exists" cannot be set
aside; and this points to the probability of such a revela-
tion as the Incarnation 218-221
We cannot always judge the past by the present   .   . 222-224
And a revelation in the past would necessarily be adapted to
the modes of thought in the past; as
E.g. The Messianic expectation   .   .   . 225
        Miracles   226-229
            The conception of the Logos .   .   . 230-231
While its present appeal to us is through the Church now
living in the world   232

CHAPTER XII

RECAPITULATION AND CONCLUSION

The teleological view of the world, though at times eclipsed
by the mechanical view, can never lose its supreme interest
for man   233-236
And it is with teleological presuppositions that we approach
the evidence for the Christian revelation.   .   . 237-240

CONTENTS

The Christian creed, moreover, does not reach us first as a
doctrine, but as a society of whose life it is the explanation   Page 240
And by the character of whose members it is commended to us   241-242
It is thus seen to be a force which enables the highest realisation
of human personality   243-245
And a realisation of which the initiative is not human but
divine   246-247
And the specific evidence for the truth of the Christian revelation is further fortified by the answer which this realisation
affords to the teleological question—"What is the end of
man?"   248-252

ILLUSTRATIVE NOTES

NOTE 1.   THE TRINITY A REVELATION   .   .   .   253

NOTE 2.   THE SOCIAL NATURE OF PERSONALITY   .   254

NOTE 3.   THE ARGUMENT FROM WORTH TO TRUTH   .   256

NOTE 4.   BUDDHISM   258

NOTE 5.   MAHOMETANISM   259

NOTE 6.   THE PATRISTIC VIEW OF DIVINE IMMANENCE.   261

NOTE 7.   REALITY   265

CHAPTER I

It is now more than the proverbial sixty years
since Newman startled the University of Oxford
with his famous sermon on the development of
Christian doctrine, in which he not only spoke of
dogma as being "evolved" with "effort, hesitation, suspense, interruptions, swayings to the
right and to the left," but also pointed out what
we should now call the dialectical nature of the
process. "One proposition necessarily leads to
another," he says, "and a second to a third; then
some limitation is required; and the combination
of these opposites occasions some fresh evolutions
from the original idea." His philosophic insight
had detected in his own department of study
the working of the general principle, whose
recognition was already in the air, and which was
subsequently destined to revolutionise the whole

E   B thought of the age; and although it was the men of science and their philosophical exponents who made the principle in question public property, it was a theologian that proclaimed it first. Thus it will be seen that the conception of evolution is no alien importation from another region into the history of theology, but was independently suggested by that history itself; but what sixty years ago seemed to many minds a questionable novelty has in the interval between that time and this become an accepted commonplace. Evolution has become the favourite category of the day. Organisms, institutions, customs, arts, sciences, societies are all studied by the historic method in the light of their development. And the same principle has naturally come to be applied to religious practice and belief, with the result that we are continually confronted with discussions of the evolution of religion in general, as well as of its various details—ritual, prayer, sacraments, ideas of God.

We have no need now, therefore, to contend for the due recognition of growth and progress in religious history. Our danger lies in the opposite direction, lest this recognition be pressed too far. For the admitted fact that Christian doctrine has undergone some kind of development is now frequently utilised to assist in explaining away the doctrines of the Trinity and the Incarnation. Christ, on this view, was merely a good man, with exceptional or unique religious insight; who was first glorified, then vaguely deified in an age of easy deification, by His disciples or their immediate successors, and finally under the influence of Greek philosophy enshrined at the heart of the Christian creed as very God of very God. There is, of course, no novelty in this opinion: it is the old unitarian position. But what is novel is the assistance which it professes to derive from our modern insight into the process of evolution. The entire Christian creed is regarded as evolved. But evolved from what? From a beginning in which on this hypothesis the germ of the subsequent development was distinctly not contained. Hence there could be no true evolution of thought in the case. For at an early stage in the process a reversal of the truth, a falsification of fact, must have taken place by which a mere man came to be regarded as God. And it was this falsehood, and not the fact behind it which was subsequently developed. We cannot, therefore, allow the falsification of fact to be vaguely slurred over as if it were a stage in a natural process of development. For all true evolution is the gradual unfolding of a germ, and is characterised by unbroken continuity. An acorn can only be developed into an oak, and not into a butterfly or a bird; and a truth into its consequences, but not its contradiction. When, therefore, men speak thus of the evolution of the Christian creed, we must insist that if the germ of the process is supposed, as it usually is supposed, to be the life of Christ, then the term evolution is not used in its scientific sense, and simply covers a confusion of thought. While, on the other hand, if the term is restricted to its proper sense, as the unfolding of a germ, then that germ is not the life of Christ, but its subsequent falsification. The evolutionary process cannot begin till the supposed mistake which it develops has been already made. To say this is merely to assert, in a particular context, what various philosophical writers have taken occasion to point out of recent years, that evolution is merely a method, and originates and can originate nothing. Whatever we find existing at the end of an evolutionary process must have existed potentially, that is to say in germ, at its beginning. The term evolution cannot be utilised like the handkerchief of a conjuror, under cover of which to substitute for one object another that is totally different in kind.

The fact is, that in becoming popular the conception of evolution has become very vague, and is commonly supposed to cover much more ground than is actually the case. Before, therefore, considering the question of its application to Christian doctrine, it may be well to make a few remarks upon evolution in general, which we will endeavour to support by quotation that we may be seen not to speak without book.

A recent philosopher, speaking of the theory of knowledge, writes to the following effect :—

" In the first place, while the theory of mental development enables us to reach a more adequate doctrine of self, it does not affect the fundamental relation that exists between the knowing subject and its objective content. Again, although the theory of development enables us to trace the genesis of such categories as space, time, and cause in the growing consciousness, it does not affect the final form of these categories or the relation they bear to the cognitive process.

In short, there is no fundamental condition or relation of knowledge that is materially affected by the notion of evolution ; but these conditions and relations remain relatively stable through the flux of change in which development works out its results. From a deeper metaphysical point of view it is the concept of evolution itself that must submit to the determination of knowledge, for it will be found that in so far as it becomes epistemologically necessary to ground relative processes in an absolute experience, just so far will it become necessary also to connect the evolutionary aspect of the world itself with a ground reality that is stable and involves the flux of change only as transcending and including it.

"Great, therefore, as has been the part which evolution has played in moulding the scientific conceptions of the time, it cannot be said with truth that it has seriously affected the fundamental problems of knowledge. The conditions of knowledge and its relation to experience remain substantially as they have been since the time of the Greeks, and as they always will be till some radical change is affected in the knowing activities themselves. This is not likely to happen, least of all through any possible extension of the concept of evolution." [1]

Two points are here to be noticed. First, that "the theory of mental development does not affect the fundamental relation that exists between the knowing subject and its objective content." A man, for example, knows more of the world than a child; but for both alike the world exists over against them, as the condition of its being known. And unless it already existed in this relation to them their growth in knowledge could never begin. Or, again, a scientific specialist knows more of his particular department of study than an ordinary man ; but only because the department already exists as part of an intelligible universe, ready to be known. Or, to change the illustration, the gradual development of our telescope and improvement of our astronomical methods has immensely increased our knowlege of the stars; but only because the stars exist, and in a cosmic order which renders them fit objects of observation. In every case alike the fundamental relation to this " objective content " is what makes the development of the subject or organ possible. Knowledge could not

---

[1] Ormond, *Foundations of Knowledge*, p. 19.

have been developed apart from an intelligible universe or telescopes evolved apart from stars. In other words, the evolution of knowledge pre-supposes a relation to an object which is itself independent of and unaffected by the evolutionary process. Or, to phrase it differently, it is an intellectual process taking place within an intelligible whole, and dependent for its possibility on the pre-existence of that intelligible whole. The second point is the necessity for " a ground reality that is stable and involves the flux of change only as transcending and including it." This—which is only the counterpart, in the field of being, of what we have just considered in the field of knowing—was plainly recognised and clearly stated both by Plato and Aristotle, and has never since been denied by any philosophy that is seriously worthy of the name. "Actuality," as Aristotle puts it, " must precede potentiality."

What this means is, that we cannot possibly conceive a literally universal evolution. We cannot possibly conceive a passage from not-being to being, as the Greeks phrased it, or from potential to actual existence except through the operation of some energy which is already actual, before the process in question begins, and adequate to produce every result in which such a process may ultimately issue. We can conceive actual being giving rise to contingent being, however unable we are to trace the mode of the occurrence. But to reverse the process, and speak as if the totality of actual being had been gradually evolved, is to use words that convey no shadow of meaning; it is literally to talk nonsense. If, therefore, we employ the term universe to signify the sum total of all being, we can conceive development within the universe, but never of the universe. And this does not mean that such a process may have taken place, though we cannot picture it; but that, if the laws of human thought are valid, such a process cannot possibly have taken place.

Moreover, what is true in this way of the whole, is true also of its parts. No result, that is to say, can be attained by any partial process of evolution which is not already contained, ideally or actually, in the ground reality of the whole. No lower form of existence can develop into a higher, except through the competence of the ground reality to produce the higher form. The seed which we describe as a potential tree or flower is packed with that potentiality from

the beginning of its existence, and its component
atoms are in well-known phrase already "manu-
factured articles." We sometimes, for example,
hear vague thinkers speak as if during the evolution of organic life animal instinct had been
developed, *proprio motu*, into human reason;
blind giving rise to conscious purpose. But no
such thing as blind or unconscious purpose is
conceivable; it is only another name for purpose-
less purpose, a plain contradiction in terms. Instinctive action, like the weaving of the spider,
or the building of the bee, purposive action—
that is to say, of whose purpose its immediate
agent is apparently unconscious, must imply conscious purpose in the ground reality behind the
immediate agent. Thus if instinct ever even
appears to pass up into reason, it can only be
because it is already itself the product of reason.
And the same thing is true of all analogous cases
of what is called evolutionary progress. Deists
of the eighteenth century viewed the world as a
machine which, when once set going, continued
to work of itself; and this fallacy has sometimes
re-appeared among writers on evolution. Whereas in fact the action of secondary causes cannot
be conceived at all without constant relation to

primary causation ; and we are compelled therefore to regard every moment of an evolutionary
process as equally related to its ground reality.

The recognition of this fact has indeed led
many independent thinkers to deny altogether
the physical derivation of one species from another
by a process of evolution ; and to see in the
resemblances between species indications not of
a physical, but of an ideal or rational connection.
One might illustrate this view from what takes
place in the case of human workmanship. When
we see specimens of any art or craft chronologically arranged in a museum, we notice that
the greatest transformations have usually been
effected by numerous gradual modifications and
improvements ; so that the beginning and end of
any series of objects are connected by a number
of intermediate links, each of which represents a
slight advance upon its predecessors. This may
easily be seen, for instance, in the history of
musical instruments, or weapons, or industrial
machinery, or means of locomotion, or means of
navigation, or instruments for measurement of
time. But there is no question of physical connection between the individual objects ; a spinet
never grew into a pianoforte, nor a flint-lock into

a breech-loader; the connection is ideal through the mind of man; and the evolution of the later from the earlier forms has from first to last been purely rational. In the same way it is at least conceivable that the resemblances between species, which have been supposed to argue the physical derivation of one from another, really represent an ideal sequence in the ground reality. But whether we adopt this particular view of evolution or no—which is immaterial to our present purpose—it is essential to remember that every stage or moment or member of any evolutionary process must be conceived as equally related to its ground reality.

The following quotation from another philosophic writer upon Theism illustrates this well :—

" Consider the production of a piece of music, say a symphony. The later parts are neither made out of the earlier parts nor produced by them; but both earlier and later parts are subject to a common musical conception and law, and root in a causality beyond themselves. If now we should ask respecting any particular note whether it be a special creation or not, the answer must be both yes and no, according to the standpoint. It is not a special creation in the sense

of being unrelated and lawless, for each note is
subject to the plan of the whole. It is a special
creation in the sense that, without a purpose and
activity including the special note, it would not
exist. Again, in such a production nothing would
be evolved out of anything, but a musical conception would be successively realised. The
antecedent notes would not imply the later as
their dynamic resultants, but both antecedents
and consequents would be produced by the com-
poser and player in accordance with the idea.
The continuity of the performance would be only
in the idea and the will and purpose of the per-
former. The same conclusions hold for any
conception of the universe as phenomenal. In
that case its evolution is but the successive manifestation of the causalty beyond the series ; and
the phases of the evolution have no dynamic
connection among themselves, any more than the
successive musical notes. Each, however, is or
is not a special creation, according to the standpoint. As subject to the law of the whole, it is
not special. As a specific and concrete fact, it is
special. In the phenomenal system, nothing is
really evolved, but an idea is successively manifested by the successive production of phenomena

that have their continuity and meaning only in the power that produces them. These considerations show . . . how ambiguous the alleged fact of evolution is. It was assumed as a matter of course that the cosmic causality lies within the cosmic series, so that the temporal antecedent dynamically determines and produces the temporal consequent. This view metaphysics definitely sets aside. The causality of the series lies beyond it; and the relations of the members are logical and teleological, not dynamic." [1]

Now this ground reality, on which philosophy insists as the necessary condition of all evolution, is of course only the abstract expression of what Theists mean by God; and we have made the foregoing quotations with a view to emphasise the fact that evolution, regarded merely in the light of philosophy, so far from superseding, only intensifies the necessity for its reference to God. It originates nothing, it invents nothing, it causes nothing. It is only a name for the gradual way in which God's purposes are unfolded in the field of existence; and the gradual way whereby in the field of knowledge they come to be recognised by man.

[1] Bowne, *Theism*, p. 107.

To return to the region of religion and theo-logy : we are very familiar by this time with the attempts that have been made to explain away the truth of our idea of God, and therewith the value of all those institutions and customs that spring from our belief in His existence and go to make up religion, on the ground that all these things have been evolved from crude and ele-mentary beginnings, and cannot really rise above the level of their origin.   But the fallacy of this appeal to evolution will be obvious after what we have said above.   There were materialists in the days of Plato, and there have been mate-rialists ever since.   But the modern materialist gains no advantage over his ancient congener by using the category of evolution, since, as we have seen, it explains no origins, and therefore cannot help his case.   The superficial—the very superficial—notion that it does so arises simply from the vague feeling that what could not happen in a moment might happen in a very long time ; whereas the metaphysical necessity by which all evolution presupposes its ground reality is obviously independent of time.   Or, to put it in other words, the length of evolutionary process cannot affect the preliminary condition

without which it could never have begun. We
may dismiss, therefore, from any further consideration this crude misconception that evolution
makes it easier to explain away the objects of
religion and theology. But there is a question
of religious importance that is raised by our
modern study of evolution. As Christians we
believe in a revelation; we believe ourselves to
possess certain truths as revealed, which we could
have obtained in no other way. And the question arises whether revealed truth can admit of
subsequent development or no. The doctrine of
the Trinity, for instance, confessedly underwent
development, as regards the language in which
it was expressed; by the adoption, for example,
of such terms as substance, person, eternal
generation, circumincession, double procession.
And such novelty of language implies some degree of novel thought. Moreover, the language
and thought were originally Greek, and arose
from the necessity of correlating the doctrine in
question with the philosophy of the age. What,
then, was the original germ of this process of
development? And was the development itself
so far legitimate, inevitable, and necessary that
its result may still be called revealed truth?

Or was it merely a human accretion, due to the temporary dominance of modes of thought which are now obsolete, and which must be stripped away if we would rediscover the original nucleus of revelation, which it has rather tended to obscure than to elucidate. Such are the questions with which we have now for some time past been confronted; and we propose to consider them in relation to the doctrine of the Trinity, with which that of the Incarnation is of course inseparably involved.

But before proceeding further it may be well to call attention to the common assumption that our modern knowledge is universally greater than that of bygone ages, and that our opinions therefore upon all subjects are more likely to be true than those of the men of old. In certain large departments of thought, such as the physical sciences, or archæology, or critical scholarship, this is of course perfectly true. But there is one region, and that for our present purpose the most important region, in which it is conspicuously untrue; and that is the region of religious experience, the spiritual history of souls—their hopes and fears, their trials and temptations, their agonies and ecstasies, their heights of faith

and depths of love.   We too have our knowledge
of these things, but it is distracted by a multiplicity of other interests, which had not dawned
upon the horizon of the earlier world; whereas
the absence of such distractions enabled the
leading minds of older days to concentrate their
attention upon the interior life and its vicissitudes.
We may be scientific, but they were spiritual
specialists.   Witness the fact that to them we
turn in our hours of spiritual need—to Job, to
the Psalms, to the Confessions of Augustine, to
St. Bernard or St. Francis, St. Catherine or St.
Theresa, to *The Divine Comedy*, *The Pilgrims'
Progress*, *The Imitation of Christ*.

Now the spiritual experience of mankind, with
all the thoughts that it suggests, is after all the
most important element in our total body of
experience, of which scientific knowledge is only
a part; while it is upon this total body of experience, and not on any isolated part of it, that our
general view of the world, our ultimate philosophy
is founded.   And it is this ultimate philosophy
that is our final court of appeal in the discussion
of religious questions; not what the physiologists
or psychologists may tell us, but our view of human
life as a whole.

We have grown so familiar with our own human nature that we are apt to think we know more about it than we really do. Hence men often take it for granted that to explain religion as a human invention, or to prove the life of Christ to be merely human, is to abolish its mystery and translate it into a language that we fully understand; whereas in fact the life of man, with its unknown origin and unknown destiny, its high capacities and tragic failures, its infinite aspirations and infinitesimal achievements, its strange intermixture of grandeur and meanness, of sanctity and sin, is the greatest mystery within our experience. *Grande profundum est homo;* and to say that a thing is human is to say that it is mysterious. Moreover, the heart of this mystery does not lie in the region of any of the sciences, in which we have made so much progress of late, but in that of religion and ultimate philosophy. The historical study of Christianity, for instance, and the criticism of its documents, leads us back in the end to our views of the probability of a revelation, and of the congruity of an incarnation with our needs, problems whose solution is little affected by our wider knowledge of the external world, but much by the interior experience of our race. On these points, therefore, we should bear in mind that we may still have much to learn from those who have gone long before us in the ways of the spiritual life.

CHAPTER II

ALL Theists would naturally admit that behind what we call the gradual evolution of religious ideas in the course of history there has been a divine element at work, an element of revelation. This is indeed only a corollary from the relation which we have seen that all processes of evolution must bear to their ground reality. But the mind of man does not act unerringly; it is liable to indolence and prejudice and presumption, and many other indefinite sources of error, partly intellectual, partly emotional and moral. Hence we cannot speak of the evolution in question as simply the human reflection of a divine revelation, because it is always a distorting reflection; the revelation struggling, if we may so say, for expression with the sinful personality by which it is continually being distorted and misread. And it is this fact that gives a superficial plausibility to the contention that the whole process is merely one of human evolution.   The human element in it seems so much more obvious than the divine. But in the Incarnation, as Christians regard it, all this is changed.

> He, the Truth, is too
>
> The Word." [1]

God Himself speaks to us through a sinless human personality, which as such has no deflecting or distorting bias, and the result is a revelation which differs not only in degree, but in kind, from all that had gone before it.   And it is only from such a revelation that we could possibly receive such knowledge of God's nature as is contained in the doctrine of the Trinity.

" God having of old time spoken unto the fathers in the prophets, by divers portions and in divers manners, hath at the end of these days spoken unto us in His Son, whom He appointed heir of all things, through whom also He made the worlds; who being the effulgence of His glory, and the very image of His substance, and upholding all things by the word of His power, when he had made purification of sins, sat down on the right hand of the Majesty on high."

[1] Browning, *Ring and the Book.*

It is a stupendous belief, we admit, but at the same time one which illuminates the equally stupendous mystery of man's original creation. For if man's life were limited to this world, he is immeasurably over-endowed for the petty part he has to play, whereas in the light of the Incarnation his original creation is at once adequately justified.

It is thus by our ultimate philosophy, founded largely, as we have seen, upon the analysis of man's spiritual nature and needs, that our acceptance of the Incarnation is mainly determined. And of that nature and its needs men like Athanasius and Augustine were, to say the least, as competent judges as any modern critic. But this philosophical predisposition does not, of course, supersede the necessity for scrutinising the historical evidence on which the fact of the Incarnation claims to rest, especially at a time when the whole of that evidence is being critically attacked. Indeed, the Christian would naturally be more anxious than any other man to sift the grounds of his own belief; in proportion as it stands for more to him than to any other man; it is his light, his hope, his life, his all; and he must needs "give a reason for the faith that is in

him." It must not be supposed, therefore, that
criticism necessarily moves in one direction only.
Its ultimate results may be constructive and positive, as well as negative and destructive.

But as construction necessarily involves the
criticism of its negations, and as those negations
were never more acutely and ably urged than in
the present day, we must direct our attention to
them for a while.

In the first place, it must be remembered that
all attempts to bring bygone history in its living
reality before us involve recourse to a certain
amount of hypothesis. And this is pre-eminently
the case with the New Testament. Lacunæ in
it have to be filled, conflicting statements reconciled, probabilities estimated, evidence balanced,
authorities appraised. And all this involves
the frequent employment of hypothesis. No
objection, therefore, can lie against the Christian
apologist for meeting the hypotheses of adverse
criticism by answers that are also in part hypothetical, since such is the necessity of the
situation.

At the same time hypotheses are always
in danger of being coloured by a subjective
element, an element due to the mental idiosyn-

crasy of their particular employer. And as the object of historical criticism is to reconstruct what actually happened, its constant aim must be to minimise this subjective interference as far as possible, and, in cases where it cannot be wholly avoided, to keep its true character constantly in mind. Whereas neither of these duties do we always find adequately practised in the present day. Cases will readily occur to anyone at all familiar with the subject, in which personal opinion has run reckless riot under the guise of scientific criticism, and others in which "facts" are quoted with a naive unconsciousness of how much theory they involve. But one or two illustrations of the point may be of use as giving it more concrete reality.

For example, to take an instance which is typical of countless others, an eminent critic,[1] after contrasting the sermon on the mount with a passage in one of the Johannine discourses, says, "It is a psychological impossibility that these two things should have proceeded from the same person." This has all the air of a scientific statement; but mark what the assertion involves —the adequate capacity of the critic to judge

[1] O. Holtzman.

what was or was not possible in another
person's mode of thought and speech.   Now
we should hardly be disposed to concede such a
degree of insight to the ablest of critics in a case
where the person criticised was a man of supreme
genius like Plato, or Shakespeare, or St. Paul ;
for it is the characteristic of such men to baffle
ordinary expectation, and scatter the prosaic tests
of weight and measure to the winds.   But would
any man with the faintest reputation for sanity
to maintain, claim this insight if he believed the
person in question to be God Incarnate, or even
possibly to be God Incarnate ?   Obviously not.
It is plain, therefore, that the Incarnation had
been ruled out of court before the assertion in
question was made.   Its impossibility or its non-
occurrence had been taken for granted.   But the
point to notice is that this negative assumption is
not explicitly put forward.   On the contrary, the
criticism in question is enunciated as if it were a
declaration of psychological science, and is subsequently used to discredit the historical character
of the Fourth Gospel, one of the great evidences,
that is to say, of the Incarnation ; whereas, we see,
the only possibility of its being made by a sane
man at all depends on his having previously

denied the occurrence of the Incarnation. In brief, an argument is used to disprove the Incarnation which presupposes that there never was an Incarnation. It is a simple and transparent instance of what logicians call begging the question (*petitio principii*).

Or take another illustration from a writer who, though a Christian apologist, is affected by the same subjective temper in his criticism.[1] There is the well-known passage in St. Matthew and St. Luke on the mutual knowledge of the Father and the Son, followed in St. Matthew by the great invitation : " Come unto Me, all ye that labour and are heavy laden, and I will give you rest. Take My yoke upon you, and learn of Me." This passage, apart from its intrinsic value, enshrined as it is at the heart of our Christian worship, is critically important on account of its close parallelism to, and consequent confirmation of, the language in the Johannine discourses. It is now said to be a reminiscence, and by one writer "a massive and close utilisation" of the last chapter of Ecclesiasticus. On the closeness of this connection, especially as regards the former part of the passage, there may perhaps be two

[1] Loisy

opinions ; but we will not pause upon this point, but pass on to notice how our critic deals with the whole passage.

"It is difficult to see in it," he says, "a literally exact expression of a declaration made by Christ to His disciples, since it is not easy to admit that Jesus would, in a spontaneous prayer or discourse, have chosen to imitate Ecclesiasticus." "It is very probable that, notwithstanding its occurrence in two Gospels, the text, in its present form at least, is a product of Christian tradition." Now, so far from its not being easy to admit, we find Christ continually utilising the language of the Old Testament, from His first conquest of temptation to His last words upon the cross. He lives in its atmosphere and breathes its spirit. He quotes it, argues from it, appropriates it again and again. And it may well be, therefore, that He was here employing the phraseology of Ecclesiasticus, but with a profound and significant alteration which makes the word "imitation" wholly inappropriate to the case. The son of Sirach confesses with what prayer and diligence he has acquired wisdom, and proceeds to invite others to share what he has gained.

" Draw near unto me, ye unlearned, and lodge in the house of instruction. . . . Put your neck under the yoke, and let your soul receive instruction : she is hard at hand to find. Behold with your eyes that I laboured but a little, and found for myself much rest."

Contrast the whole tone of this with the language of St. Matthew. " All things have been delivered unto Me of My Father . . . neither doth any know the Father save the Son, and He to whomsoever the Son willeth to reveal Him. Come unto Me, all ye that labour and are heavy laden, and I will give you rest. Take My yoke upon you, and learn of Me. . . . For my yoke is easy, and My burden is light." If the phrases here used were suggested by Ecclesiasticus, their incidence is completely changed. Christ does not speak as the student, but as the source—the personal source of wisdom, and of the rest which it conveys. And the use of the old language, with this change of application, is the very best means that could have been chosen to emphasise the fact that He taught " with authority, and not as the scribes." And yet this tremendous transformation is called an imitation of the earlier passage, such as Jesus would not have chosen to make! And on the strength of this hypothetical improbability we are asked to surrender the authenticity of a passage which is of the utmost theological importance. We welcome scientific criticism ; but this is not scientific criticism. For when a man of science invents a hypothesis, it is that he may afterwards verify it by comparison with facts ; and he never proceeds to base further reasoning upon it until after it has been verified. But here no such verification is possible. The judgment remains subjective from beginning to end ; and yet in all its subjectivity it is used as a basis for attaining further critical results.

We have chosen these two instances as both bearing on the Fourth Gospel, which we shall subsequently have to consider. But they are specimens not only of many others, but of an entire method which is far too freely employed and too readily admitted in modern criticism. Dr. Newman, in an interesting passage written more than thirty years ago, contrasts the opinions of a number of expert writers on the early history of Greece and Rome, and asks, ' Why do they differ so much from each other whether in their estimate of . . . testimonies, or of . . . facts?

Because that estimate is simply their own, coming of their own judgment; and that judgment coming of assumptions of their own, explicit or implicit; and those assumptions spontaneously issuing out of the state of thought respectively belonging to each of them; and all these successive processes of minute reasoning superintended and directed by an intellectual instrument far too subtle and spiritual to be scientific." [1]   And the same may be said of many of our modern critics of the New Testament.   Much of their method is too personal to themselves, too idiosyncratic to be scientific; and this is illustrated by the endless differences of detail to which it leads; as, for instance, when we find one critic considering the history of the Fourth Gospel to be more genuine than its discourses, and another maintaining with equal confidence that its discourses are more genuine than its history.   It is not in the face of science, therefore, but in the name of science that we hold such criticism to be of little account.

Further, there lies behind all attempts at criticism of this kind a fundamental assumption, which the Christian Church in ages when it was

[1] *Grammar of Assent.*

capable of collective utterance would have refused
to admit, and which the great majority of Christian
people would, at the present day, repudiate. That
assumption is that we can best attain to a right
understanding of the New Testament by separat-
ing it from the society which existed before it
and created it, and treating it like any literary
relic which archælogy may have unearthed.

Whereas how does the matter really stand?
The Christian Church is an aggressive, a missionary society, which claims to have been
founded by God Incarnate in the person of
Christ Jesus, and to be sustained and guided,
amid all its human imperfections, by His Holy
Spirit. Its mission is to invite men, as it has
done for nineteen centuries, into communion with
itself, in order that they may live in the power
and die under the consolation of its creed. And
for this work it has an equipment of ministers,
and sacraments, sacred Scriptures, and a sacred
day. Its Scriptures are thus only a portion, and,
strictly speaking, not an original portion, of its
total organisation. But at the same time they
are inseparably connected with that organisation,
as having been written for the use of the Christian
Church by the most inspired of its members,

selected and set apart by others under similar inspiration, and invested with applicability to the souls of each succeeding generation of men by the same Spirit, as Christians believe, that controlled their original composition and selection.

Such was historically the relation of the Church to the New Testament till the Reformation ; but at the Reformation various changes occurred. In the first place, the unity of the Church and therewith the unity of its interpretation of Scripture disappeared. Secondly, the New Testament passed from being, as it were, the private property of the Church into the public possession of the world. And thirdly, a theory arose that the Church was founded on the New Testament, rather than the New Testament on the Church ; that the Church existed to expound the Scriptures, instead of the Scriptures to subserve the Church. We need not pause to disentangle the good and evil which were almost inextricably involved in these various changes. Our present point is merely that they caused the Bible to be studied in isolation from an essential part of its original context ; and that by an almost inevitable necessity of the case, since the unity of the Bible remained, while the unity of its historical context was gone, and confusion reigned in the whole ecclesiastical situation.   The first consequence of this was the investiture of the Bible with an undue degree of infallibility ; the Bible alone being credited with what was really the office and work of the Bible and Church together. Hence in turn came the natural reaction, of which we are feeling the full force at the present day, in the claim of intellectual criticism to treat the Bible like any other book.   This claim is of course legitimate exactly in proportion as the Bible actually is like any other book ; but, when we examine the facts of the case, this is not, without qualification, the conclusion that they suggest.   For what do we find ?   If we are told that the Meditations of Aurelius, or the sayings of Epictetus, or " any other book " is as profitable to read as the New Testament, we must search the catalogue of some large library to discover where they are to be found, and possibly then be at some pains to procure them.

Whereas the New Testament confronts us at every turn.   There is no escaping from its presence.   Its history is inwoven into the whole history of the world for nineteen centuries. Martyrs innumerable have attested its power, and died with its language on their lips. Saints have spent ascetic lives, and scholars laboured on the study of its pages. Great intellectual movements have been concerned with its interpretation. Secular policy has again and again been profoundly modified by its existence. While, above all, it has been the secret stimulus of those countless hidden lives which have been the true salt of the earth and source of all its spiritual progress. And go where we may, and do what we will, it rises in evidence before us. We cannot travel through an English county or walk along a London street without being arrested by the sight of stately buildings which exist to impress it upon the world. A merchant cannot date a letter, nor a swindler forge a cheque, without implicit reference to the gospel story.

In other words, the New Testament is an integral part of a great living religion, and therefore lives at the present moment in a totally different sense from that in which Plato's dialogues or the plays of Shakespeare may be said to live. There is something of a fallacy therefore in supposing that it can be critically treated quite like any other book. It is not a question of the lawfulness of such treatment, but of its

logical possibility.   For in approaching any other
piece of literary criticism, we start from common
premises which are generally accepted, and could
not hope, of course, unless we did so to reach
any generally acceptable conclusions.   But critics
of the New Testament are, by the very nature
of their case, fundamentally divided in their premises before ever they begin their task; for they
either have the Christian belief in the reality of
the Incarnation or they have it not.   It may be
said that there is a third alternative possible—
that is, to have an open mind upon the question.
But this is not really a third alternative; for the
man who has an open mind in this particular case,
is *ipso facto* at the time an unbeliever, since he
cannot be basing his life upon the Incarnation in
the Christian sense.   It is not vital to him.   It
is not the cause and condition of his living as he
does.   Now this belief or disbelief must radically
affect our judgment of all the most important
problems which the New Testament presents.
Hence the Christian and unchristian critic, even
when they use common language, are not really
upon common ground.   For example, at the
very outset they both appeal to history, and yet
they mean by history two different things.   The

Christian Church has always regarded the life
and death and resurrection of Jesus Christ as
equally historical facts, because they have been
transmitted by a continuous tradition, dating
ultimately from the testimony of eye-witnesses,
recorded and emphasised in practically contemporary documents—documents, that is to say,
either written by or in close connection with the
eye-witnesses themselves : the testimony of these
witnesses being further accredited by their character and conduct, their sobriety, their original
slowness to believe, their subsequent readiness
to die for their belief, and by dying to convince
the world of their veracity and the intensity of
their conviction. Of course the modern Christian
reads all this in the light of what Christianity has
been to himself and others, and is predisposed
by his experience of a supernatural power now at
work in the world, to accept the account of its
supernatural initiation. But he none the less
regards that initiation as a fact of history in the
ordinary sense of the word—that is to say, as a
series of events recorded by those who took part
in them, and whose testimony for a variety of
reasons, which Paley, among others, has so well
expressed, is exceptionally strong.

Now the unchristian critic rejects this testimony not on the ground of its weakness, considered as testimony, but on the ground that the events to which it testifies are incongruous with our present experience or present estimate of what is probable—that is to say, he makes probability and not testimony the ultimate criterion of historical truth ; and further assumes that our present experience may be taken as a sufficient standard of all possible experience, an assumption which more or less vitiates all attempts to reconstruct the past by present lights. Here, then, we have two very different conceptions of history ; and we may remark in passing that if the term "scientific" is to be applied to either of them, it would seem more justly to belong to the Christian, who appeals to facts of evidence, than to his opponent who qualifies his facts in obedience to a theory which is essentially *a priori*.

But there are now a number of critics who claim to believe in the reality of the Incarnation, and yet who seem to make some confusion between these two views of history. They speak of the resurrection as a spiritual fact, and maintain that it belongs to the region of faith and not of history, on account of its supernatural character.

Whereas the Christian contention has always expressly been that when the Word was made Flesh, a supernatural Being entered what we call the order of nature with the ultimate view of lifting that order to a level which at present we call supernatural; and that the Resurrection was the first manifestation of this change, in the exhibition of a body which, while capable of human recognition and human intercourse, had become the free and unfettered and adequate organ of a supernatural person. Of the mode in which this took place we can know nothing; but our only reason for believing that it took place at all lies in the records handed down by the Church. We cannot therefore believe in it and yet at the same time disbelieve in the records on which it rests. And the records plainly show that the belief was due not to an invention of the credulous, but a conviction of the incredulous. True : the risen Christ only appeared to those who had previously put faith in Him, and thereby merited the further confirmation of their faith. But He appeared, not through any co-operation of their faith, but precisely when that faith had failed, by the sole operation of His own will and power. No one saw, or was able to see, Him until He showed

Himself.   Such is the plain statement of all the accounts.   The appearances, as described, were neither spiritual, in the sense of ghostly, nor spiritual, in the sense of being confined to the hearts or minds of the disciples.   They were in the fullest degree objective, in our modern use of this term.   And we cannot therefore deny them the name of historical, simply for being new facts in history, of however strange a kind.   To do so is, as we saw above, to base history not on testimony, but on probability—on what we now think likely to have occurred.   Nor must we for a moment imagine such a procedure to be scientific.   For it is precisely against such *a priori* repudiation of novelties that science has made all its progress, and therefore perpetually protests.

Moreover, the crowning feature and climax of the Incarnation was Christ's triumph over death ; and the mere conviction of His continued existence would have constituted no such triumph. Its evidence consisted in the objective manifestation to witnesses of His human person in its risen and glorified condition.   And the extreme importance attached by those witnesses to their function as such, with all the further emphasis laid upon it by St. Paul, can have no meaning but that they witnessed to a fact as having happened, or, in other words, as being historical. It was the inevitable and inseparable conclusion of the personal entrance of God into history which the Incarnation means.   And the faith of the Christian Church is not merely faith in the continued presence of Christ ; but also in the fact that this presence was originally certified by witnesses chosen before of God after He rose from the dead.

The foregoing illustrations may suffice to give some notion of the part played by subjective pre-possessions in much current criticism of the New Testament.   And as a rule what are called the most advanced critics are those in whom this element is largest, and who require therefore to be estimated with the greatest amount of caution. Whereas in the popular discussion of the subject in question, the very converse is often assumed to be the case ; and the critic of extreme views is supposed to be the superior critic.   This is merely another instance of the way in which eccentricity of any kind, from the fashion of a man's coat to the profession of his opinions, is apt to catch the public eye, quite irrespectively of what may be its value. And though notoriety of this kind does not mislead the serious student, it necessitates by its existence an amount of apparent attention on his part, which is apt in turn to mislead public opinion, by seeming to confirm its mistaken estimate.

CHAPTER III

IT is now usual in tracing Christian origins to begin with St. Paul, as he carries us up to the earliest date. It was also usual, till lately, to begin with those four of his epistles whose authenticity and genuineness were universally admitted, at least by all critics whose opinions could be called of any weight. But it should be remarked in passing that this limitation is an extreme concession to adverse criticism. It is an *argumentum ad hominem* to conciliate critical opponents by meeting them on common ground ; but not in the least an admission that the remaining epistles or the majority of them cannot with reason be attributed to St. Paul, as they now are by all the conservative critics, as well as by some of their advanced opponents. Now the epistles in question — those, namely, to the Romans, Corinthians, and Galatians—were written, roughly speaking, before the year 60 A.D. But two things are perfectly plain from their contents : first, that there had been no fundamental change in St. Paul's gospel since he began to preach, and therefore that what we find written in 60 A.D. was in its essence what he taught in 40 A.D., or within ten years of the Crucifixion ; and, secondly, that this teaching was in substantial accord with that of James, Cephas, and John. This latter point is implied as distinctly as possible by St. Paul himself in the Epistle to the Galatians ; and again in the Corinthians, where he says, " Whether it be I or they, so we preach and so ye believed "; and again by the tone which he adopts in writing to Churches which he had not personally founded ; while it is further so strongly corroborated in the Acts of the Apostles as to have given rise to the Tübingen theory that the Acts was a later book, written with the express purpose of harmonising the supposed divergences between Petrine and Pauline doctrine. But the early date and historical accuracy of the Acts has been amply revindicated of late, and therewith the value of its evidence on the present point. What, then, do we find in these epistles ?

Not only is Jesus Christ continually spoken of

as the Lord and the Son of God in an unique
sense, "His own Son," as contrasted with sons
by adoption; but St. Paul's entire relation to
Him throughout these epistles is not that of a
man to a human master, but to a Being of wholly
other than mere human rank; through whom
"God will judge the secret things of men," and
before whose judgment-seat all men "must needs
appear." Thus the whole tone and implication
of the epistles prepare us for the passage in the
Romans in which Christ is expressly termed
"over all God blessed for ever." And there is
not the faintest reason for altering the punctuation
of the passage which both our English versions
have retained, with practically the whole of anti-
quity behind them, though some modern critics
have attempted to do so in two different ways;
affording a fresh instance of the arbitrary methods
that we have been considering above.

St. Paul's precise conception of the Spirit
would be less easy to define from these epistles,
as he speaks variously of the Spirit of God, the
Spirit of Christ, the Holy Spirit, the Lord the
Spirit, or the Lord of the Spirit, and once says
the Lord is the Spirit. But distinct activities are
attributed to the Spirit. "The Spirit searcheth

all things, yea, even the deep things of God."
" The Spirit Himself beareth witness (αὐτὸ τὸ
πνεῦμα) with our spirit, that we are the sons of
God." He " dwelleth in us," " helpeth our
infirmities," " maketh intercession for us with
groanings that cannot be uttered." We are " led
by the Spirit of God." Our bodies are the
temples of the Holy Ghost, and " He who raised
up Jesus from the dead shall also quicken our
mortal bodies through His Spirit that dwelleth
in you." Finally, the distinction of agency which
is implied in these expressions is definitely recognised in the concluding words of the Second
Epistle to the Corinthians : " The grace of the
Lord Jesus Christ, and the love of God, and the
communion of the Holy Ghost, be with you all."

We find, then, the distinction of Father, Son,
and Holy Spirit being taught by St. Paul,
presumably within ten or twelve years of the
Crucifixion, and presumably in agreement with
the other apostles ; both these presumptions, it
should be noticed, being of no far - fetched or
subjective kind, but practically of the nature of
moral certainties ; and we find this by merely
critical methods. And when we remember how
many apostles were alive during those few years,

to bear witness to what they had seen and heard; and how much weight was subsequently attached to this apostolic tradition; we cannot conceive a profound alteration of the Christian doctrine to have taken place, and that during the time of its first and most earnest propagation. And we naturally conclude that this common doctrine was derived from Christ Himself.

It is possible to limit our appeal to a minimum of St. Paul's epistles, for the sake of starting from a position which practically all accept. But when Christian apologists with mistaken courtesy allow the Fourth Gospel to be put out of court, they are doing more than this; for they are deferring to a critical judgment which as a body they do not accept. And it is time that this should be clearly recognised. For the problem of the Fourth Gospel has been by this time so exhaustively discussed that we know its every turn by heart. We are almost weary of the various arguments; so familiar have they become. And the result is a definite difference of opinion, mainly due to religious and philosophical presuppositions. We have already given an instance of this in which the premiss of a particular argument against the authenticity of the gospel obviously presupposed the rejection of the Incarnation. And so it is throughout. Disbelievers in the Incarnation must in some way neutralise the evidence of the Fourth Gospel, and may be perfectly sincere in doing so. But a number of Christian thinkers, that is, believers in the Incarnation, are now convinced of its authenticity and genuineness ; not because they have not weighed the case, but because they have weighed it thoroughly and consider the external evidence as strong as need be expected, and the internal evidence overwhelming. Of course, in saying this one includes among such thinkers many who without having published their views upon the subject, have satisfied their own minds upon it ; as is abundantly shown by the fact that in their preaching and teaching they take the Johannine authorship for granted ; in a way that outsiders may think uncritical, but which is really the result of criticism. In making a statement of this kind it is necessary to be well within the mark ; and therefore not to speak of more than "a number of Christian thinkers," though probably, as far at any rate as England is concerned, " a great majority " would be the truer expression.

Our object in saying this is not, of course, to

prejudice a critical question by an appeal to authority, but simply to show, in a compendious way, the weight which the conservative solution of that question actually possesses, without enumerating all the well-known arguments for it at length. There is, however, one argument on which it may be well to pause; because its force has been blunted in many minds of recent years, by what is merely a popular confusion of thought. We are now familiar with the fact that the canons and customs of Hebrew and other Oriental authorship differ considerably from our own; and that the various grades of pseudony-mous literature, in which a later writing is either produced as or incorporated with the work of an earlier or greater name, need not imply any dis-honesty either of intention or of effect. Hence there has arisen a vague idea in many minds that the Fourth Gospel may be viewed in this way. But this is, of course, simply and utterly impossible. For the Fourth Gospel stakes everything upon its authorship. It claims to be written by a witness, who had seen and handled, expressly because he was a witness and had seen and handled; the last expression, according to tradition, of that witness which had been the

E

very heart and core of the apostolic preaching, uttered, as Browning phrases it, in presence of the thought, " How will it be when none more saith, ' I saw ' ? "

This was forcibly put by Renan in the thirteenth edition of his " Life of Christ "; and his words may be worth quoting, for the clearness with which they put the dilemma on the point.

" One or other of these two alternatives must be true. Either the author of the Fourth Gospel is a disciple of Jesus, an intimate disciple from the earliest date ; or the author, in order to carry weight, has employed an artifice from beginning to end of his book, calculated to suggest that he was an exceptionally qualified witness to the truth of his facts. . . . We must therefore choose between two hypotheses : either to recognise John the son of Zebedee as the author of the Fourth Gospel, or to regard that Gospel as an apocryphal writing composed by an individual who desired to pass it off as the work of John the son of Zebedee. There is, in fact, no question here of legends, popular creations for which no one is responsible. A man who, to gain credence for what he relates, deceives the public not only as to his name but also as to the value of his

testimony, is not a legend-monger—but a forger."
" Moreover, this would not be the only fraud of
the kind which the author in question must have
committed," he continues, since the author of
the gospel is almost certainly identical with the
author of the First Epistle of St. John, where
again "he represents himself as an eye-witness
of the evangelical history, and a well-known man
of high consideration in the Church."

Now the real weight of this dilemma lies not
in the critical improbability that such a forgery
could have succeeded, though that is extreme ;
but in the moral and spiritual impossibility that
the Fourth Gospel could be such a forgery at all,
when we reflect upon what that gospel is,—the
spiritual gospel, the absolutely central book of
the world's religious history, the great literary
sacrament of the Christian Church,—the very
expression of the Incarnation in terms of human
language ;—no faintest taint of insincerity is conceivable in such a book.

We have enlarged upon this particular point,
on account of its being so often obscured in
popular thought ; but, of course, it is only one
of the many convergent arguments which confirm
what is after all the greatest of all arguments, the

constant tradition of the Christian Church that the gospel was written by St. John.

But if so, the probability which we inferred from St. Paul becomes a certainty ; namely, that the distinction and relation of Father, Son, and Spirit was taught by Christ Himself. For this teaching, in simple, vivid, pictorial phraseology, is plainly so ascribed, and can be easily distinguished from anything which we may attribute to the later reflections of St. John, or the possible effect of familiarity with St. Paul. Moreover, the language of St. John, as regards the relation of the Father and the Son, corroborates, and is corroborated by the well-known passages in St. Matthew and St. Luke which we reviewed above ; the far-fetched extravagance of the arguments against them, being of themselves sufficient to show how little ground there is, in sober reason, for their rejection ; against the evidence of two gospels.

Then there is the explicit baptismal formula in St. Matthew. It is now suggested that this formula does not convey Christ's own words ; on the ground that it sounds more technical than His usual language, and represents a more developed doctrine than He personally proclaimed; while the most primitive practice of baptism would seem, from its earlier records, to have been in the name of Christ, rather than the Trinity, which could hardly have been the case had the command in question been His own. But as against this it may be reasonably maintained that the language is no more technical or developed than that expressly attributed to Christ, again and again, by St. John. While the baptism into the name of Christ need not be construed, and certainly cannot be proved, to mean more than baptism into a Christian community, or baptism as a Christian. And had the original form,—the form, that is, which had all the weight of apostolic tradition behind it, been "in the name of Christ," it is difficult to imagine how or why it should have been universally altered. But probabilities of this slight and subtle kind, when so evenly balanced, hardly justify the rejection of a passage which has all the authority of the manuscripts in its favour. Moreover, the words are attributed to Christ after His resurrection—a point to which we shall return.

These, then, are the most prominent instances of what is implied throughout the whole New

Testament; every book of which speaks of the unique dignity of Christ, and His close relation to the Father, while most of them make further and frequent mention of the Spirit.

Christians, therefore, have sufficient justification, from their own point of view, for believing that the existence of the Trinity was taught by Christ Himself. This is, of course, in direct contradiction of the modern opinion, according to which Jesus Christ only by degrees came to regard Himself as the Messiah, and never allowed even this to be proclaimed till the very end of His career; while, further, he was only preached at first as Messiah, according to the earlier chapters of the Acts, all else being due to subsequent development.

But this view, which is thought by many to be critically established, suggests various criticisms upon itself.

In the first place, no believer in the reality of the Incarnation would dream it possible to reconstruct, and much less to reconstruct out of our fragmentary records, the inner history of the mind of Christ. We read that He grew in wisdom, and are obliged to believe in such a degree of self-limitation or self-emptying (κένωσις) as would enable Him to pass through a truly human experience of life.   But the degrees and details of this limitation are and must, from the nature of the case, for ever remain unknown to us; while any attempt to trace them, on the part of critics who do not believe in the Incarnation, are, it need hardly be said, valueless for the Christian mind.

Secondly, though the character of Messiah was that under which Jesus presented Himself, as was natural, to the Jews, He coupled this at times with an intimation of an august and eternal personality, uniquely related to His Father.   He claimed to be a Son, where the highest of the prophets had been but servants.   And He spoke, as reported by the synoptists, quite as plainly as by St. John, "with authority and not as the scribes"; an authority in relation to the law, and the Sabbath, and the destiny of the human race, which would be unintelligible unless it were divine.   It would, of course, be natural that such sayings should be but dimly understood during His earthly career; and we are expressly told that such was the case, and that their significance was only realised after He had risen from the dead.

And this brings us to another point, the effect of the resurrection, and of their intercourse with the risen Lord, upon the disciples. It is evident that, up to the resurrection, the disciples did not realise, nor could they indeed have realised, whatever He might say, that Jesus Christ was God incarnate. But after the resurrection the whole situation was changed. The immense prominence given by the apostles in their preaching to the resurrection must have been the reflection of its effect upon themselves. And this is no more than we should expect. The resurrection was a stupendous fact, the witnessing of it a stupendous experience which, of itself, must have gone far to create that wonderful transformation in the character of the apostles which the subsequent illumination by the Spirit confirmed. Not only those, therefore, who deny the resurrection, but those who palliate the extreme surprise of it to the apostles, leave one of the most important factors in the history of Christianity unaccounted for. That factor was the sudden development of courageous enthusiasm in the previously faint-hearted apostles.

Paley, it will be remembered, has drawn a powerful picture of the trials which the original preachers of Christianity naturally had to expect, and actually underwent—"labours," as he says, "dangers, and sufferings, voluntarily undergone in attestation of the accounts which they delivered, and solely in consequence of their belief of those accounts."   And it might be well sometimes to recur to Paley's vigorous presentation of the tremendous moral miracle herein involved—the common-sense view of a man of the world—by way of a corrective to the many thin and facile explanations that are now offered to us of how Christianity glided, as it were, into existence, explanations that savour much more of the study than the market-place, arguing more knowledge of books than of men.

The change which enabled the apostles to face these difficulties and dangers is the greatest moral miracle of the early Christian Church; and this change must have been largely due to the alteration which the resurrection made in their whole conception of their Master.   He whom Peter had not formerly feared to rebuke has now become "my Lord and my God."   This difference of attitude is plainly perceptible in all the accounts of Christ's appearances after His resurrection, constituting, as it does, one of the subtle indications of their truth. And it would be upon this new and awful realisation of His august personality that the illumination of the Holy Spirit worked, as He had promised. " He shall glorify Me; for He shall take of Mine, and shall declare it unto you." "All things whatsoever the Father hath are mine : therefore said I, that He taketh of Mine, and shall declare it unto you." Nor is this all. We read in the Acts that " He was received up after that He had given commandment through the Holy Ghost to the apostles whom He had chosen," and again that " He shewed himself . . . appearing by the space of forty days, and speaking the things concerning the kingdom of God," and in St. Luke's Gospel that " He opened their mind, that they might understand the Scriptures." We need not pause upon the question whether, when St. Luke wrote the condensed last chapter of his gospel, he was unaware of the longer period afterwards mentioned in the Acts, nor upon the suggestion of myth, which is supposed by many to be inherent in the number forty. For St. Luke has been proved to be an accurate historian, and had access, as he tells us, to eye-witnesses ; and the accounts in St. John's Gospel

are to the same effect.   We cannot doubt, therefore, that the apostolic tradition bore witness to
an intercourse with the risen Christ which extended, at least, over a considerable number of
occasions and days; nor can we believe that this
tradition, being that of the eye-witnesses themselves, could by any possibility be incorrect.   But
our point is the subject of this intercourse—
"things concerning the kingdom of God."   If, as
we have been assuming, the discourses recorded
by St. John were already lingering in the minds
of the disciples, though imperfectly understood,
it is reasonable to suppose that their meaning
would acquire fuller development, when, with
all the authority of His great change upon Him,
Christ "opened their mind, that they might
understand the Scriptures."   If so, the doctrines
of the Trinity and the Incarnation, which we find
taught at so early a date by St. Paul, may at this
time have come explicitly home to the apostles;
in which case the words in St. Matthew that we
considered above, and which are attributed, be it
remembered, to the end of this period, may well
have closed and summarised its teaching, and
been, naturally and appropriately, spoken by
Christ Himself.

As against this view a great deal is made by some critics of the absence of any express doctrine of the incarnation from the earlier discourses recorded in the Acts. But this certainly need not imply more, and therefore cannot be quoted as implying more than that the apostles began their work by endeavouring to lead the Jews, in the same way that they had themselves been led, to recognise in Jesus the Messiah, the Christ. While it is obvious that St. Luke, who had already written his gospel, could not have seen anything incompatible with it, in what he himself records as its historic continuation.

In fact, the conception of a merely human Christ, who was afterwards deified, can only be attained in this way by an extraordinarily arbitrary selection of every passage which, if taken out of the context of its occurrence, might make in favour of such a conception, but which actually occurs in a context of the very opposite tendency; while there is a simplicity and naturalness about the gospel narratives as we have them which should convince all, who do not presuppose the impossibility of miracle, that they cannot be thus dismembered.

Indeed the remarks of Paley on this point are

as applicable to-day as when he made them, and, as they are becoming unfamiliar, may be worth quotation.

" Now, that the original story," he says, " the story delivered by the first preachers of the institution, should have died away so entirely as to have left no record or memorial of its exist- ence, although so many records of the time and transaction remain ; and that another story should have stepped into its place, and gained exclusive possession of the belief of all who professed themselves disciples of the institution, is beyond any example of the corruption of even oral tradi- tion, and still less consistent with the experience of written history : and this improbability, which is very great, is rendered still greater by the reflec- tion that no such change as the oblivion of one story and the substitution of another took place in any future period of the Christian era. Chris- tianity hath travelled through dark and turbulent ages ; nevertheless it came out of the cloud and the storm such, in substance, as it entered in. Many additions were made to the primitive his- tory, and these entitled to different degrees of credit ; many doctrinal errors also were from time to time grafted into the public creed, but still the

original story remained and remained the same."
And he adds an important consideration.

"Among the proofs that the story which we
have *now* is, in substance, the story which the
Christians had *then*, or, in other words, that the
accounts in our gospels are, as to their principal
parts at least, the accounts which the apostles
and original teachers of the religion delivered,
one arises from observing that it appears by the
gospels themselves, that the story was public at
the time, that the Christian community was
already in possession of the substance and principal parts of the narrative. The gospels were
not the original cause of the Christian history
being believed, but were themselves among the
consequences of that belief."

He then refers to St. Luke's expression,
"Those things which are most surely believed
among us, even as they delivered them unto us,
which from the beginning were eye-witnesses and
ministers of the Word." And again, "Those
things wherein thou hast been instructed."

When we compare the emphasis laid here and
elsewhere in the New Testament on eye-witness
with the emphasis laid in the sub-apostolic and
subsequent ages upon apostolic tradition, it

becomes impossible to suppose a gap between the two through which any substantial change could have crept in.

Briefly to resume, then : the Christian Church existed and taught a gospel from the days of Jesus Christ, and in process of time committed portions of this teaching to writing, in the form of letters and memoirs. The especial claim of its earliest teachers was to have had personal evidence of what they taught, and the especial claim of their successors was to have preserved the substance of this evidence intact. And all because it was a revelation, something that had come to them without their asking, and beyond their power of imagining ; yet of which, when once revealed, they were so certain that they gladly died for its sake. We have written evidence that this teaching included the doctrines of a trinity and an incarnation as early as St. Paul wrote his epistles ; that is to say, within thirty years of its origin. And it is an inevitable inference from his own words that the same doctrines had been taught by him from the first, that is, from a date about twenty years earlier, and in common with the other apostles, while both doctrines are attributed to Christ Himself by St. John. These are the most salient features of the situation ; but they are supported by others, into which it has not seemed necessary for our immediate purpose to digress, such as the whole character and teaching of Christ as depicted in the synoptic gospels, as well as arguments from the Apocalypse and the other various epistles. All point to the same conclusion—that the two doctrines in question are an original element of the gospel of Christ, revealed, that is to say, by Himself as and when His disciples were able to bear them, but with sufficient clearness to ensure and justify their becoming objects of subsequent reflection, and therefore of such development as reflection must inevitably involve.

CHAPTER IV

THE TRINITY IN PATRISTIC TRADITION

WE have alluded above to the tradition by which the apostolic eye-witness was handed on; but the subject demands some further emphasis in view of the fact that its importance is apt to be very much underrated by many of the critics in the present day. To begin with, we must remember the conditions of its origin. The Jews were accustomed to oral teaching of a kind that trained them in tenacity of memory, and consequent capacity for the accurate transmission of details, and their standard of fidelity was extremely high. The apostles, therefore, naturally taught after the manner of their time and country, while the matter of their teaching was what they had seen and heard. This teaching was further extended by catechists as the Church increased, whose oral instructions prepared the way for the written gospels. And from the second century onwards we find the greatest possible importance attached to the accurate preservation of this apostolic tradition, as the following quotations may show :—

"We have not," says Irenæus, "received the knowledge of the way of our salvation by any others than those by whom the Gospel has been brought to us. Which Gospel they first preached, and afterwards, by the will of God, committed to writing, that it might be for time to come the foundation and pillar of our faith. For after that our Lord rose from the dead, and they (the Apostles) were endowed from above with the power of the Holy Ghost coming down upon them, they received a perfect knowledge of all things. They then went forth to all the ends of the earth . . . having all of them and every one alike the Gospel of God." "The tradition of the Apostles hath spread itself over the whole world ; and all they who search after the sources of truth will find this tradition to be held sacred in every church. We might enumerate all those who have been appointed bishops to these churches by the Apostles, and all their successors up to our days. It is by this uninterrupted succession that we have received the tradition which actually exists in the Church."

Again, Clement of Alexandria writes as follows: —" My memoranda are stored up against old age as a remedy against forgetfulness, truly an image and outline of those vigorous and animated discourses which I was privileged to hear, and of blessed and truly remarkable men."

. . . . . .

"Well, they preserving the tradition of the blessed doctrine derived directly from the holy Apostles Peter, James, John, and Paul, the son receiving it from the father (but few were like the fathers), came by God's will to us also to deposit those ancestral and apostolic seeds. And well I know they will exult; I do not mean be delighted with this tribute, but solely on account of the preservation of the truth, according as they delivered it. For such a sketch as this will, I think, be agreeable to a soul desirous of preserving from escape the blessed tradition." [1]

Origen speaks to the same effect: "Since many of those who profess to believe in Christ differ from each other, not only in small and trifling matters, but also on subjects of the

---

[1] Clem. Alex. *Storm.* i. i.

highest importance . . . it seems on that account necessary first of all to fix a definite limit and to lay down an unmistakable rule regarding each one of these. . . . For as we ceased to seek for truth (notwithstanding the professions of many among Greeks and barbarians to make it known) among all who claimed it for erroneous opinions, after we had come to believe that Christ was the Son of God, and were persuaded that we must learn it from Himself; so, seeing there are many who think they hold the opinions of Christ, and yet some of these think differently from their predecessors, yet as the teaching of the Church, transmitted in orderly succession from the apostles, and remaining in the churches to the present day, is still preserved, that alone is to be accepted as truth which differs in no respect from ecclesiastical and apostolical tradition." [1]

And again Athanasius :—" There is no fellowship whatever between the words of the saints and the fancies of human invention ; for the saints are the ministers of the truth, preaching the kingdom of heaven. . . . For as each of the saints has received, that they impart without alteration, for

[1] Orig. *De Prin*. Pref.

the confirmation of the doctrine of the mysteries. Of these the (divine) Word would have us disciples, and these should of right be our teachers, and to them only is it necessary to give heed, for of them only is 'the word faithful and worthy of all acceptation'; these not being disciples because they heard from others, but being eye-witnesses and ministers of the Word, that which they had heard from Him have they handed down."[1]

The contents of this apostolic tradition which was the nucleus of the subsequent creeds came to be called the canon or rule of faith, of which Tertullian says that it is "descended from the beginning of the gospel" (*ab initio evangelii*), and is "wholly one, changeless, unalterable." And the mental attitude of the early Church towards it was afterwards summed up in the well-known Vincentian maxim, *Quod semper, quod ubique, quod ab omnibus* : "That which has always been received, and everywhere, and by all."

Now the word "tradition" is often taken to imply a blind following of custom ; but this tradition was the very reverse of blind : it was, if one may so say, acutely self-conscious ; it understood its own character.   Moreover, it reflects light

[1] Athanasius, *Festal Letter*, ii.

back upon the apostolic teaching. Their teaching was thus preserved, because they had taught
that it should be so ; and that, again, because they
were not transmitting theories that could be modified, but describing facts that they had witnessed,
and of which as witnesses they themselves were
a part.   It was of the essence of the Christian
life to be founded on fact—the fact of the life
and death and resurrection and teaching of Jesus
Christ.   This made that moral revolution possible
to which the apologists continually appeal, as the
great practical proof of Christianity.   This made
St. Paul succeed where Seneca hopelessly failed.
And tradition simply meant the maintenance
that these facts were facts.   It is the natural
correlative of witness, as witness is the correlative of revelation.   But a tradition like this, of
which the evidence is so plain and palpable, is
incompatible with the kind of development which
many critics assume to have taken place ; a
development in which alien elements gradually
filtered into and became incorporated with primitive Christianity, till they had altered it past all
recognition.   The Christian society was too
obviously aware of itself and its own essential
principles for this ; for it was daily making use

of those principles to fashion the lives of its individual members, and proving in the process their more than human power; their unique and utterly unparalleled ability to save men in life and sustain them in death, and that the death of martyrdom—*Christiani ad leones.*

In fact, the history of religion often raises the same question that occurs, as we saw above, in connection with the origin of species, as to how far similarities of structure or function necessarily imply a causal connection within the phenomenal order. And whatever we may think about physical organisms, it is very certain that in religious history similarity does not of necessity imply connection, and must never hastily be assumed so to do. For example, it is a striking fact that in the records of three great religions we have accounts of the temptation of their respective founders—Zarathustra, Buddha, Jesus Christ. The accounts of the two former immediately remind us, both by their likeness and their contrast, of the latter. Yet it would be nothing less than a critical absurdity to suppose the latter connected with the earlier history. The temptation of Christ stands out as unique as His entire personality, and is vitally connected with the whole of His subsequent life and work. We can never doubt, when once we have read it, that it actually occurred. And what of the other two? Stripped of their mythological embellishments, they must also have occurred; they could not have failed to occur, simply because human nature is what it is. Every man has to fight temptation on entering his life's work, and if that work is to be the founding of a great religion, its prefatory temptation will be correspondingly great. And if the Buddha and Zarathustra were both historical personages, they must necessarily have undergone some such spiritual conflicts as are recorded of them; similarity of situation producing similitude of experience, without any causal connection whatever.

We have quoted the above case as a very simple instance of a phenomenon which the comparison of religions continually presents. And the scholar, when he meets with such parallelisms, in the abstract seclusion of his study, is very liable to be misled into supposing connections between them for which no real evidence exists. And so we are told with much confidence that the essential idea of our eucharist came from Mithraism, and that the substitution of Sunday for

the Sabbath was due to the influence of a Baby-
lonian sect ; and many like things, wherever a
correspondence of any kind can be unearthed.
Whereas in fact the very multiplicity of such
correspondences should of itself suggest the
extreme improbability of their being instances
of causal connection, rather than analogous results
of analogous circumstances acting on a common
human nature.

It is of course quite true that in the course of
time the Christian Church absorbed into itself
many customs and practices and symbols and
phrases that had come down from earlier days ;
but it did so precisely in virtue of its own master-
ful vitality, like a strong man sweeping weaker
wills into the service of his own.   And any
reaction which these alien elements had upon
the Church is utterly incomparable to the reaction
which the Church had upon them.   They did not
impair its identity ; but it identified them with
itself, assimilated, utilised, elevated them to loftier
ends than they first subserved, and fuller meanings than they first possessed.   While in strong
contrast to all those minor accidents of its
existence, the central and essential faith of the
Church stands out unique, positive, self-conscious,

appealing in evidence of its unalloyed identity to its continuous tradition.

We have referred to this subject because the doctrine of the Trinity is sometimes explained away by a similar misuse of the comparative method. Trinitarian modes of thought have historically been of frequent occurrence. There were trinities, in the sense of threefold groups among the gods of India; and again among those of ancient Babylonia; and again in Egypt. A philosophic trinity occurs in Plato, and is very prominent in Neo-platonic thought. And it is an obvious suggestion that the Christian Trinity was borrowed from one or other of these sources, or from the general atmosphere into which they had all entered; making Trinitarianism a common mode of Thought. The possibility of such a supposition was further facilitated by assigning an extravagantly late date to all the writings in the New Testament which bear upon the point. For the result of this was to involve the whole first century of Christian history in a degree of darkness that allowed time for any amount of alien influence to invade its original creed. And the Pauline and Johannine writings, as we call them, could then be easily regarded as reflecting the issue of a long process of intellectual development, during which the doctrine of the Trinity had been gradually incorporated with the primitive religion of Jesus Christ.

But it is now a familiar fact that this radical attempt upon the dates of the documents in question has been abandoned, by all critics who are worthy of the name. The majority of what are called advanced critics concede more epistles to St. Paul than did their predecessors, as well as a much earlier date to the Fourth Gospel; with the embarrassing result that it becomes much more difficult to attribute their contents to development. But what is really of more importance is that, as a result of the whole discussion, conservative critics—those, that is to say, who, broadly speaking, uphold the traditional view of the Church on the New Testament—have felt the intellectual strength of their position to be considerably augmented. And this for two reasons. In the first place, the essentially unscientific nature of the more extreme negative criticism has become increasingly apparent, from the number of subjective, arbitrary, and improbable hypotheses that it is seen to involve. Its self-confidence is discovered to be unjustified by

any adequate solidity of argument; and its whole
effect, as an attack on the Christian position,
is thereby discredited. And, secondly, it has
become abundantly clear that criticism does not
always lead in one direction. For in the sifting
process of critical controversy many fresh details
have come to light which fortify the Christian position. To quote a single case in point: the assertion that St. Paul neither knew nor cared for the
historic details of the human life of Jesus Christ,
has given occasion for a searching re-examination
of the Pauline Epistles. And the result has been
to show the high probability, amounting to moral
certainty, that he makes allusion to many of those
details, and was therefore personally acquainted
with more; while he further presupposes the like
knowledge on the part of those to whom he
writes, in a way to show that it must have formed
a part of their original instruction. We are not
here arguing this question, but merely quote it
as an illustration of the way in which the critical
attack has materially strengthened the confidence
of the defence in the strength of its own position.
The same result has occurred in relation to the
historical accuracy of the Acts; and many other
cases might be quoted. Thus the traditional view

of the New Testament can not only be retained against criticism, but critically retained,—retained, that is, by adequate counter-criticism ; and is all the stronger therefore for the very number of the attacks that it has met and answered.

But when once St. Paul and St. John are restored to their traditional place, the century of darkness, during which alien ideas could have crept into the Church, disappears ; and the contention of our previous chapter reasserts itself. That is to say, we find the existence of the three Divine Persons plainly recognised, at a time and in a way which irresistibly suggest that it was taught by Christ Himself. And this conclusion is confirmed by the rest of the New Testament. And it is not taught by Christ, as reflected in the gospels, in a way that would possibly admit of its being borrowed by Him from alien sources. It comes from Him with that note of authority which was " not as the scribes," and is intimately connected with His presentation of His own person to the world, and with His assertion of His own claim to its allegiance. While it is repeated by St. Paul in the same way, not as a speculative doctrine, but as the practical and actual presupposition of the Incarnation ; that condition of the Godhead which first enabled the Incarnation and its consequent atonement to take place, and then enabled its meaning and efficacy to be brought home to the souls of men. And the continuous tradition of the Church, repeated by father after father was that this doctrine had come directly through the apostles from Christ.

This is plainly assumed throughout the First Epistle of Clement to the Corinthians, near the end of the first century.

"The apostles have preached to us," he says, "from our Lord Jesus Christ; Jesus Christ from God. . . . For having received their command, and being thoroughly assured by the resurrection of our Lord Jesus Christ; and convinced by the Word of God, with the fulness of the Holy Spirit, they went abroad, publishing that the kingdom of God was at hand."

Again, probably only a few years later, Ignatius writes to the Magnesians: "Study therefore to be confirmed in the doctrine of our Lord and of His apostles; that so . . . ye may prosper both in body and spirit, . . . in the Son, and in the Father, and in the Holy Spirit. Be subject to your bishop, and to one another, as Jesus Christ to the Father, according to the flesh; and the apostles both to Christ, and to the Father, and to the Holy Ghost."

Again, he tells the Ephesians that they are "the stones of the temple of the Father, prepared for His building, and drawn up on high by the cross of Christ, as by an engine, using the Holy Ghost as the rope."

There is no special inculcation of the doctrine in question, it will be noticed, in either of these writers; it is presupposed, assumed, taken for granted; with a perfect naturalness that is extremely significant when their early date is borne in mind. We are undoubtedly carried back to apostolic times. While, on the other hand, if we compare these passages with the more explicit statements of a century later, the substantial identity of their teaching on the subject is plain. This may perhaps best be shown by a quotation from Origen; because Origen, as is well known, speculated freely, whenever he felt himself free to speculate; and this makes his adherence to tradition, on the present point, all the more emphatic.

"It ought to be known," says Origen, "that the holy apostles, in preaching the faith of Christ, delivered themselves with the utmost clearness on certain points which they believed to be necessary to every one, even to those who might be dullest in the investigation of divine knowledge. . . . The particular points clearly delivered in the teaching of the apostles are as follows :— *First*, that there is one God, who created and arranged all things. . . . God from the creation and foundation of the world, . . . and that this God in the last days, as He had announced beforehand by His prophets, sent our Lord Jesus Christ to call, in the first place, Israel to Himself; and, in the second place, the Gentiles. . . . *Secondly*, that Jesus Christ who came, was born of the Father before all creatures; that, after He had been the servant of the Father in the creation of all things—' For by Him were all things made'—He, in the last times, divesting Himself (of His glory) became a man, and was incarnate although God, and while made a man remained the God which He was. . . . that He assumed a body born of a virgin and of the Holy Spirit. . . . Then, *thirdly*, the apostles related that the Holy Spirit was associated in honour and dignity with the Father and the Son." [1]

[1] Origen, *De Prin.* Pref. 3, 4.

We must remember, moreover, that this tradition, which is so scrupulous to preserve its own identity, was not a thing handed on by merely a few individuals, but by the whole body of Christians. It does not really depend upon things like the fact that Irenæus overlapped Polycarp, and Polycarp St. John; but was the common possession of a great society, which was conspicuously living in dependence upon this creed; and must have been transmitted by the lips of thousands who emphasised and consecrated its transmission, by the saintly lives and heroic deaths which were its fruit.

Finally, we would recur to the fact, that the tradition in question does not date from a time when the origin of its content had been forgotten, and has nothing in common with the many stereotyped traditions of that kind. On the contrary, its express claim is to be accurately aware of the origin of its own content. It practically touches the New Testament; and their joint evidence precludes the possibility of any foreign source being admitted for the Christian doctrine of the Trinity; for we can trace it to its fountain-head. In saying this we are not, of course, referring to the theological terminology in which the doctrine was subsequently expressed; but to its essence, that is, the distinct though correlative existence and agency of Father, Son, and Holy Spirit.

Moreover, this doctrine in its simplicity does not really resemble any of the foreign sources from which it is supposed to have been derived. We have examples in the gnostic systems of the kind of result produced by an eclectic syncretism of oriental and philosophic elements of thought, and nothing could be in stronger contrast to the Christian doctrine; it is like the difference between fairy-tale and fact.

In brief, then, to conclude: the Christian tradition is too clear and too authoritative to be lightly set aside; and that tradition interprets and confirms the obvious evidence of the New Testament, to the effect that the real essence of the doctrine of the Trinity — beside which all subsequent modes of its expression are of wholly secondary importance — came as a revelation from Jesus Christ Himself.

In the words of St. Basil: " In delivering the formula of the Father, the Son, and the Holy Ghost, our Lord did not connect the gift with number. He did not say, 'into First, Second, and Third,' nor yet into One, Two, and Three, but He gave us the boon of the knowledge of the faith which leads to salvation, by means of holy names." [1]

[1] Basil, *De Spir.* 44.

CHAPTER V

No characteristic of the early Church is more prominent in the Acts and the Epistles than its sense of guidance by the Holy Spirit. This guidance, we read in the Gospels, had been promised by Christ Himself, and one of its especial objects was to be a fuller understanding of His own significance. "The Comforter, even the Holy Spirit, whom the Father will send in My name, He shall teach you all things, and bring to your remembrance all that I said unto you." "When the Comforter is come, whom I will send unto you from the Father, even the Spirit of Truth, which proceedeth from the Father, He shall bear witness of Me." "I have yet many things to say unto you, but ye cannot bear them now. Howbeit when He, the Spirit of Truth, is come, He shall guide you into all the truth . . . He shall glorify Me; for He shall take of Mine, and shall declare it unto you."

The more negative critics both deny the authenticity of these promises and regard the corresponding sense of guidance in the Church as an illusion. But the Christian, believing both the promises and their fulfilment, finds therein the key to the subsequent development of the Church's life and doctrine. " It seemed good to the Holy Spirit and to us." But to read that development aright we must remember both the terms of this statement—" the Holy Ghost," the infallible spirit, and " us," His fallible human instruments. For the history of the Church is the resultant of these two forces : the One inspiring, illuminating, guiding ; the other co-operating indeed, but always in some degree limiting the effect of the inspiration and the guidance, by the fact of its own inevitable limitations. Christians in all ages, as we know from their biographies, illustrated by our own experience, have been conscious of this dual control of their personal lives. They have felt the presence of the quickening Spirit, with a certainty that is beyond doubt ; but they have also felt how His power has been checked by their own ignorance, unreadiness, lack of courage, lack of faith, and general inheritance of sinful tendency. And the history of the Church is only the history of its individual members writ large. There have been lives of sanctity and ages of faith in which the hindering influence of the human medium has reached its minimum; and dark ages again, with wickedness in the high places of the Church, when the light of the Spirit has seemed well nigh quenched. But His presence may even then be detected in hidden lives and lonely places, and with His presence, His power to quicken, to restore, to revive.

Our present concern, however, is confined to one detail of this guidance—the formulation of the doctrine of the Trinity. The essence of that doctrine, we have seen reason to believe, must have come from Christ Himself, who alone could declare it with the necessary authority. For, as St. Thomas Aquinas truly says: "It is impossible for the natural reason to arrive at the knowledge of the divine persons. By natural reason we may know those things that pertain to the unity of the divine essence, but not those which pertain to the distinction of the divine persons";[1] a position in which his acute critic Duns Scotus is also fully

[1] *Summa*, i. 32. 1.

at one with him.[1]   Had the doctrine in question, therefore, originated with St. Paul or St. John, or any other mere man, however inspired, it could not have appealed to the Church as more than a human speculation or mystic intuition; whereas it has always been regarded, in sharp distinction from this, as a fact of revelation.   But confessedly St. Paul and St. John clothed it in new phraseology, and thereby brought it into a new relation to the thought of their age.   And in so doing they not only initiated a process of development which was continued by the subsequent councils of the Church, but became also the two great authorities to which those councils appealed.

Now the result of this process—the final definition of the doctrine of the Trinity—has hitherto been accepted by the Church as authoritative. Whereas it is nowadays often contended that this definition was expressed in the terms of a philosophy that we have outgrown, implying modes of thought that are no longer ours, and need not therefore be accepted by Christians of the present day.   Of course if we considered the councils of the Church to have been infallibly guided, this question would be foreclosed; but the Holy

[1] See Note I.

Spirit acts, as we have seen, through human instruments, and to that extent is limited by their capacity. We have learned to see this human element in the Bible, which we no longer regard therefore as verbally inspired. St. Paul himself draws an express distinction between his own speech and that of the Lord ; and when we read the history of the councils we are naturally prepared to find a similar situation in them. We have still therefore to consider the question on its own merits.

Let us take as a particular instance the employment of the term " Logos," or " Word," by St. John, as being at once the most striking innovation of language within the New Testament itself, and also the most profoundly influential upon subsequent thought. The term, as is well known, had both Greek and Jewish antecedents, which meet in Philo, and probably met not in Philo alone but in the general intellectual atmosphere of which he was a representative product. It is linked on the one hand with that poetic personification of the Wisdom or Word of the Lord which had grown increasingly articulate in later Jewish literature ; while on the other hand it mounts up through the immanent

or seminal reason of the Stoics to the Aristotelian
"forms" and the Platonic "ideas," and through
them again to various expressions that we find
used among the pre-Socratic thinkers, to describe
the rationality and order of the world.   St. John
would probably have thought more of the Jewish
affinities of the term, though in subsequent use
its Greek aspect became more prominent.   Now
it may be perfectly true that we now neither
personify wisdom nor hold the Platonic or Stoic
doctrine of ideas.   But this fact does not render
the term borrowed from them obsolete.   For the
truth is that the new faith fashioned a new thing
out of them, and that this new thing belonged
thenceforward not to them, but to itself.   We
may, to a certain extent, illustrate the case from
the use of the term "Messiah."   By adopting
that name Jesus Christ set His seal upon the
remarkable messianic expectations of the Jews,
as being in their essence true; while at the same
time He profoundly modified the form which
those expectations had assumed in the popular
mind.   And when "Christ" came to be preached
to races that had no Jewish antecedents, this was
virtually a new name with a novel connotation.   It
arose out of the Jewish past, but superseded and

transformed that past in the process of so doing ; showing Judaism to have been a preparation for a thing quite other than itself.   And there is an analogy in this to what took place in regard to the term " Logos."   Its adoption justified the Greek tendency to ascribe the rationality and harmony and order of the world to divine ideas ; and at the same time justified the Jewish tendency to describe those ideas in terms of personal agency, as the wisdom or word of the Lord.   But while thus implying that both these tendencies had been moving in a right direction, it carried them forward to a conclusion far other than their own ; and fashioned out of their language a new name for a new fact in the world's history—the Incarnation of the Son of God.   Thus the term was, so to speak, taken out of its old associations, to be employed thenceforward as a Christian symbol.   And its present use does not commit us to agreement with the theories once connected with its origin, but simply with the Christianity to which it now belongs.   Of course if we did not believe in the Incarnation the case would be totally different. For then it would be true, as is so often said, that the use of the term involved the importation into primitive Christianity of metaphysical ideas that were not its own, and are now, in that particular form, obsolete. But, given our belief in the Incarnation, the phrase involves no addition to that belief; but only an additional description of it, explanatory of its relation to the past. Its use is equivalent to saying, "This was the reality which Jewish and Greek philosophy had alike been feeling after; and whose appearance has now rendered all their bygone phases obsolete, while absorbing the elements of truth which they contained into its greater self." And as regards the retention of an ancient term to describe this fact; one might compare it to the preservation of an antique vestment for ceremonial use in church or court; it may be no longer in the fashion of the day, but for that very reason connotes continuity with the past, and therefore appropriately symbolises the inner identity of present with bygone life.

This then is a typical instance of what we mean by the development of Christian doctrine. It is not the inculcation of new articles of faith, but the translation of our original articles of faith into new language, to meet the requirements of a new situation. The existence, that is to say, of the Trinity and the significance of His own advent had, as we believe, been taught by Christ Himself.   And no addition was made to this revelation, nor could, as far as we can conceive, be made by any human interpreter.   At the same time, we believe this work of interpretation to have been guided by the Holy Spirit, leading men to a fuller insight into the meaning of the original revelation, and in that sense, to new truth.   " He shall lead you into all truth."   Our belief, of course, in this spiritual guidance, is itself an act of faith, and we cannot press its acceptance upon adverse critics ; though, for ourselves, we may consider it an essentially rational and probable faith, which we are fully justified in trusting.   We must further bear in mind that the operation of the Holy Spirit does not obliterate the individuality of its human instruments ; and we should infer from the gospels that there were very different degrees of intelli-gence among the apostles themselves.   It is quite possible therefore that they may have had very different degrees of insight into the full meaning of their own message.   Even St. Paul had made a great advance in his theological thought, between the date of his writing to the

Thessalonians and Galatians, and his writing to
the Colossians and Ephesians, while St. John, as
we believe, produced his "spiritual gospel" at
the end of an exceptionally long life-time, spent
in its meditation.   Even if we were disposed
therefore to concede as a fact—which is very far
from necessary—that some of the apostles had a
more limited conception than others, of the scope
of their new creed, this would be its explanation.
It would not imply that the revelation of Father,
Son, and Holy Spirit did not come from Christ
Himself, but merely that some minds were slower
than others to grasp all that this implied.   The
limitation would, in our modern use of the terms,
be subjective, not objective.   While if the guidance of the Holy Spirit was a reality, it would be
those who saw most, and not least, in the meaning of the original revelation, that would be its
truest interpreters.   It would be quite true therefore to regard St. Paul and St. John as the two
chief creators of Christian theology ; not, however,
in the sense of being its inventors, but of being
its first and most inspired exponents.

There was, indeed, at one time a tendency to
credit the apostles, as a whole, with too complete

an intelligence of the original deposit of faith (*depositum fidei*), combined with, and consequently obscured by, reserve in its communication (*disciplina arcani*). But such a theory is psychologically improbable, and does not tally with what we know of the facts. Development of apprehension and interpretation there certainly was, and must have been, from the moment that Christianity passed from its Jewish cradle, and, claiming to be a universal, a catholic religion, came into immediate contact with all the intellectual, religious, and social forces of the age. For its attitude to all these forces had of necessity to be defined; an attitude which involved the selective assimilation and consequent consecration of many current customs and institutions and ideas; together with the total rejection and condemnation of others. And in this gradual definition of its relation to contemporary thought the Church trusted to the guidance of the Holy Spirit. The belief in this guidance was, of course, as essential a part of Christianity as belief in the Incarnation itself; and therein lies the sufficient answer to all such critics as would draw negative deductions from the silence of Christ. The subjects to which Christ, as re-

ported in our fragmentary records, never alluded,
or on which He laid no emphasis, were, these
critics imagine, beyond His ken.   Thus He did
not foresee or intend the wider social and intellectual developments of His preaching.   But of
course such criticism is only part and parcel of
the general humanitarian view of Christ's person
and work.   In the view of the Church, on the
contrary, the work of Christ and the work of the
Spirit were co-essential factors in a religious life
which was one continuous indissoluble whole.
Christ had lived, and taught, and died, and risen,
and chosen and commissioned human agents to
continue His work in the world ; with the express
promise that, in so doing, they should be illumi-
nated and supported by His Spirit ; and thenceforth the presence of that Spirit became the very
constitutive condition of the Church.   "We,"
says Athanasius, "apart from the Spirit, are
strange and distant from God, and by the
participation of the Spirit we are knit into the
Godhead ; so that our being in the Father is not
ours, but the Spirit's, which is in us and abides
in us."[1]   And such has been the belief of the
Christian Church at every period of its history.

[1] *Contra Arian.* iii. 25.

Now, many modern critics, as we noticed above, in their reconstruction of Christian history, entirely ignore this continuous belief of the Church, or rather presuppose that it is untrue, by representing the development of doctrine, as well as of other modes of ecclesiastical life, as a perversion of the primitive gospel. As a rule, this view begins with a denial of the Incarnation, and regards the gospel as consisting solely in the ethical teaching of Christ, and not in His personality and claim upon the personal allegiance of the world. All that is not explicitly present in that teaching—as well as much, it must be added, that we believe it to contain—is then ruled out of court, as an accretion, an unwarranted addition, a corruption of the unsophisticated gospel, by the importation of alien elements from external sources, whereby it was converted into a sacramental system and a metaphysical creed.

We have already had occasion to allude to these and similar views in another connection; and merely refer to them here to point out their utter incompatibility with that belief in the guidance of the Holy Spirit which we are now considering, and their consequent antagonism to what has always been and always must be the Christian view of Christian history. It is important to notice this because the views in question are sometimes presented to us by men of great historical erudition, and we may consequently be liable in our just and due deference to their superior knowledge of historical facts to overlook the absolutely fundamental character of our divergence from their theory of history.

For they regard Christianity as transformed by a succession of external forces, whereas we regard those forces as themselves transformed by the internal, assimilative power of Christianity. In saying this, we refer to central and essential doctrines, such as that of the Trinity, with which we are at present concerned. For it is, of course, undeniably true that, in the lapse of ages, many alien customs and opinions crept into the popular practice and belief of Christians, with various degrees of sanction from those in authority. It is, moreover, very difficult to trace the exact date and origin of these infiltrations, or to say precisely at what point they passed from being useful appropriations into harmful corruptions. But still a broad line of demarcation can easily be drawn between all such cases, in which the

play of human motives, and those often ignorant
or superstitious motives, was obviously dominant,
and the deliberate, authoritative, conscious,
prayerful determination by the Church in council
of its own essential creed. And to group such
different things crudely together, as manifestations of a common process, merely because in
both cases there was an assimilation of ideas that
were of secular origin, is an utterly uncritical
way of writing history.

The Christian Church, then, emphatically believed its progressive formulation of doctrine to
have been guided by the Holy Spirit. But, at
the same time, it regarded this process as one of
interpretation, and not of innovation; the adaptation of its original creed to new intellectual
situations; the fuller explanation of its meaning
to new critics that arose; but never an addition
to that original creed—never the imposition of a
new article of faith.

This is nowhere better illustrated than in the
description that Athanasius gives of the Council
of Nicaea; the more so in that both he and the
council are identified with the introduction of a
conspicuously new piece of terminology into the
creed. Certain Arians, he explains, had held a

council, from which they had issued a creed with
its date affixed. On this Athanasius exclaims:
" Ursanius and Valens and Germinius and their
friends have done what never took place, never
was heard of among Christians. After putting
into writing what it pleased them to believe, they
prefix to it the consulate, and the month and the
day of the current year; thereby to show all
sensible men, that their faith dates, not from of
old, but now from the reign of Constantius."
With this he then goes on to contrast the procedure of the Council of Nicaea, which issued its
decrees without any date affixed; and first, in
making an ecclesiastical rule, to regulate the date
of Easter, employed the phrase, " It seemed good."
" But about the faith," he continues, " they wrote
not ' It seemed good,' but ' Thus believes the
Catholic Church,' and therefore they confessed
how they believed, in order to show that their
own sentiments were not novel, but Apostolical;
and what they wrote down was no discovery of
theirs, but is the same as was taught by the
Apostles."[1]

No words could make it plainer that Athanasius
and the Council of Nicaea conceived themselves

---

[1] Athan. *De Synodis*, i. 35.

to be guarding an heirloom, and not introducing any novelty by their definition. And though, of course, a new term cannot be used without some suggestion of new thought, this thought was clearly intended to be no more than an explanation of what Christians had previously believed. Such was undoubtedly the view taken of the formulation of the doctrine of the Trinity by those at whose hands it took place.

Briefly, to resume then what we have been saying : our belief in the Church's guidance by the Holy Spirit is co-ordinate with our belief in the Incarnation. But our confidence that any given action is the result of that guidance, while always an act of faith which we cannot expect opponents to share, must vary with the particular circumstances of the case. Now, in the cases of St. Paul and St. John we believe the element of divine guidance to have been, so to speak, at its maximum, and the element of human hindrance at its minimum. Consequently, we believe them to have been divinely guided in their selection of new language to throw new light upon the significance of the Incarnation, and therefore incidentally of the Trinity. This need not imply any theory of verbal inspiration or dictation.

The apostles chose their language in a human way, as human beings make their choice; but they were inspired men, and therefore they chose aright; they selected the best terms that the intellectual situation of the day afforded. And in so doing they took these terms out of their local and temporary context, and appropriated them to the expression of specifically Christian ideas; thereby rendering their use as permanent as the truths that were so expressed. St. Paul and St. John thus became the two chief pioneers of Christian theology; and the fathers who followed them believed themselves to be imitating this apostolic method, under the same spiritual guidance; with the sole object of further explaining what the apostles had taught. Thus the teaching of St. Paul and St. John constitutes a development of Christian doctrine, in the sense of being an inspired explanation of what was implicit, but never an addition to what was implicit in the teaching of Christ Himself.

CHAPTER VI

DOCTRINAL DEVELOPMENT IN THE FATHERS

WE saw in our last chapter that the terms used by St. Paul and St. John in speaking of the Trinity became by that use a part of the permanent terminology of the Church; whose employment commits us to no retention of any obsolete modes of thought, but simply to the Christian creed. We now pass on to consider whether the same may be said of their successors. And, in the first place, it may be well to call attention to the emphatic distinction which the Christian fathers continually draw between the knowledge of God's existence and the knowledge of His nature; and as this is not perhaps as generally known as it should be, a few typical quotations may be of use.

Clement of Alexandria quotes with approval the saying of Plato: " It is a difficult task to discover the Father and Maker of this universe;

and when we have found Him, it is impossible to declare Him to all; since expression, such as we use in other instruction, is here impossible." He then himself continues, " No one can rightly express Him wholly. For on account of His greatness He is ranked as the All, and is the Father of the Universe. Nor are any parts to be predicated of Him. For the One is indivisible —without form and name. And if we name it, we do not do so properly, terming it either the One, or the Good, or Mind, or Absolute Being, or Father, or God, or Creator, or Lord. We speak not as supplying His name; but for want we use good names, in order that the mind may have these as points of support. . . . It remains then that we understand the Unknown by divine grace, and by the word alone that proceeds from Him." While, even in union with Christ, " we only reach in a measure to the conception of God, knowing not what He is, but what He is not." [1]

To the same effect Origen writes : " According-ing to strict truth God is incomprehensible and inestimable. . . . For among all intelligent, that is, incorporeal beings, what is so superior to all

---

[1] Clem. Alex. *Strom.* v. 12 ; v. 11.

others—so unspeakably and incalculably superior —as God, whose nature cannot be grasped or seen by the power of any human understanding, even the purest and brightest?"[1]

And again, commenting on the above passage from Plato:

"For ourselves, we maintain that human nature is in no way able to seek after God, or to attain a clear knowledge of Him, without the help of Him whom it seeks. He makes Himself known to those who after doing all that their powers will allow, confess that they need help from Him, who discovers Himself to those whom He approves, in so far as it is possible for man and the soul still dwelling in the body to know God."[2]

Such is the language of the two first great philosophical theologians of the Church; and it is echoed a century later by Athanasius, who is popularly credited rather with confidence than diffidence of thought: "God, Maker of all and King of all, that has His being beyond our substance and human discovery . . . made through His own Word . . . the human race after His own image."[3]

---

[1] Orig. *De Prin.* I.   [2] Orig. *Contr. Cel.* vii. 42.
[3] Athan. *Contr. Gent.* 2.

"For God . . . since He is by nature invisible and incomprehensible, having His being beyond all created existence, . . . by His own Word gave the universe the order that it has, in order that since He is by nature invisible, men might be able to know Him at any rate by His works."[1]

"God . . . when He was making the race of man through His own Word, seeing the weakness of their nature, that it was not sufficient of itself to know its Maker, nor to attain to any idea at all of God, . . . gives them a share in His own image, . . . and makes them after His own image, and after His likeness; so that perceiving the image that is the Word of the Father they may be able through Him to attain to an idea of the Father."[2]

"Although it be impossible to comprehend what God is, yet it is possible to say what He is not."[3]

He is followed, again, by the great Cappadocian group—Basil and the two Gregories,—who all speak to the same effect.

"That God is, I know," says Basil; "but

---

[1] Athan. *Contr. Gent.* **2**. 35.   [2] *De Incar.* 11.

[3] *Ep. ad Monachos*, i. 2.

what His essence is, I hold to be above reason,
. . . faith is competent to know that God is, not
what He is." [1]   "With regard to the Creator of
the world," says Gregory of Nyssa, "we know
that He is, but deny not that we are ignorant of
the definition of His essence." [2]

And again, Gregory Nazianzen : "A theologian
among the Greeks has said in his philosophy
that to conceive God is difficult, to express Him
is impossible. . . . But I say that it is impossible
to express Him, and more impossible to conceive Him." [3]

And if we turn from the Greek to the Latin
fathers, we find similar language used ; notably
by Hilary of Poictiers, and Augustine, who both
wrote special treatises upon the Trinity.

Hilary writes : "There can be no comparison
between God and earthly things. . . . We must,
therefore, regard any comparison as helpful to
man rather than as descriptive of God, since it
suggests rather than exhausts the sense we seek.
. . . Neither the speech of man, nor the analogy
of human nature can give us a full insight into
the things of God.   The ineffable cannot submit

[1] Basil, *Adv. Eun.* i. 12.   [2] Greg. Nys. *Adv. Eun. orat.* 12.
[3] Greg. Naz. *Orat.* 34.

to the bounds and limitations of definition. . . .
God is a simple Being: we must understand
Him by devotion, and confess Him by reverence.
He is to be worshipped, not pursued by our
senses, for a conditioned and weak nature cannot
grasp with the guesses of its imagination the
mystery of an infinite and omnipotent nature. . . .
What presumption to suppose that words can
adequately describe His nature, when thought
is often too deep for words, and His nature
transcends even the conception of thought."[1]

The same thought continually recurs in
Augustine; who repeatedly speaks of the in-
adequacy of human language. " God must not,"
he says, "even be described as unspeakable
(*inaffabilis*), since by the very use of this term,
something is spoken. . . . Yet God, since nothing
can be worthily spoken of Him, accepts the
service of the human voice, and wills us to
rejoice in praising Him with words of our own."[2]
And again: " Our thoughts of God are truer
than our words, and His existence is truer than
our thoughts." (*Verius cogitatur Deus, quam
dicitur, et verius est quam cogitatur.*)[3] And again:

---

[1] Hil. *De Trin.* i. 19; iv. 2; ix. 72; xi. 44.
[2] Aug. *De Doct. Christ.* i. 6.   [3] *Id. De Trin.* vii. 7.

"We say three persons, not as being satisfied with this expression, but because we must use some expression." (*Non ut illud diceretur, sed ne taceretur.*)[1]

And again : "God is erroneously called substance, as a familiar synonym for essence, which is the truer and more proper term to use."[2]

These quotations are all, it will be seen, from leading thinkers of their day ; and they might be multiplied indefinitely from others of less note. But we will merely conclude them with a reference to John of Damascus, who, at the end of the patristic age gave a general summary of what was commonly held to be the orthodox belief of the Church. He writes as follows:—
"Neither do we know, nor can we tell what the essence of God is. . . . It is not, therefore, within our capacity to say anything about God, or even to think of Him, beyond the things which have been divinely revealed to us. It is plain that there is a God. But what He is in His essence and nature is absolutely incomprehensible and unknowable."[3]

Now the view thus described is not analogous

---

[1] Aug. *De Trin.* v. 9.   [2] *Ibid.* vii. 10.
[3] John Damas. *De F. O.* i. 2, 4.

to the modern agnostic position, as some of the language in which it is expressed might seem at first sight to imply. For the fathers attach the fullest value to the various arguments of natural theology for God's existence, and for our ability to know something of His character from the beauty and harmony and purpose in the world ; while Augustine, in especial, elaborates the ontological argument in various ways. But, further, and this is still more important, they were all profoundly religious men. Their religion was their life. They lived in the full conviction of their personal dependence upon God, and of their need for conscious communion with Him. And the same Augustine who says that God cannot even be named, says also : "Thou hast made us, O God, for Thyself, and our souls are restless till they rest in Thee."

The language, therefore, that we have been quoting, is not that of intellectual agnosticism, but of religious awe—awe intensified not by the thought of God's remoteness, but by the conviction and experience of His intimate nearness to men. It is thus much more akin to the reverential abstinence from the use of God's name, which characterised later Judaism, than to any sympathy with the Neo-Platonic exaggeration of His transcendence, — His aloofness from the world.

Now it is plain that the men who habitually used such language as this would be the last to attempt independent speculation on the divine nature. And this is precisely what we find to be the case. Their constant profession is, as we saw above, to preserve the apostolic tradition; and their constant appeal for its interpretation is to Scripture; while their main charge against heretical opinions is that of being innovations. "For, what our fathers have delivered," says Athanasius, "this is truly doctrine; and this is truly the token of doctors, to confess the same thing with each other, and to vary neither from themselves, nor from their fathers."[1]

It will suffice for our present purpose to quote one or two of the many theologians who contributed to the gradual formulation of the doctrine of the Trinity; and of these none were more prominent nor more important than Origen and Athanasius; the former being specially connected with the thought of the eternal generation of the Son; and the latter with the final adoption

[1] Athan. *De Decretis*. ii. 4.

of the term "consubstantial" by the Church.
Let us see how they worked.

"We have always held," says Origen, "that
God is the Father of His only begotten Son,
who was born indeed of Him, and derives from
Him what He is, but without any beginning. . . .
John says, in the beginning of his gospel, when
defining God by a special definition to be the
Word, 'And God was the Word, and this was in
the beginning with God.'   Let him, then, who
assigns a beginning to the Word or Wisdom of
God, take care that he be not guilty of impiety
against the Unbegotten Father Himself, seeing
that he denies that He had always been a Father,
and had generated the Word."   And after en-
larging on this topic, he continues : " Let us now
ascertain how those statements which we have
advanced are supported by the authority of holy
Scripture.   The Apostle Paul says, that the only
begotten Son is 'the image of the invisible God,'
and 'the first-born of every creature.'   And
when writing to the Hebrews, he says of Him,
that He is 'the brightness of His glory, and the
express image of His Person.'"[1]   And, again :

"'The Son of God, the first-born of all crea-

---

[1] Orig. *De Prin.* i. 2 ; ii. 3-5.

tion,' although He seemed recently to have become incarnate, is not by any means on that account recent. For the holy Scriptures know Him to be the most ancient of all the works of creation; for it was to Him that God said, regarding the creation of man, ' Let us make man in our image, after our likeness.' " [1]   And, again, in answer to an objection of Celsus :

" We do not ' reverence beyond measure one who has but lately appeared' as though He did not exist before; for we believe Himself when He says ' Before Abraham was, I am.' "

" We have learned who the Son of God is, and know that He is ' the brightness of His glory and the express image of His person.' " [2]

Notice that these passages, which all bear upon the eternal generation of the Son, constantly refer to Scripture, and in this they are typical of Origen's whole method. At the end of his treatise on first principles he writes :

" As it is not sufficient in the discussion of matters of such importance to entrust the decision to the human senses, and to the human understanding . . . we must, in order to establish the positions which we have laid down, adduce the

Orig. *C. Cels.* v. 37.   [2] *De Prin.* iv. 1.

testimony of Holy Scripture. And that this testimony may produce a sure and unhesitating belief . . . it seems necessary to show . . . that the Scriptures themselves are divine, that is, were inspired by the Spirit of God."[1]

Accordingly, he is before all things biblical; his whole atmosphere is biblical; he leans more on mystical interpretation, at times, than we should do, and draws arguments from the sapiential books, where we should perhaps not draw more than illustrations; but his main emphasis is, precisely as our own would be, upon St. Paul and St. John. Thus we feel, as we read him, that with all his Greek learning, he is moving wholly within the current of the Jewish and Christian tradition—a point which is well brought out when Celsus alleges the superiority of Plato, whereon he exclaims:

"Observe now the difference between the fine phrases of Plato respecting the 'chief good' and the declarations of our prophets regarding the 'light' of the blessed; and notice that the truth as it is contained in Plato concerning this subject, did not at all help his readers to attain to a pure worship of God, not even himself who could

---

[1] Orig. *De Prin*. iv. 1.

I

philosophise so grandly about 'the chief good,' whereas the simple language of the Holy Scriptures has led to their honest readers being filled with a divine spirit." [1]

Origen had a profound influence on some of the greatest of his successors—as notably upon the three great Cappadocians — Basil, and the two Gregories,—and thus upon the general theology of the Church.   But, before making further comment on him, we will pass to Athanasius, who was the leading spirit in the Council of Nicaea, at which the term " consubstantial " or " co - essential " (ὁμοούσιος) was adopted, and he subsequently wrote a letter in its defence. Here again we meet with the same scriptural tone.

" We have learned from divine Scripture, that the Son of God is the very Word and Wisdom of the Father.   For the Apostle says, ' Christ the power of God, and the Wisdom of God.' And John, after saying, ' And the Word was made flesh,' at once adds, 'and we saw His glory, the glory as of the only begotten of the Father, full of grace and truth.' . . . If, then, they (the Arians) deny Scripture, they are at once aliens

---

[1] Orig. *C. Cel.* vi. 5.

to their name. . . . But if they agree with us that the sayings of the Scripture are divinely inspired, let them dare to say openly what they think in secret." [1]

But the Arian party charged the Council with the introduction of unscriptural language ; whereon Athanasius explains that the Council "wished to do away with the irreligious phrases of the Arians, and to use instead the acknowledged words of the Scripture that the Son is not from nothing, but 'from God.'" Finding, however, that this expression was misinterpreted by their opponents—

"The fathers . . . were forced to express more distinctly the sense of the words 'from God.' Accordingly they wrote 'from the essence of God,' in order that 'from God' might not be considered common and equal, in the Son, and in things originate, but that all others might be acknowledged as creatures, and the Word alone as from the Father." [2]

"It behoved," say his opponents, "as regards our Lord . . . to state from the Scriptures what is there written of Him, and not to introduce non-scriptural expressions." "Yes," he answers,

---

[1] Athan. *De Decr.* 15.   [2] *Ib.* 19.

" it behoves, say I too; for the tokens of truth
are more exact as drawn from Scripture than
from other sources; but . . . the irreligion of
Eusebius and his fellows, compelled the Bishops,
as I said before, to publish more distinctly the
terms which overthrew their irreligion." [1]

He further quotes in the same letter a catena
of authorities mounting up to Origen, of whom
he says :

" Concerning the everlasting co-existence of
the Word with the Father, and that He is not
of another essence or subsistence, but proper to
the Father's, as the Bishops in the Council said,
you may hear again from the labour - loving
Origen. . . . See, we are proving that this view
has been transmitted from father to father . . .
that which from the beginning those who were
eye-witnesses and ministers of the Word have
handed down to us." [2]

Again, in another letter to the Bishops of
Egypt, he writes as follows :—

" The New Testament arose out of the Old,
and bears witness to the Old. . . . Thus Paul
was an apostle of the Gospel 'which God promised afore, by His prophets in the Holy

---

[1] Athan. *De Decr*. 32.   [2] *Ib*. 27.

Scriptures'; and our Lord Himself said, 'Ye search the Scriptures, for they are they which testify of Me.' How then shall they confess the Lord unless they first search the Scriptures which are written concerning Him?"

"Since Holy Scripture is of all things most sufficient for us, therefore recommending to those who desire to know more of these matters, to read the Divine Word, I pass on." [1]

So far we have been considering the doctrine of the Son. And the case is similar with the doctrine of the Spirit. The operation of the Holy Spirit was, as we have seen, part of the apostolic tradition; but His personality and divinity are not as explicitly stated in Scripture as in the case of the Son. This fact led to a great deal of hesitation and uncertainty with many of the fathers, when the formulation of their doctrine became necessary. And even at as late a date as when Gregory Nazianzen was appointed to the see of Constantinople we find him saying, that some men regard the Holy Spirit 'as an energy; others think that He is a creature; others again that He is God; while others do not know which of these opinions to adopt,

---

[1] Athan. *Ad Episc. Aegypt.* 4.

out of reverence for the Scriputres (αἰδοῖ τῆς γραφῆς)." [1]   The last point is noteworthy as show- ing how entirely the whole question was regarded as one of scriptural interpretation.   And this is nowhere better brought out than by St. Hilary, in his treatise on the Trinity.   Speaking of some who held heretical opinions, more especially on this point, he says : " Their treason involves us in the difficult and dangerous position of having to make a definite pronouncement, beyond the statements of Scripture, upon this grave and abstruse matter.   The Lord said that the nations were to be baptised in the name of the Father, and of the Son, and of the Holy Ghost.   The words of the faith are clear ; the heretics do their utmost to involve the meaning in doubt.   We may not on this account add to the appointed form, yet we must set a limit to their license of interpretation. . . . But the subject is in- exhaustible.   I can see no limit to my venture of speaking concerning God in terms more pre- cise than He Himself has used.   He has as- signed the names—Father, Son, and Holy Ghost —which are our information of the divine nature. Words cannot express, or feeling embrace, or

[1] Greg. Naz. *Orat. Theol.* v. 5.

reason apprehend the results of enquiry carried further; all is ineffable, unattainable, incomprehensible." [1]

And again in the prayer with which he concludes his treatise : " Thy Holy Spirit, as the Apostle says, searches and knows Thy deep things, and as intercessor for me speaks to Thee words I could not utter. . . . Nothing, except what belongs to Thee penetrates into Thee ; nor can the agency of a power foreign and strange to Thee measure the depth of Thy boundless majesty . . . Paul . . . thought that the description was sufficient, when he called Him Thy Spirit. With these men, peculiarly Thine elect, I will think in these matters . . . I will not trespass beyond that which human intellect can know about Thy Holy Spirit, but simply declare that He is Thy Spirit." [2]

The same thing is briefly expressed by another, less-known writer as follows :—

" It is sufficient for the faithful to know that while the Son is begotten, the Spirit proceeds from the Father ; and that we use the very words which the divine Scripture willed us to use ; . . .

---

[1] Hil. *De Trin.* ii. 5.　　　　[2] *Ib.* xii. 55, 56.

but of what sort or kind that procession may be, it is permitted to none to know."[1]

It was in this temper that the Synod of Constantinople (A.D. 381) declared the Holy Spirit to be "the Lord and Giver of Life, that proceedeth from the Father, that with the Father and the Son together is worshipped and glorified, that spake by the prophets."

Our quotations have grown so numerous as to need some apology. But quotation is the only means of creating the kind of impression that we wish to convey. Yet even so, no amount of quotations can adequately show the scale and proportion of scriptural influence on the fathers. We read page after page, chapter after chapter, treatise after treatise, father after father; and meet everywhere the same constant reference to both Old and New Testaments; the same transparent intention to interpret, and never do more than interpret the latter, for dogmatic purposes, in what is believed to be its original and traditional sense.

We have quoted a few only of these leaders in the movement by which Christian theology was in process of being defined; but they may fairly

---

[1] Nicetas (Migne, *P. L.* lii. 856).

be taken as typical, in their method, of the whole patristic attitude towards the faith.   What kind of development, then, do we here find?   A very profound and erroneous one indeed, if we disbelieve the doctrine of the Trinity to start with. But if, on the contrary, we believe the sufficient germ of that doctrine to have come from Christ Himself, there is no other development in the fathers than we found in St. Paul and St. John; no other than they themselves explicitly profess; a development—that is to say, of authoritative interpretation and expression, but no addition to the articles of faith.   In other words, we find a development of doctrine, or teaching, in the sense of a new mode of stating the old truth; but not in the sense of the invention or proclamation of any new truth; and though this distinction may sound subtle it is profoundly real.   And then as regards the new form of expression, the case is precisely similar to that of St. John.   " Consubstantial " and " co-essential " are Greek terms, fashioned out of the current philosophical language of the day.   But their use commits us to no acceptance of any obsolete system of thought. People sometimes speak vaguely about Christian dogma having been involved with Greek metaphysics; much as if it were something parallel to being involved with the Ptolemaic astronomy or any other ancient theory which the world has now outgrown. But, in fact, nothing of the kind is the case. The terms in question were simply adopted as those best calculated to express the specifically Christian idea that Jesus Christ is really God. They do not even carry with them any particular theory of what "essence" or "substance" may be; as is plain from the fact that those very men who insisted on the use of the term "co-essential" insisted equally, as we saw above, upon our utter inability to know what the essence of God is. The words, in short, as employed by the Christian fathers, were stripped of any alien connotation, and simply utilised to denote a particular point of Christian belief; and they are therefore as applicable now as ever, if we retain the patristic creed.

The various forms of Gnosticism, though they contain too much of the Oriental fairy-tale to be called strictly philosophical, still show us the kind of thing that would have resulted from the incorporation of Greek ideas into Christianity, as distinct from the mere utilisation of Greek words. Whereas, in sharp contrast to all this the whole process of patristic definition lies open before us; and we can plainly see that at no point did any substantially Greek influence come in. On the contrary, the fathers are full, from beginning to end, of the thought that Christianity was not only the lineal descendant, but also the climax and completion of Judaism. We are reminded, as we read them, of a jesse window; by the way in which one continuous development is traced through successive stages from its earliest Jewish root. The various theophanies, or divine manifestations, in the Old Testament are ascribed to the Word who finally became incarnate. The passage from the Hebrews is quoted on Moses preferring the reproach of Christ. The intrinsic superiority of the Jewish Scriptures to other literature is a favourite theme. While what we should call the inspiration of Plato—and this is almost more significant—is urged as evidence that he must have been acquainted with the writings of Moses. The Jewish revelation has expanded with the advent of Christ, to embrace the world, and become the Catholic Church; but it remained in origin exclusively Jewish; and the fathers gloried in the fact. We should expect them, therefore, to be the last men who would consciously incorporate Hellenic elements in their creed; nor did they, as regards the central doctrine we are considering, unconsciously admit them.

The fact is that the action of environment is often exaggerated; and it has been so in the present case. In biology we know that the nature of their environment modifies organisms; but it only does so by stimulating their internal energy to respond to itself. Environment does not and cannot create, but it elicits new characteristics in a plant or animal; while the creative capacity comes from within. And the growth of the early Church both in doctrine and practice was analogous to this. It possessed an intense individuality, an intense vitality, an intense identity of its own. And when brought into contact with Greek and Roman life and thought, it lost none of this identity by the fact; but only appropriated what was best and truest in the surrounding life and thought to its own purposes; thus utilising the alien environment as a means of increased self-realisation. At a later date than that of which we are speaking this would not, of course, be equally true. Corrupt and ignorant times came, and with them foreign ideas and practices crept in.   But during the ages when the doctrine of the Trinity was in process of formulation, and in respect of that process, it is true to say that the fathers never intended to do more than transmit the apostolic tradition which they had received, more especially from St. Paul and St. John ; and that in their method of doing so, they relied upon the continuance of the promised guidance of the Holy Ghost.

CHAPTER VII

OMNIA EXEUNT IN MYSTERIUM

THE foregoing chapters have briefly summarised our reasons for retaining the traditional Christian belief that the vital essence of what came to be called the doctrine of the Trinity was revealed by Christ Himself as God Incarnate. And, of course, in retaining this position we are influenced by all the complex and cumulative arguments which favour the Incarnation, and therefore traverse the criticism that starts with the assumption of its incredibility. Further, the same reasons which predispose us to believe in the Incarnation prepare us also to recognise the continued action of the Holy Spirit in its interpretation. Hence we believe the subsequent definition of the doctrine, though the work of fallible human agents, to have been divinely guided in a right direction. And to this guidance we would attribute the substantial agreement that is to be found, in the midst and in spite of the infinitely various shades of personal opinion. Such leading theologians, for example, as Athanasius and Augustine, differ widely in their exposition of the doctrine. Yet both are equally anxious to avoid Tritheism on the one hand, the belief in three gods; and Sabellianism on the other, the belief in three aspects of one God; both, that is to say, have the Trinity in Unity really at heart. It has been said indeed, with probable truth, that no two men have the same conception of God; and this would perhaps be truer still of the Trinity; whence the various shades of opinion that are disclosed in the history of its definition. Indeed it was this very variety that necessitated the definition. For individuals continually tended to translate the Christian revelation into terms of their own; to rationalise, to explain it; to bring it more within human comprehension, as they thought. And as against this tendency the desire of the Church, as we have seen above, was to transmit the revelation, as it had been revealed. For a revelation of God to man must, of necessity, be partial. We can see into it, but we cannot see around it; we view its earthly, but not its heavenly side. Hence

the clearest revelation remains framed in mystery,
the illimitable mystery of the Being of God.   We
cannot go beyond what has been revealed, or
infer from it more than has been revealed, and
if it is our duty to transmit it, we must transmit
it as nearly as possible in its original form.   This
then was the object of dogmatic definition ; to
transmit the tradition of what the original revelation had been taken by Christians to mean.   We
have traced the efforts of the fathers to be true
to this object ; and if we believe in the original
revelation as a fact, we cannot help believing
further, that those to whom it was made would be
guided to interpret it aright.

It accords with this that the whole spirit of
their definition should be largely negative, as has
been so often pointed out—a refusal, that is, to
allow explanations to be given of what could not
be explained.   For the purpose of the Christian
Church was practical ; to enable its members to
realise their sonship to the Father, their fellowship with the Son, and their sanctification by
the Spirit, with all that this involved.   And the
doctrine of the Trinity was to ensure the permanent possibility of this realisation ; to enable
each successive generation to enter afresh into

its power. Athanasius and Augustine did not claim a greater knowledge of God than that of St. Paul and St. John, because they formulated common knowledge in more technical terms. But each generation needed training to live by the same knowledge, and dogma was the condition of the sameness. It has the inevitable aridity of all abstract statement, and bears no more likeness to its Object than a botanical description bears to a lily or a rose, or a musical score to a symphony of sound. But it keeps the existence of that Object before us; that we may each in our day enter afresh into the experience of its living power, and so hand the symbol of that power on—the grace of our Lord Jesus Christ, and the love of God, and the fellowship of the Holy Ghost. And it is on this ground that we still claim validity for the Patristic definition; the ground that it represents no more than the spiritually guided interpretation of what Christ Himself had taught His disciples. Terms like "personality" and "substance" may have somewhat changed their connotation with the progress of the ages; but not in a way to make their present significance inconsistent with their past, of which it is no more than the natural development.

K

And we can still employ them to express the doctrine which the Church has always taught— the Trinity in Unity which on the one hand is not Sabellianism, nor Tritheism on the other.

This doctrine, in the form in which we believe it to have been revealed by Christ, is quite distinct from the many artificially arranged triads that we meet with, like that of Brahma, Siva, and Vishnu in India; and also from the divine families like that of Osiris, Isis, and Horus in Egypt; while it still less resembles the trinity of reason, the creator, and the world, which was read into Plato by a post-Christian commentator; and is altogether earlier than Neo-Platonism, whose founder, Ammonius Sarcas, it should be remembered, had originally been educated by Christian parents as a Christian. Nor again did it originate in any of the psychological analyses by which it was subsequently illustrated. In a word, it was not invented but revealed. "Ye have not chosen Me, but I have chosen you."

On the other hand, if the doctrine is true—if there is Trinity in that Godhead by which the world and mankind were created, we should expect to find adumbrations of it present in creation, as we believe divine attributes to be reflected in the beauty and order and purpose of the world, and in the justice and love and holiness of man. When therefore we see that the unit of human society, the family, is essentially a trinity of father, mother, and child, and that there is a psychological trinity involved in the very structure of the human mind, we may well regard these things as the created reflections of a Triune Creator, not causes that suggested an untrue doctrine, but effects of the fact that it is true.

Intellectual objections to this doctrine on the ground of its mystery have been often urged. It has been thought to import fresh difficulty into the already difficult conception of God. But is this so? Can this be so? Can anything increase that difficulty? We have already seen how unanimously the fathers, with their firm convictions of God's existence, confess their utter inability, apart from revelation, to conceive His nature. And this same inability lies at the root of our modern Agnosticism. Natural theology has but two sources of information, the material world and the mind of man. And both are baffling. While they emphatically reveal a Creator, they seem also at times to conceal Him. Our imagination is paralysed in the effort to conceive a Being whose infinite power guides the stars in their stupendous courses, while His infinitesimal care directs the sea-shell's curves, and paints the insect's wing. And while the order, the bene- ficence, the beauty of creation are leading our thoughts in one direction, we are arrested by the spectacle of noxious animals and "nature red in tooth and claw"—the universal life of prey.

> Conjecture of the worker by the work :
> Is there strength there ? enough : intelligence ?
> Ample : but goodness in a like degree ?
> Not to the human eye in the present state.[1]

Nor, as we have already had occasion to point out in another context, is the spectacle of human history less perplexing. When we reflect on the long preparation of the earth for man's inheri- tance, or the marvellous mechanism of his body, and still more wonderful powers of his mind, we are led to expect great things of him ; but we do not find them ; sin and sorrow, failure and frustration everywhere take their place.

> What is the course of the life
> Of mortal man on the earth ?—
> Most men eddy about

---

[1] Browning, *Ring and the Book*.

> Here and there—eat and drink,
> Chatter and love and hate,
> Gather and squander, are raised
> Aloft, are hurl'd in the dust,
> Striving blindly, achieving
> Nothing ; and then they die—
> Perish ;—and no one asks
> Who or what they have been,
> More than he asks what waves,
> In the moonlit solitude mild
> Of the midmost Ocean, have swell'd,
> Foam'd for a moment, and gone.[1]

Man's equipment is out of all proportion to his achievement, and suggests, at least in its superficial aspect, a design that has failed.   There are times with most of us when we could echo the language of Tennyson's dying Arthur—

> I found Him in the shining of the stars,
> I mark'd Him in the flowering of His fields,
> But in His ways with men I find Him not.[2]

These difficulties do not annul the positive arguments of natural theology, but they seriously obscure and complicate the picture that it presents ; and in the face of them we cannot claim to attain, by the light of nature, any clear and consistent conception of God.   There are thinkers at the present day who advocate pluralism, which

---

[1] M. Arnold, "Rugby Chapel."   [2] Tennyson, *Idylls of the King*.

would be equivalent to a philosophical reconstruction of polytheism. While others, again,
incline to recur, as Mill in the last century antici-
pated, to a dualism of antagonistic principles,
like the Persians of old. We may fairly conclude,
therefore, that, apart from Christianity and the
systems of thought which Christianity has influenced, the modern is very little in advance of
the ancient world. It is wholly untrue, therefore, to suppose that natural theology supplies
us with any standard of intelligibility or clearness by which we can test the Christian conception of God to its disadvantage. And in the
present day we may go further and say the same
of physical science. There was a time when
physical science, because it dealt with things
that we can see and touch and verify by sensible
experience, tended to claim superiority to the
intangible conceptions of metaphysics. But such a
claim can nowadays no longer be maintained. For
the further scientific men pursue their enquiries
into the ultimate nature of energy and matter, the
more remote do their theories become, not only
from the capability of experimental verification,
but even from the possibility of imaginative
conception. The various speculations on the

constitution of that ether, which is the fundamental postulate of modern physics, are a sufficient
illustration of this fact.　All phenomena—matter,
energy, electricity—are supposed to depend on
this ether; yet it cannot itself be otherwise described than by symbolical terms, which even
baffle our ordinary powers of conception, and may
still, it is admitted, be remote from the truth.
Here as elsewhere *omnia exeunt in mysterium,*
as the schoolmen said of old,—" all things end in
mystery,"—when we try to think them out.　Thus
science, which can weigh and measure and test
what we call phenomena, things that fall within
the region of sensible experience, so surely, can
supply no correspondingly clear conception of
the ultimate conditions on which that experience
depends.　It can utilise the laws of gravitation,
but cannot explain them.　It can employ electricity for a hundred purposes, but cannot tell what
electricity is.　Hence the man of science can no
longer afford to criticise the metaphysician for failing to conform to his standard of clearness, since he
himself loses all standard of clearness on approaching the confines of ultimate things.　Thought
must then for both alike become symbolical, hint-
ing at realities that it cannot adequately grasp.

No system of thought, therefore, can reasonably claim for its ultimate conceptions, any greater simplicity or clearness than the Christian ; for all, in the last resort, are wrapped in mystery alike. But we go further, and claim for the Christian conception of God, that it throws at least more light than others, even upon the "obstinate questionings" of intellectual speculation. That conception, as we have seen, was in no wise of speculative origin ; but simply due to the practical revelation by Christ of the Father, Son, and Spirit ; while the express intention of those who further defined it was to keep this "revealed" and "practical" character in view. This is historic fact that we cannot allow to be gainsaid. Yet, when confronted with human philosophy, the doctrine of the Trinity assumes a speculative value ; for it seems at least to indicate the direction in which the solution of some of our most perplexing problems may lie.

There has always been a double difficulty, one metaphysical and the other moral, in conceiving the absoluteness of God. A person is primarily and essentially a self-conscious subject ; and if we are to think of God as personal, He too must be, metaphysically speaking, a subject. But a subject

means a subject of experience, one who under-
goes experience, or for whom experience exists,
and therefore implies as his correlative an object
or objects of experience. And the metaphysician
is compelled to ask, what can this object be, in
the case of God? For if we suppose the universe to be this object, we must either regard
God as dependent for His realisation upon something which is other than Himself; and, in that
case, His absoluteness vanishes; He ceases to be
God: or we must view the universe as a mode
of Himself, in a way that leads to Pantheism, in
which personality is lost. We are driven, therefore, to the conclusion that, if there be an
absolute, eternal subject, He must have a
correspondingly absolute object, an eternal
experience, if His proper absoluteness is to be
maintained.

Now, any one unacquainted with the history of
thought might easily suppose that we are here
describing an intellectual situation, which really
arose out of reflection on the doctrine of the
Trinity, in order then to show how that doctrine suits it; and are, therefore, merely arguing
in a circle. But, of course, the very converse
is the case. The difficulty in question was

first discussed by Plato and Aristotle, as
pure metaphysicians, long before the Christian
era. And Aristotle, who, in his aristocratic
Greek way, views philosophic contemplation as
the noblest occupation, and therefore the most
appropriate to God—proceeds to ask what does
God contemplate, since He cannot be adequately
occupied with relative and finite things; and
concludes that He must contemplate Himself
(νοεῖ ἄρα ἑαυτόν), or, as we should say, be His
own Object. This conception of divine existence
is thus reached by Aristotle, the "master of
those who know," as a necessity of pure thought.
But he does not develop it further; nor had he
the means. When, therefore, philosophic thinkers
who had been trained in the atmosphere of the
Greek schools became Christian, it was natural
that they should find in the doctrine of the
Trinity an intellectual illumination. For, like
the telescopic discovery of a star, which mathe-
matical calculations have already prophesied, it
was a revelation at once of the possibility and
the reality of what philosophy had said must be;
—relations in the Godhead, which do not disturb
Its absoluteness, because they are internal to
Itself. At the same time, the thinkers in ques-

tion were clearly conscious, as we have shown above, that their doctrine had not come to them by the way of philosophy but of revelation; and that the primary purpose of that revelation was not philosophic, but practical and moral. They in no way, therefore, distorted their religion into a philosophy or confused its sharp outlines with an intellectual haze. Men like Origen and Athanasius were plain and simple Christians before all things. But, because they were also thinkers, they could not but see what a new light their creed threw upon a recognised perplexity of thought.

But metaphysic, after all, is ever an unpopular subject; and to say that a doctrine has metaphysical value is almost to disparage it in ordinary eyes. We will turn, therefore, to what is really only a particular case of the abstract difficulty above mentioned, but as being a particular case, is somewhat more concrete and obvious; that is our difficulty in conceiving the moral absoluteness of God. We think of God as absolutely holy; of holiness as being, one might almost say, His most essential and divine characteristic. This is the lesson which the Jews so laboriously learned from their prophets, and which once learned has become the permanent possession of the world. " God hath spoken in His holiness," " I am the Lord thy God, the Holy One of Israel thy saviour." " The Lord is Holy in all His works." " The Lord of Hosts is His name, the Holy One of Israel." " They have no rest day and night, saying, Holy, holy, holy, is the Lord God Almighty." Familiar and full of meaning as these words have become to us, if we ask a simple theist, that is, a monistic or unitarian theist, what they mean, he is landed in a difficulty at once. For it is, of course, from their human application that we borrow the terms " holiness " and " righteousness " to apply them to God ; and man is essentially a social being, whose moral character is mainly determined by his various relations to society. There are, indeed, certain personal or self - regarding virtues, as they are called, consisting chiefly in habits of propriety and self-control ; but these are rather preliminary to the true moral life, which involves relations with others ;—relations of truthfulness, justice, benevolence, service, sympathy, self - sacrificing love. It is the old story of the subject requiring an object, recurring in the moral sphere. The moral life, then, as we know it, being essentially a social life, the question arises—how can we apply moral attributes to God? Are they only applicable in virtue of His relation to men, or other created beings? Do they merely mean that He is just, and benevolent, and loving to His creatures? In that case God's righteousness would only be potential, apart from His creation, and need the existence of the creature before it could become actual or real. But this is equivalent to saying that He is dependent upon the creature for His realisation of those very attributes which we most inevitably regard as essentially divine; those attributes which especially constitute for us the very meaning of the word God; and thus His moral absoluteness vanishes. This is no fanciful difficulty: Aristotle recognised it, in the place to which we referred above, and declined to apply moral attributes to God on the express ground of their relative and contingent nature; with the result that His divine being, while retaining absoluteness, remains coldly metaphysical, in lonely contemplation of Himself alone. Nor is this all. Not only does our conception of God become confused and unintelligible, but our morality at the same time loses its essential basis; for in all the

nobler ethical systems of the world, that basis
has been the divine character. Man's duty, said
Plato long ago, "is to grow as like as may be to
God; and that means to become holy, and just,
and wise." And all the highest moralists after
him have thus grounded man's goodness in that
of God. There have, it is true, been theologians
now and again who, like Duns Scotus, have
attributed moral distinctions to the mere fiat of
the divine will, maintaining that goodness is
simply good because God so wills it to be. But
this has never been more than an eccentric
opinion; nor does it contain really much meaning when analysed; since we cannot really think
of God's will as anything else than the expression
of His essential nature. "The essence of God,
and His volition," as St. Thomas puts it, "are
the same."

The agnostic, of course, who considers God
unknowable, and the empirical moralist who bases
ethics upon utility, happiness, or the like, are
both unaffected by the above-menticned difficulties; but they constitute a serious problem to
the strictly unitarian theist, if he really attempts
to think out his creed. But the doctrine of the
Trinity, of co-eternal persons within the God-

head, throws new light upon the subject, however much it may be a "light that no man can approach unto." For this doctrine enables us to think of God, as, if the term be guarded from any tritheistic connotation, a social being, or society; or, to use what is perhaps safer language, as existing in a mode of which the family, the unit of human society, is the created and faint reflection. And so it becomes possible to conceive of the various relations which constitute righteousness, and especially of love, in which they culminate, as internal to the Godhead; and of holiness, therefore, as the eternal, essential characteristic of God; and the consequent source of that "categorical imperative," that awful, unqualified, absolute authority with which the moral law addresses the conscience of mankind. "Ye shall therefore be holy: for I am holy." "Be ye therefore perfect, even as your Father which is in heaven is perfect."

This question of divine holiness is, indeed, only a particular instance or aspect of what we must mean, what we cannot help meaning by divine personality. If we are to think of God as personal at all, we must of necessity involve some kind of plurality in the conception; for personality implies this. A person is as essentially a social, as he is an individual, being; he cannot be realised, he cannot become his true self, apart from society; and personality having this plural implication, solitary personality is a contradiction in terms.[1]

Our object has been to indicate that, so far from increasing our intellectual perplexities, the doctrine of the Trinity tends rather to their relief. At the same time, when saying this, one must finally repeat that we should shrink from following even what seem to be necessities of human thought, into the high and awful region of which we have been speaking; were it not for our conviction that a revelation of that region has been made to us. The Christian Church, as we have seen, first accepted that revelation in its practical simplicity, as a message to the heart and will; and only by degrees discovered its incidental illumination of the world of thought. In like manner we only venture to recur to that illumination in the present day, because we believe it to have reached us, in the first instance, independently of human invention, as a message from above.

[1] See Note 2.

CHAPTER VIII

PRACTICAL POWER OF THE DOCTRINE

WATERLAND, the great defender of the Trinitarian doctrine in the eighteenth century, maintains, first, that it is sufficiently clear; and, secondly, that it is sufficiently practical. And though the form of his arguments was better adapted to his own generation than it would be to ours, we may well borrow from him this distinction; and, having already touched upon the point of clearness, proceed to consider the practicality of our doctrine; in the sense of the practical effect which it is calculated to exercise, and, as a matter of history, has exercised upon the world. Waterland well strikes the key-note of the matter in his opening sentence:

"A right knowledge of God, and a practice conformable to it . . . are not *speculative* or *indifferent* matters, but matters properly practical and of infinite concernment. If *religious* practice in any measure depends upon a previous *knowledge* of *God* (as undoubtedly it does), then certainly, for the like reason, the *perfection* of that practice depends upon the perfection of such knowledge. A general and confused notion of God may produce as general and confused rules of demeanour to Him; while a more particular and explicit apprehension of the Deity will, of course, produce a more particular and explicit service."[1]

Now, it will hardly be denied in any quarter that the conception of God, which we find among the Jews after their exile, was the highest attained by any race in the pre-Christian world; its nearest competitor, the Persian, being less truly spiritual, and further hampered by dualism. And this conception resulted in the correspondingly high and spiritual morality which is reflected for us to-day in the later Psalms.

It was to this, then, that the doctrine of the Trinity in Unity lineally succeeded. It was proclaimed in its essence, as we have seen reason to believe, by Him in whom the long line of Jewish prophets culminated and ceased; and was, in this regard, the last word of the prophetic

[1] Waterland, *Doctrine of the Trinity*, chap. ii.

revelation.   It thus arose out of the most practical religion of the past; the religion with the
clearest conviction of divine holiness and human
duty.   And, in its turn, it surpassed Judaism in
both these points.   Its revelation of God, however mysterious, was fuller and more concrete;
and its correlative illumination of human duty
more complete.

In saying this we cannot, of course, really
separate the Trinity from the Incarnation.   For
the existence of the Trinity is the presupposition,
the necessary condition of the Incarnation; and
the practicality of the doctrine, its bearing on
practice, essentially consists in this fact; that it
enables us, in a measure, to conceive the possibility of the Incarnation.   It is in and through
the Incarnation that we have attained to our
deepest knowledge of the relations between God
and man; and all the intense practicality, which
belongs to our belief in the Incarnation, must
therefore attach also to the conception of God,
which lies at the base of that belief.   Hence the
total effect upon the world of the doctrine of the
Incarnation is equally and inseparably the effect
of the doctrine of the Trinity.

When now we say that this doctrine increased

our knowledge of God, we must remember that it is not of its abstract expression by councils that we are speaking, but of its concrete and pictorial presentation by Christ. For the former only existed, as we have seen, to enable the perpetual renewal of the latter, in its vivid appeal to the hearts and minds of men.

"God so loved the world, that He gave His only begotten Son."

"I came forth from the Father, and am come into the world: again, I leave the world, and go to the Father."

"When the Comforter is come, whom I will send unto you from the Father, even the Spirit of Truth, which proceedeth from the Father, He shall testify of Me." "When He, the Spirit of Truth, is come, He shall guide you into all truth."

"No man hath seen God at any time; the only begotten Son, which is in the bosom of the Father, He hath declared Him."

"God was in Christ, reconciling the world unto Himself."

"The Spirit itself beareth witness with our spirit, that we are the sons of God."

"The Spirit itself maketh intercession for us with groanings which cannot be uttered."

Here are no theological abstractions; all is vivid, concrete, pictorial; and it is in this form that the doctrine has influenced the world. The personality of Jesus Christ, and the personal character of His mutual relations with the Father and the Spirit, however much it may perplex the metaphysician, has enabled ordinary men to realise in heart and conscience that the God with whom we have to do is personal. And this sense of divine personality, little understood but profoundly felt, has been the dominant factor in the spiritual development of Christendom. It has affected, that is to say, the national histories no less than the individual lives of all those who have hitherto proved themselves the progressive races of the world.

It may be worth while to consider this in a little further detail. In the first place the Father-hood of God was more profoundly conceived than ever before. "Like as a father pitieth his own children, even so is the Lord merciful to them that fear Him." That had been the utmost utterance of Judaism, "like as a father." But Christianity went beyond this in its doctrine of One who is eternally and essentially a Father, in that He has eternally and essentially a

Son.   Here, again, Athanasius may be worth quoting :

"In the instance of the Godhead only," he says, "have the names Father and Son fixity and permanence ; for of men, if any one be called father, yet he has been son of another ; and if he be called son, yet is he called father of another ; so that in the case of man the names father and son do not properly hold."[1]   "Thus it belongs to the Godhead alone, that the Father is properly (κυρίως) Father, and the Son properly Son, and in Them and Them only does it hold that the Father is ever Father and the Son ever Son."[2]

And again : "It is more pious and more accurate to signify God from the Son and to call Him Father, than to name Him from His works only, and call Him Unoriginate.   For the latter title does nothing more than signify all the works, individually and collectively, which have come to be through the will of God through the Word ; but the title Father has its significance and its bearing only from the Son.   'Unoriginate' is a word of the Greeks, who know not the Son ; but 'Father' has been acknowledged

[1] Athan. *Ad Serap.* i. 16.   [2] *Contr. Ar.* i. 21.

and vouchsafed by our Lord. For He, knowing Himself whose Son He was, said, 'I am in the Father, and the Father is in Me'; and 'He that hath seen Me hath seen the Father,' and 'I and the Father are One'; moreover when He teaches us to pray He says '. . . say, Our Father.'"[1]

And again: "We are creatures by nature, and God is our Creator through the Word; but afterwards we were made sons, and thenceforward God the Creator becomes our Father also. . . . We are not sons by nature, but the Son who is in us . . . and God is not our Father by nature, but of that Word in us, in Whom and because of Whom we cry 'Abba, Father.' So the Father calls them His sons in whomsoever He sees His own Son, and says 'I begat'; since begetting is significant of a son, and making is significant of the works. And thus it is that we are not begotten first but made; . . . but afterwards, on receiving the grace of the Spirit, we are said thenceforth to be begotten also."[2]

It should be noticed in passing that these passages again illustrate that profoundly scriptural character of patristic thought, to which we have already referred. But our present concern

---

[1] Athan. *Contr. Ar.* i. 34.   [2] *Ibid.* ii. 59.

is with the conception of divine fatherhood which they convey. Not only is that conception itself an advance on the Jewish, and all other that had gone before, in concreteness, in completeness, in vivid reality; but at the same time this advanced conception has become common property—master and servant, old and young, rich and poor, sage and simple, all alike pray "Our Father," with a new sense of the full meaning of the words. And from this "more particular and explicit" conception of God's fatherhood would naturally flow a clearer sense of our correlative relation to Him as such. The vague sense of our dependence upon God becomes, in this light, conscious trust; the awe of His omnipotence is tempered by the conviction of His love. Obedience and disobedience to the moral law carry a more personal implication. The performance of our duty is recognised as the keeping of His commandments, and patience in adversity that we cannot alleviate as the acceptance of His will. Thus the Christian belief in God the Father is intensely practical. It brings the conviction of God's personality out of the region of speculative theory into close, intimate, immediate contact with the affairs of our daily life; while it invests those affairs, in consequence, with a new significance and dignity as being the object of our Father's care.

But the consciousness of dependence upon God, under which the above-mentioned acts and feelings may be classed, does not exhaust the demands of our religious instinct.   Man further yearns, and has yearned from the earliest days when we can trace his spiritual history, for some degree of intercourse, communion, fellowship with God, while, at the same time, conscious of his own moral unfitness therefor.   This has led him not only to prayer, but also, and perhaps earlier, to the outward embodiment of prayer, in ceremonial worship, and sacrifice, and sacrament. He has felt an instinctive or a conscious need to include his body in his religion, while dimly or acutely aware the while that his body is the instrument of all his sin.   Hence have followed endless efforts after purification and atonement that should sanctify the body as well as the soul. We need not enlarge upon these things, with which the comparative study of religions has of late years made us all familiar.   Our present purpose is only to recall to mind the important place which they have historically occupied in the practical religion of the world—the desire for communion with God, and the widespread use as a means thereto of ceremonial worship, sacramental meals, and expiatory sacrifices, rude or refined. Now it may seem almost superfluous to point out how this great demand of the religious instinct was met and purified and sanctified by the belief in the Incarnation of the Eternal Son. But the Incarnation is, as we have seen, an inseparable part of the total Christian doctrine of the Trinity, and our present object is to show how intensely practical that doctrine, for all its mystery, has been. First, then, there is the simple aspect of the Incarnation as a divine condescension to human capacity.

"As a kind teacher who cares for his pupils, if some of them cannot profit by high studies, comes down to their level and so succeeds in teaching them by simpler means; so also did the Word of God. For seeing that men . . . had turned away from the contemplation of God . . . and were seeking about for Him in nature and the world of sense . . . the Word of God takes to Himself a body, and as a Man walks among men and meets their senses half-way; to the end that they may, from what the Lord does with His body, learn the truth, and through Him come to know the Father." [1]

So writes Athanasius; and we may compare with him the well - known words of our own poet :

> For Wisdom dealt with mortal powers,
>   Where truth in closest words shall fail,
>   When truth embodied in a tale
> Shall enter in at lowly doors.
>
> And so the Word had breath, and wrought
>   With human hands the creed of creeds
>   In loveliness of perfect deeds,
> More strong than all poetic thought ;
>
> Which he may read that binds the sheaf,
>   Or builds the house, or digs the grave,
>   And those wild eyes that watch the wave
> In roarings round the coral reef. [2]

The significance of this comparison lies in the centuries that it covers. The truth for which Athanasius contended, after nineteen centuries of pervasive influence, persists, in spite of scorn and hatred, with undiminished power in the world to-day.

But the secret of this power has lain not merely in the fact of the Incarnation, but especially in its atoning aspect. And it is important in this connection to remember that Christianity did not

---

[1] Athan. *De Incar. Verb.* 16.   [2] Tennyson, *In Memoriam.*

invent the notion of atonement; it is no solecism in history, as its opponents often seem to suppose. On the contrary, history is full of it: every great religion, every earnest generation of men has been pre-occupied with the sense of sin, and the struggle for its abolition, either by ascetic or sacrificial expiation. And it was to this great world-want that the Christian atonement appealed. In speaking of the Atonement we must always bear in mind that the Christian Church has never authorised any one special theory on the subject of its nature. On the contrary, many such theories or modifications of theory have been current from time to time; and it was regarded by Gregory Nazianzen, a leading theologian of the early Church, as one of those speculative questions, on which we might hold mistaken opinions without serious danger to our Christian life. But whatever our thoughts on the matter, two points should be kept in mind. The first is that the love of the Father for sinners is plainly recognised in the New Testament as the cause of the coming of Christ. "God so loved the world, that He gave His only begotten Son, that whosoever believeth in Him should not perish, but have everlasting life." "God was in Christ, reconciling the world to Himself." "While we were enemies, we were reconciled to God through the death of His Son." And this was fully felt in the early Church. "When the measure," says the unknown author of the beautiful epistle to Diognetus; "when the measure of our wickedness was full and its natural consequence of punishment and death was to be expected . . . God did not hate us, or repel us, or remember our sins against us, but was long-suffering and pitiful, and in mercy took (ἀνεδέξατο) our sins upon Himself, and Himself gave His own Son as a ransom for us, the sinless for the sinful, the just for the unjust. For what else but His righteousness had power to cover our sins?" Any theory, therefore, which conflicts with this cardinal truth is unscriptural, un-patristic, and however much it may be held by Christians, essentially un-Christian; while it is such theories that have brought the whole doctrine in question, and with it the Christian religion, into disrepute in many minds.

The second point to be remembered is that the vicariousness of Christ's sacrifice must never be divorced or considered in abstraction from the correlative truth of His progressive union with believers; enabling them ultimately to make what He has done for them in a very real sense their own. "For whom He justified, them He also sanctified." "If Christ be in you, the body is dead because of sin; but the Spirit is life because of righteousness." "The Spirit Himself beareth witness with our spirit, that we are children of God: and if children, then heirs; heirs of God, and joint-heirs with Christ; if so be that we suffer with Him, that we may also be glorified with Him." It is necessary in speaking of the Atonement to mention these two points, because they have been the subject of so much misconception and misrepresentation as often to make the doctrine seem irrational and incredible. But beyond this we are not now concerned with any discussion of the doctrine itself, but simply with its practical effect upon the world. It has, as a matter of history, lifted the burden of sin from countless human hearts, and made the path of new life possible. Generation after generation of men have felt its reality in their own experience; and simple souls, who could least explain it have lived most fully in its power. It has brought the faith in God's love home to man, in a way that nothing else could do; firing the hearts of martyrs and missionaries in its cause; and quickening the spiritual life of innumerable men; while it is impossible to estimate the debt which the secular progress of the world owes to the secret influence which by renewing human nature at its core, has liberated and intensified all its noblest energies.

Thus the Incarnation, with its atoning consequence, met and satisfied the age-long craving of the human heart for pardon and peace in communion and fellowship with God. But its influence was not confined to the spiritual side of man's nature alone. For it gave rise to a worship and sacraments which took up and raised to a new level and clothed with a new meaning all of the like nature that had ever gone before; leading men to present their bodies, in "reasonable, holy, and lively sacrifice" to God, with all the profound and far-reaching results that such sacrifice involved. We can easily trace and criticise the controversies and the conflicts that have arisen out of Christian worship, and raged around the Eucharist; but we cannot see the other side of the picture that is "hid with Christ in God," the power of the Eucharist in the spiritual history of the world; what it was to the martyrs ere they faced the lions; what it was to the lonely missionary in the northern forests; what it was to the long line of ascetics in their warfare with the flesh; what it was to the teachers and preachers who contended for the faith; what it has been throughout the ages to penitent sinners and holy and humble men of heart, "a great multitude whom no man can number"; what it is to-day to countless lives of which the outer world can only recognise the practical efficiency, and not its secret source. Yet all this has to be weighed and reckoned with if we would estimate the power which belief in the Incarnation, and therefore in the doctrine which lies behind the Incarnation, has exerted in the world.

Once more, there is yet another element in the religious consciousness which has played an important part in the history of the world, and that is the belief in, or the sense of, divine inspiration. We meet with it among rude races in the form of religious excitement or phrensy, a kind of possession by which the proper personality of its subject was for the time superseded. We find it attributed in a higher form to poets like the Vedic hymn-writers, or to great religious leaders or reformers. While its highest exhibition in pre-Christian times is, of course, in the consciousness of the Hebrew prophets, with their mysterious experience so often repeated, "The Word of the Lord came unto me." This element of religion, again, was at once elevated and emphasised by the Christian doctrine of the Holy Ghost, in a way that was supremely practical. In the first place, the gift of the Spirit was proclaimed to be no longer an exceptional, but for Christians, a normal thing; a thing which every Christian as such was to share. Secondly, it was the Holy Spirit, the Spirit of Holiness, rendering men's bodies "temples of the Holy Ghost," and their actions "fruits of the Spirit." This consciousness gave that new intensity and solemnity and confidence to the moral life of Christians, which first enabled it to triumph over the laxity of the Greco-Roman world; and has subsequently sustained it, amid all adverse conditions, as the real salt of the earth, the real preservative of society from the successive inroads of corruption. Thirdly, the operation of the Spirit, while a divine indwelling, was the very converse of pantheistic possession. It did not suspend or supersede, but on the contrary accentuated the

M

proper individuality of its subject. "There are diversities of gifts," says St. Paul, "but the same Spirit." "For to one is given through the Spirit the word of wisdom ; and to another the word of knowledge according to the same Spirit ; to another faith . . . to another gifts of healing . . . to another working of miracles . . . to another prophecy . . . to another discerning of spirits . . . to another divers kinds of tongues . . . to another the interpretation of tongues . . . but all these worketh the one and the same Spirit, dividing to each one severally as He will." And the same has been the case throughout Christian history. All the great saints have been men and women of marked individuality. Yet while thus intensifying the individual side of character, the unity of the Spirit has been the bond of peace, the bond which has held individual lives together in the closest social union. "For by one Spirit we are all baptised into one body." Other forces indeed, in the course of history, have interfered with the realisation of this union, till it cannot now be called more than an ideal, as regards the Christian world at large. But within the separate sections of that world we can trace the unifying action of the Spirit as a real force affecting conduct, and quickening the aspiration for its own fuller realisation in a way that has many practical results.

Nor does this personal indwelling exhaust the operations which Christians attribute to the Spirit. There is the inspiration of Scripture. No words are needed to emphasise what the Bible has been, considered simply as a force in human history; and that force has been due not merely to its intrinsic contents, but to the belief that those contents spoke with the awful authority of the Spirit's inspiration. "The Word of the Lord came unto me saying . . ."

And once again there is the kindred belief in the inspiration of the Church. The function of the Church for twenty centuries has been to uphold unpopular truths before the world. Its history has been an age-long passion, an age-long warfare against discouragement of every kind—tyrannous oppression, intellectual criticism, barbarous invasion, cultured contempt; complicated often by the paralysing presence of internal corruption, and doctrinal discord, and failure of faith. And when we read the lives of the men and women who have so maintained the fight against those odds that the faith is still

alive, while its successive foes are dead and gone,
we realise that the secret of their success lay in
their confident reliance upon the promised permanence of the Spirit's presence in the Church.
Here again, therefore, the Christian doctrine was
eminently practical.

Now it may be thought that all which we
have been saying in this chapter is very obvious
—too obvious, in fact, to need such restatement.
But familiarity, as we all know, is apt to breed
contempt; and familiar truths may come to lose
all their meaning from their very obviousness.
So in the present case, the essential dependence
of the facts, that we have passed in review, upon
the doctrine that lies behind them is, as a rule,
entirely forgotten.   Our object, therefore, has
been to point out that the Christian doctrine of
the Trinity has, as a matter of fact, been intensely
practical.   Each of its constituent elements has,
as we have seen, brought the thought of God
in a different way home—closely and effectually
home—to the human heart; while together they
embrace and satisfy all the demands of our
religious instinct.   And further, man's religion,
when real, is never an isolated thing, but intimately connected with all his secular energies.

And thus the power which has guided the religious, has also profoundly influenced the secular development of Christendom — its poetry, its painting, its music, its philosophy, its literature, its law, the gradual improvement of its social and political institutions; and this not merely or mainly by guiding men's ideals, but still more by restoring to them the moral freedom, without which ideals would beckon in vain. The advance of what we call the progressive peoples of the world may no doubt have been partly due to their racial characteristics; but it is impossible to read history without seeing that it was in a far greater degree the result of their religion; not the controversial religion, which is all that the external critic sees, but the inner religion which has renewed men's lives in each successive generation, and so given their best energies free scope.

When, therefore, objections are urged against the doctrine of the Trinity, on the ground of its metaphysical and abstract character, we may point with confidence to the concrete magnitude of its results. It may not indeed be more comprehensible than any other conception of what is essentially beyond our comprehension. But it has enabled a more vivid apprehension than any other of God's various relations to men; and proved in consequence, if we look beneath the surface of history, the most practical of powers.

CHAPTER IX

ITS WORTH A PRESUMPTION OF ITS TRUTH

THE purport of our last chapter was to point out that, as a fact of history, the doctrine of the Trinity has been the form in which Theism has gained its closest and most effective hold upon human life; with the implication that this fact constitutes a strong presumption of the truth of the doctrine; as being the result which we should naturally expect a revelation to have. But this touches upon a question, whereon it may be well to pause for a while, as it is one much discussed at the present day,—the question, namely, of the relation between value and truth. How far can we argue from a thing's value to its validity? Is worth any indication of truth?

The distinction, with which we are now so familiar, between judgments of value and judgments of truth, dates from Kant's severance of the pure and the practical reason. This led

Lotze to distinguish between our æsthetic and ethical aims, on the one hand, which lead us to form judgments of value or worth; and our intellectual aims, on the other, which lead us to form judgments of truth. Thus a judgment of truth is a statement of what a thing means for the intellect, or, in other words, of what we know about it; while a judgment of worth or value is a statement of what a thing means for the feelings and the will, or, in other words, of how much we care about it. The former judgment, therefore, when established and verified, tends to become impersonal,—independent, that is to say, of any particular mind; but the latter must always imply personal reference to a self or selves. To take an illustration from our present subject: "Jesus Christ was crucified under Pontius Pilate" would be a judgment of truth; of historic truth, commanding general assent; an impersonal statement of fact. Whereas "Christ died for us" would be a judgment of worth; a statement of the significance of His death for us, which could only be made by a personal believer.

From Lotze, Ritschl took over this distinction, and, as is well known, emphasised its theological significance; maintaining that the conception of

God can only be represented in judgments of value; and that only of such judgments, therefore, should theology consist. We are not now concerned with his particular system, but only with some reflections, which the distinction that he thus popularised suggests.

In the first place, it has long been recognised that Kant's severance of the pure from the practical reason was far too complete. And the same may be said of this distinction of judgments to which it gave rise. In the abstract they may be separate, but in the concrete thought of actual life they interpenetrate each other. Knowledge, for instance, springs from curiosity, and seeks its satisfaction; but both the initial curiosity, the unsatisfied desire, and the final satisfaction, the rest in its fulfilment, are in the last analysis emotional states; while the whole of the intellectual interval between these involves ceaseless energy of will. So, on the other hand, any estimate of a work of art, or deed of heroism, if it is to be more than fanciful, must include an intellectual—a strictly intellectual—appreciation of its conditions, and its content. Thus the distinction in question is not so much between two different kinds of judgment, as between the different proportions in which the various ingredients common to all judgments are combined. For all judgments are naturally, and in ultimate analysis, personal; they proceed, that is, from the action of the whole personality. But whereas in the more abstract sciences the personal element is at a minimum, and can be artificially eliminated, in concrete affairs it is at a maximum, and influentially affects our results. And nothing is more concrete than religion, with its claim on the allegiance of every faculty of our being.

It is quite true, therefore, to say that the personal faith of the believer is essential to the right apprehension of theological doctrine. Indeed, it is a truth that cannot be too strongly emphasised, in face of the facile criticism of theology by its opponents to which we are so accustomed in the present day. "Without holiness, no man can see the Lord." A man must both "will to believe" and "will to do," if he would "know of the doctrine." But neither the "will to believe" nor the "will to do" act blindly; they have intellectual judgments behind them, and it is their constant aim and object to make those judgments more secure. True, the only knowledge of God which will avail us is the experience of our personal relation to Him; and when that goal is attained we need not retraverse the road whereby we reached it. But we could never have started upon that road at all without presuppositions which are essentially intellectual, however little the majority of believers may be able to put them into words. "For he that cometh to God must believe that He is, and that He is a rewarder of all them that diligently seek Him." The young and the simple may indeed accept this and the like truths upon authority, but this does not alter their intellectual character; any more than when the average layman accepts scientific discoveries, in the same way, at second hand. Moreover, the Christian society is educative and missionary; a great part of its work is to bring others within the range of a spiritual experience, which, as yet, they confessedly do not possess. And this necessarily involves the intellectual presentation of doctrine; which must consequently be patient of such presentation; it must be reasonable, as well as valuable, and, in many cases, reasonable before its value can be tested.

It would seem, therefore, a serious exaggeration to speak of Christian doctrine as founded exclusively upon judgments of value, though the exaggeration of an important truth. That truth, however, is no novelty, but as old as Christianity. "He that willeth to do . . . shall know of the doctrine." "The word of hearing did not profit them, because they were not united by faith with them that heard." Not only is the intellectual appreciation of doctrine valueless, when divorced from the faith that enables us to translate it into personal experience and so make it true for ourselves; but faith is also an important element even in its right intellectual appreciation. For example, faith in the person of Christ, as divine, conditions our whole view of His life and teaching, considered as a revelation; and faith in the guidance of the Church by the Holy Spirit our whole view of doctrinal development. It furnishes us with presuppositions, and principles of interpretation that we should not otherwise possess.

This leads us to the further question, that is now often asked. How far are judgments of value, or judgments into which faith enters as a constituent element, any evidence that their contents are real and true; independently, that is, or what is now commonly called objectively real and true? For instance, is the fact that my belief in God is of the greatest present value to me any proof that God exists? or, again, is the value of Christ to the world any proof that He is God? And here we at once see the danger arising from that abstract treatment of the judgments of value to which we alluded above—the malign inheritance of Kant's severance of pure from practical reason. For if judgments of value were really devoid of all metaphysical implication, if they were strictly and literally predications of value and nothing else, they could not, of course, logically carry us a single step beyond themselves. For the fact that a given belief is useful, cannot, in abstract logic, prove that it is true. But are judgments of value, as they occur in real life, ever truly of this abstract nature? Are they not always implicated in a context which is ultimately metaphysical? To begin with, as we have already said, they are personal, they are the judgments of a person or self. And a person who reflects upon himself finds that he is a rational being in a rational or intelligible world. There are, of course, a minority of sceptics who deny the rationality of the world, and the consequent possibility of knowledge. But in the face of modern science such scepticism is even much less tenable than when Plato and Aristotle opposed it long ago. For science can only exist on the assumption that the world is intelligible and can therefore be known; and it proves the truth of this assumption every time that it issues a prediction that is subsequently verified, as in the famous discovery of Uranus; every time that it turns freshly found secrets of nature to human use; every time that it makes a machine which works, or employs a chemical with foreseen effect. These are practical proofs, of continual occurrence, that the material world is intelligible or rationally ordered; and on the strength of them the scientific man is perfectly assured that all the regions of nature still unknown may be ultimately reduced to knowledge.

But the same person who thus finds himself to be rational, and the inhabitant of a material world which is rationally ordered, finds himself also to be a moral and spiritual being; with a conscience, however acquired, that distinguishes right from wrong; and with a desire for spiritual communion with other persons, and, in its deepest analysis, with God. Moreover, these moral and spiritual characteristics are inextricably intertwined with his reason; they are inseparable elements in the self-same personality, over the whole of which reason plays. And the demand of reason to meet with rationality is necessarily the same in every field. Reason demands, or assumes, therefore, that the moral and spiritual world should be as rationally ordered as the material. And this can only be the case if our moral and spiritual aspirations are ultimately realised, and therefore justified. For if human nature, the highest thing in all the nature that we know, existed only to be frustrated, and frustrated in respect of those very characteristics by which it excels the rest of nature, the world would be indeed irrational, and purposelessness the end of all its seeming purpose. But a part of nature, the material order, we already know to be rational; and reason is thereby justified in assuming the same of the whole. It is indeed the very function of reason to make this assumption. It would not be reason otherwise. Moreover, the assumption admits of a partial—if very partial—verification here and now. For every life of noble endeavour or saintly experience is a proof that human personality is capable, as far as our present limitations allow, of realising what ought to be, or, in other words, what reason demands, and so becoming truly rational, or conformable to reason. And so we are led, step by step, to conclude that there must be a God, to enable the complete realisation of our moral ideals, and to justify our aspirations for communion with Himself. And the process of our reasoning, it should be noticed, is closely parallel to that by which the man of science concludes from his partial knowledge of natural phenomena, that, given time and opportunity, all can be ultimately and adequately known.

We have not intended to do more than briefly allude to this familiar argument in outline; because our present concern is not with what it proves, but with the nature of its proof; and its bearing on the inference from value or worth, to reality or truth. For it will be seen at once, from what we have been saying, that, in real life, we do not deal with value in the abstract, but with value in a particular context, the context of a rational and teleologically ordered world; or, to put it otherwise, value as estimated by a person who is essentially rational, and whose reason necessarily permeates and qualifies all his judgments.

Thus the moral argument in question for the

existence of God is not the blind postulate of a
working hypothesis with which human life cannot
dispense; but a veritable process of reasoning,
whose major premiss is the rationality of the world.
For if the world is rationally ordered, as we
believe that it is, then the value of God to our
moral and spiritual life, or, in other words, the
necessity for His existence, if that life is ever to
attain the complete realisation which reason
demands for it, affords the strongest possible
presumption that He does exist. Thus in this
particular case we do argue from value to
validity, or from worth to truth, or from importance to reality; and we do so by a strictly
rational process, which does not indeed amount
to a demonstration, but affords a degree of probability which many would be willing to regard
as moral certainty. Other arguments from value
to reality may not be so convincing as this; but
the point that we would emphasise is that,
whenever the value of a thing can be shown to
be closely connected with the rationality of the
world as a whole, this fact justifies a rational
presumption, as distinct from a mere postulate
of its reality or truth.[1]

[1] See Note 3.

N

We may now return to the point from which we started, the value or importance which the doctrine of the Trinity has, as a matter of history, possessed for the world, as briefly indicated in our last chapter ; with the inference that we would draw from this fact. The doctine of the Trinity, as being a form of Theism, has behind it and is supported by all the complex and cumulative arguments that make for Theism. Theism, again, considered in connection with man's world-wide and age-long desire for communion with God, creates an immense presumption in favour of the occurrence of such a revelation as would make that communion possible, in its utmost degree. We can only conceive such a revelation to be made through human personality ; and the fullest form that a revelation through human personality could possibly take would be an Incarnation of God. The Christian Church has always believed Jesus Christ to be God Incarnate, on the ground of the claim which He personally made ; as interpreted by the society which He founded, and to which He promised spiritual guidance into all truth. Jesus Christ, in the belief of the Church, revealed the existence of Father, Son, and Spirit in the Godhead; which revelation the Church subsequently formulated, for the purpose of transmission, as the doctrine of the Trinity in Unity. These are the intellectual presuppositions, this is the philosophic and historic context, in relation to which we have to estimate the importance or value which the doctrine has possessed for mankind. We may sum that importance up in a phrase by saying that the doctrine lies at the very root of the existence of the Christian Church;—the Christian Church which has brought home to its true members in every age, and brings home to them with equal efficiency to-day, precisely that conviction of communion with God, and consequent consecration and confirmation of life, which it would be the object of a revelation to bring. "Hereby *know* we that we abide in Him, and He in us, because He hath given us of His Spirit."

Now we have seen above that the satisfaction of our moral and spiritual aspirations must be a condition of the rationality of the world. If they are doomed for ever to frustration, then our reason lies. We may fairly argue, therefore, that the only religion which has rationally and really satisfied these aspirations, as far as our earthly limitations allow, and which promises with an authority authenticated by its past and present power, their adequate fulfilment hereafter;—we may fairly argue that such a religion, even other arguments apart, may be presumed from the connection of its human value with the rationality of the world to be true.

It is sometimes objected to this line of argument that it in technical language "proves too much," since other religions have been equally satisfactory to their adherents, and should therefore, if this be any argument, be equally true. Buddhism and Mahometanism are the two systems most frequently and familiarly quoted to this effect. It should be noted, therefore, in the first place, that we can in no way isolate the appeal to "satisfaction" or "value" from its rational context. We merely regard it as one factor among many in a complex proof; one element in a cumulative argument which tends to corroborate, while in turn it is corroborated by the rest. And, in the next place, it will be noticed that we have spoken of "the rational and the real" satisfaction of our religious aspirations and desires, meaning one which reason approves, and which issues in practical results that are conformable to reason.

And this qualification is essential to our argument. For we do not merely mean that the Christian has a subjective sensation of satisfaction in his creed, but that he has a satisfying conviction, that is justified by the reasonableness of the grounds on which it rests ; and that produces a character which reason emphatically affirms "ought to be," as representing the most rational realisation of human personality. Now when we turn to Buddhism we do not find these requirements there met. We find indeed self-control and purity both inculcated and practised, and an attitude of calm and gentle amiability to all the world. And herein we may well recognise the operation of a Spirit greater than its subjects suspect. But upon what intellectual foundation does it all rest, and what therefore is its ultimate character? It rests upon pessimism ; upon the conviction of the irrationality of the world, and consequent need for "the great renunciation." Conscious individuality is regarded as the cause of all pain and sorrow ; and this conscious individual existence is due to the presence of desire in the heart, which, as long as it continues, leads to endless re-births. The enlightened man who, understanding this, purges himself from all desire, thereby enters into the peace of Nirvana ; and with the death of his body will cease from all conscious individual existence.

> Long have I wandered ! Long !
> Bound by the Chain of Life,
> Through many births :
> Seeking thus long, in vain,
> "Whence comes this Life in man, his Consciousness,
> his Pain !"
> And hard to bear is Birth,
> When pain and death but lead to Birth again.
>
> Found ! It is found !
> O cause of individuality !
> No longer shalt thou make a house for me :
> Broken are all thy beams.
> Thy ridge-pole shattered !
> Into Nirvana now my mind has past :
> The end of cravings has been reached at last.[1]

Such a system may satisfy its adherents in the sense of helping them to make the best of an intolerable situation ; but this is not the kind of satisfaction that reason demands or can approve. For reason affirms that the world is rational, that it "means intensely and means well"; and the only adequate goal of conscious personality must consist in the actual realisation of all its latent capacities ; while sin and sorrow arise, not from

[1] Trans. by Rhys Davids, *Buddhist Birth Stories.*

the desire for fulness of life, which is of the very
essence of life itself, but from the action of
specifically evil desires upon the will.   In the
one case all is positive ; in the other all negation.
The one view stimulates human progress in
every direction—art, science, literature, com-
merce, social and political advance.   The other
renounces everything simply for the sake of its
renunciation.   Above all, the ethical aim of the
one is to realise the good, and is therefore
essentially unselfish and altruistic ; that of the
other merely to escape the evil in a way which,
in the last analysis, is selfish and immoral.[1]   And
what is true of Buddhism is true of all systems of
religion which aim at or expect the obliteration
of personal individuality whether by annihilation
or pantheistic absorption.   They destroy the
whole value of life considered as a school of
character, whose development is prophetic of its
continuance, and therewith all the moral meaning
which reason recognises in the world.

Mahometanism is in very different case, for
Mahometanism is very much, as Dante viewed
it, a Christian or Judeo-Christian heresy, with a
firm belief in God, and a future life in which vice

[1] See Note 4.

and virtue are respectively punished and rewarded.
Many also of its moral and religious precepts and
practices are noble, and represent a great advance
on the previous condition of the Arabian races.
But when every allowance has been made for all
that can possibly be said under these heads, and
apart from all criticism of the many details which
invite criticism, there is one broad fact which
adversely differentiates Mahometanism from
Christian morality. And that is, that Mahometanism does not recognise the inherent value of
personality as such; its claim to be an end in
itself, and never to be regarded as a means to
an end.

> Our life is turned
> Out of her course, wherever Man is made
> An offering, or a sacrifice, a tool
> Or implement, a passive Thing employed
> As a brute mean, without acknowledgment
> Of common right or interest in the end;
> Used or abused, as selfishness may prompt.[1]

And though this phraseology may sound very
Kantian and therefore recent, the truth that it
expresses was older than Mahomet, and lay at
the very root of the religion which he claimed to
supersede. "There can be neither Jew nor

---

[1] Wordsworth's *Excursion*, bk. ix.

Greek, there can be neither bond nor free, there can be no male or female : for ye are all one *man* in Christ Jesus." As against this Mahometanism sanctions both polygamy and slavery, and thus denies the human dignity of the majority of mankind. And nothing that can be pleaded as to the relative expediency of such a sanction for a given race or age, can alter the fact that it disallows an inalienable right with which reason invests personality. And this defective treatment of the human person, with its many disastrous historical results, was undoubtedly connected with the rigid unitarianism of Mahomet's theology. It has often been pointed out that as a matter of history the Incarnation, with its closer union of the human and the divine had the greatest influence in developing and intensifying the significance of human personality, and with it the actual characters of men. And it was in the light thrown on them by the Incarnation that the Fathers constantly harp upon the words of Genesis : " In the image of God created He him ; male and female created He them."

The tendency of Mahomet's monotheism, on the other hand, was to emphasise exclusively the infinitude of the gulf between the Creator and

His creatures, without any adequate recognition of their correlation. The Creator is regarded simply in His transcendence; as the Author of absolute decrees; and the creature remains in all his creaturely infirmity. There is no mediator between the two, nor anything analogous to the Christian doctrine of the Holy Spirit, whose in-dwelling presence is a perpetual principle of progressive development. No such injunction, therefore, as " Be ye perfect," no presentation of an absolute standard is possible. Morality remains relative and stereotyped in its rela-tivity, with no higher sanction than that of ultimate rewards and punishments of a purely relative and human type. There is thus no scope for that progressive development or realisation of our personality, that attainment of reality through personal union with the absolute source of reality which is alike the demand of reason and the promise of Christ. " As Thou, Father, art in Me, and I in Thee, that they also may be one in Us." " It doth not yet appear what we shall be : but we know that, when He shall appear, we shall be like Him : for we shall see Him as He is." [1]

[1] See Note 5.

And what is true of the two religious systems of which we have spoken is true of all others, when compared with Christianity. They lack precisely that which the doctrines of the Trinity and the Incarnation profess to supply—a power that can educate our personality to what reason shall recognise to be its true perfection, and also secure for it the actual attainment, fulfilment, realisation of all that such perfection implies.

> Thy power can fill the heart that Thy power expands.

In a word, all others are relative religions, and as such cannot claim to have their truth involved in the rationality of the world, while the claim of Christianity is to be the absolute religion which alone can finally satisfy the reason. " Heaven and earth shall pass away, but My words shall not pass away." And this claim justifies our arguing from its value to its truth, in a world where, if our reason is to be adequately satisfied, truth and goodness must ultimately coincide, and the Truth be also the Life.

CHAPTER X

Our last two chapters have been concerned with the value as exhibited in history, which the doctrine of the Trinity has possessed for life, the spiritual and moral and therefore practical life of men. But we incidentally alluded in a previous chapter to its value also for thought; the way in which it helps rather than hinders us in thinking about God, and His relation to the world. We will now return to consider this value for thought in a little further detail. We have already seen that the doctrine of the Trinity throws light upon the absoluteness of God. All Theists regard God as absolute in the sense of being self-contained and independent of all necessary relation to finite persons or things, meaning by this that finite persons and things are in no way essential to His being what He is, in no way contributary to, or constitutive of His Godhead. Yet when we proceed, as all Theists do, to think further of this absolute Being as personal and good and loving, we recognise that these characteristics imply and involve relationships. It is a distinct help to our thought, therefore, as we have already seen, to be told that such relationships exist within the Godhead, and thus do not detract from its absoluteness or independence of all other than Itself. We may not see far, but we see farther than we should otherwise have done; for we catch a glimpse into a Life that is no abstraction, like the impersonal absolute of some philosophers, but rich and concrete with the fulness of eternal relationships—relationships which again contain the potency of Its further relations with finite things. When men speak of an impersonal "Absolute," difficulties at once arise as to the nature of its connection with the relative world of finite and changing things; since it must either exclude all relations and so fade into a mere abstraction, or include all relations and so disperse into a vague generalisation that can lead us to no profitable thought. But from the Christian point of view these difficulties do not occur. For we have nothing to do with an impersonal absolute, but with an absolute God; and

we regard the existence of finite things and processes and persons as due to His voluntary creation. Though therefore in a sense created nature
may be said to limit God's absoluteness, as in
the case of finite freewill, it is with no essential
limitation, but only a contingent one,—contingent
on the Divine will itself. In other words, it is a
self-limitation consequent on God's will to create ;
but such voluntary self - limitation comes from
within and not from without, whereas it is only
limitation from without, limitation by another,
which would be incompatible with the proper
absoluteness that we attribute to God. A king
does not diminish his authority by delegating its
exercise to his ministers.

Moreover, when we look more closely at
the matter, we see that in the case of human
personality, self-limitation is the necessary condition of its highest excellence. For sin is always
transgression, the over-stepping of due bounds,
the refusal to be limited by the " Thou shalt not,"
whether of divine or human law. And the sinner
tends in consequence to lose his clear-cut outline
in a way to which words like dissipation and
dissoluteness point. He progressively merges
his distinct individuality in mere membership of

a class, the class that is addicted to, and at last identified with his particular type of sin or crime. Madness, prison, suicide may be the end, and all equally symbolise the destruction of proper personality, or, to use a modern term, the depersonalisation, to which transgression leads.

Whereas virtue is rooted in self-control, self-discipline, that is, voluntary self-limitation, the effect of which is not to obliterate but to intensify and emphasise personality both in its individual and universal aspect; since the more individual a man is, and therefore the more distinct his function, the more important a factor does he become in the social whole; his difference from others constitutes his usefulness to others, and their correlative need of him. We are familiar with this fact in the case of the great statesman, or lawyer, or general, or artist; and it is even truer in the case of the great saint. Thus voluntary self-limitation is plainly the means, and the only means, by which human personality can ever attain to its highest degree of individual excellence and universal worth. In a word, self-limitation is the sole condition of self-realisation. And we see this best of all where virtue culminates in love. For "greater love hath no man than this, that a man lay down his life for his friends." Here the very same act is at once the climax of all possible self-limitation and the supreme realisation of the highest self. Thus self-limitation proves, upon analysis, only to be an abstract description of what in concrete reality is self-determination; and the noblest characteristic of personality as we know it is self-determination, of which the motive is love. If, therefore, we are to think of three persons in the Trinity, united by a bond of eternal love, we should suppose this characteristic to have some high analogue within the Godhead, and thence to be reflected in God's relation to created persons and things, without any consequent infringement of His absolute character.

All this may sound abstract and academic; but it needs saying since it indicates the direction wherein lies our answer to an objection that is actually raised. Moreover, it is only the abstract statement of a truth that is vital to practical religion, and not more vital for the intellect than for the heart and will.

> Change and decay in all around I see :
> O Thou who changest not, abide with me.

It is only our sense of God's absolute independence of us, if we may so express it, that enables us entirely to depend on Him; and that dependence is the very root of our religion. Our reason demands an absolute Being, to make relative and finite existence intelligible. Our will or moral nature demands an absolute God, to make the ultimate realisation of our ethical ideals possible. Our affections demand an absolute Love in which they may permanently rest. In a word, our personality, which is essentially dependent upon others, demands beyond all finite and fleeting others an absolute other personality as its only adequate object and end.

"O Lord, thy word endureth for ever in heaven. Thy truth also remaineth from one generation to another."

"Before the mountains were brought forth, or ever the earth and the world were made; thou art God from everlasting, and world without end."

"Thy righteousness standeth like the strong mountains: thy judgments are like the great deep."

"The Lord is loving unto every man; his mercy is over all his works."

"My soul is athirst for God: yea, even for the living God."

This is the basal, the fundamental utterance

of the religious consciousness, on which all else depends; and as such it is naturally the one which we find emphasised in Judaism, with its ultimate fear of even naming the Holy Name. This consciousness is not originally a creation of pure reason.   It is partly instinctive, partly intuitive, partly traditional, partly inferential.   But the process of its evolution or education, though psychologically interesting, does not affect the reality of its Object, any more than the evolution of the eye affects the physical nature of light.   And that reality is affirmed by reason, upon analysis, to be no mere practical postulate, but a necessary implication of all our thoughts.   And upon this absolute reality the doctrine of the Trinity throws, as we have seen, still further light; which again reason did not originate, but can recognise, when revealed, as rational.

To think of God in this way is to think of Him, in modern phrase, as transcendent, as above and beyond all relative and finite existence; the High and Holy One that inhabiteth eternity, "dwelling in the light that no man can approach unto."   But this does not exhaust the content of the religious consciousness.   For we also think of God, as immanent in creation; that is, as omnipresent, indwelling, upholding, sustaining, controlling, guiding the universe in all its ways; and finally informing and inspiring men with the knowledge of Himself. This line of thought has historically come down to us from Greek rather than from Jewish sources, and was, as is well known, emphasised in the Greek theology of the Alexandrian Fathers. It represents an important aspect of religious truth, and one that, from various causes, has assumed great prominence in the present day.

Now it is theoretically possible to isolate either of these aspects of the Divine and regard it as the whole truth; to conceive of God as simply transcendent, or simply immanent in the world; but in each case with disastrous results. For if we isolate the transcendence, or lay such predominant emphasis upon it as practically to exclude all else, we come to think of God only in His remoteness, or distinction from the world; and are on the road that leads, through the various forms of Deism, with its distant God and mechanical universe, to the logical end of Agnosticism, the mere recognition of an unknown and unknowable power. And this satisfies neither our heart nor our head; it is an intellectually untenable and morally useless position, against which our whole personality revolts.

On the other hand, we may isolate the conception of divine immanence, and think of God as dwelling in the universe, without in any way transcending it. This means pantheism of one kind or another; which regards the material universe as God's bodily manifestation, and God as the universal soul or life. Hence the various processes of the world, such as evolution, are not merely controlled by God, but identified with Him, and He with them. He comes to consciousness in man, and is the source of all human activity; with the logical consequence that He must be conceived to be the cause of evil as well as good. For directly we allow Him any moral distinction from the universal life we tacitly reintroduce the conception of transcendence; and this is probably what most professors of pantheism unconsciously do. Thus a doctrine of mere divine immanence or pantheism is for all practical intents and purposes, indistinguishable from materialism, with its recognition of universal energy. And God thus conceived is neither the God which our religious consciousness demands, nor a God that our reason can recognise or receive.

Hence it will be obvious that divine immanence and divine transcendence are not mutually exclusive, but essentially correlative conceptions, which must be held together to satisfy the requirements either of reason or religion. Judaism, for example, as we have said above, lays especial stress upon the divine transcendence; but it fully recognises all that is religiously essential in the correlative conception; that is to say, God's intimate nearness to human affairs.

"For thus saith the high and lofty One that inhabiteth eternity, I dwell in the high and holy place, with him also that is of a contrite and humble spirit, to revive the spirit of the humble, and to revive the heart of the contrite ones." "For though the Lord be high, yet hath he respect unto the lowly." "O Lord, thou hast searched me out, and known me: thou knowest my downsitting and mine uprising; thou understandest my thoughts long before. Thou art about my path and about my bed, and spiest out all my ways. For lo, there is not a word in my tongue, but Thou, O Lord, knowest it altogether. . . . Such knowledge is too wonderful and excellent for me; I cannot attain unto it. Whither shall I go then from thy Spirit, or whither shall I go

then from thy presence? . . . If I take the wings
of the morning, and remain in the uttermost
parts of the sea ; even there also shall thy hand
lead me, and thy right hand shall hold me."

Here we have the two thoughts in immediate
juxtaposition ; as indeed they are throughout the
Old Testament ; and we feel at once as we know
also, in our own personal experience, that the
thought of God's nearness derives all its religious
significance from the opposite thought of His
greatness.   He "who is not far from every one
of us" is yet "the High and Holy One," "The
Rock that is higher than I," The Lord "who
sitteth above the water floods," The Lord "who
remaineth a king for ever."   He is at once so
near that we can instantly turn to Him ; and yet
so supreme that we turn with the confident
assurance that the "Lord is a great God and a
great king above all gods."   It is because he is
so essentially Other than ourselves that we can
securely "abide under the shadow of the
Almighty" : with

The submission of man's nothing perfect to God's all-complete,
As by each new obeisance in spirit I climb to His feet.[1]

Even in our own human relationships the

---

[1] Browning, *Saul.*

element of otherness is essential. It is because
my friend is other than myself, and as such independent of my personal sin or sorrow, that I can
turn to him in time of trouble to support my
weakness by his strength. It is because those
who love me are other than myself, better, or
greater, or holier, or lovelier, that I feel my whole
being enriched and expanded by the gift of their
love. And all true union among men is attained,
not by the obliteration, but by the emphasis of
their individuality, or peculiar difference; enabling
each man to perform his function—that which
in Plato's phrase, "he alone can do, or can
do best"—for the common good of the social
whole.

In religion this principle culminates. For in
religion we seek union with Another who is all
that we are not, and can supply therefore all that
we lack. But this union must be a moral union,
an union of free persons ultimately self determined;
and the possibility of moral union ceases directly
metaphysical confusion begins. If there is no
determinate outline between the creature and the
Creator; if our being is metaphysically involved
in that of God, or His in ours, we lose, together
with our personal distinction, our capacity for

spiritual communion.   Thus however much stress
we lay upon God's immanence, or intimate presence in the world, and inspiring guidance of the
minds of men ; this immanence gains its whole
significance and character from the fact that it is
the immanence of the Transcendent One, the
Eternal, the All-Holy, the Almighty.

Judaism, as we have seen, while emphatically
asserting God's transcendence, combines it with
a sense of His spiritual nearness to mankind, and
providential government of the world ; but it did
not develop this into a general doctrine of divine
immanence.   That doctrine, on the other hand,
was prominent in the Indian and Stoic philoso-
phies ; but in a form which always tended to pantheism, even if it was not in all cases thoroughly
pantheistic, with the unsatisfactory consequences
that we have noticed above.   Here therefore
again the doctrine of the Trinity assists our
thought ; at least to the extent of throwing a
suggestive light upon the combination of immanence with transcendence.   For that doctrine, as
taught by the fathers, after St. Paul and St. John,
represents the Son, viewed as the Word (Λόγος),
to be the eternal expression or manifestation of
the Father—the Father who is the sole source of

Godhead, as they expressed it ($\pi\eta\gamma\grave{\eta}\ \theta\epsilon\acute{o}\tau\eta\tau\sigma\varsigma$)
—and to be consequently His instrument and
mediator in the creation of the world.   It may
perhaps be allowable to illustrate this thought by
a human analogy, provided that it be not pressed
too far.   Our own inner, invisible self, our
personality, is manifested through our body, with
its looks, and tones, and gestures; our body is,
as regards this world, our permanent and more
or less adequate manifestation; our person, as
it is often called.   But precisely because it is so
it becomes the natural and inevitable instrument
or organ of all our other temporary manifestations,
the words that we speak, the deeds that we do,
the statues, the pictures, the poems, the machinery
that we create.   These things are voluntary
manifestations of different aspects of our central
self: we are free to make them or to leave them
unmade; they are partial and particular and
transient; they do not express us essentially and
permanently as our body does; but their possibility entirely depends upon the fact that we
possess in our body a permanent principle of self-
manifestation.   And on this analogy we may
conceive that He who is God's essential and
eternal manifestation would also be the agent, as

such, of His temporal and contingent manifestation in creation.

We are thus enabled to think of the Father whom no man hath seen at any time as God in His eternal transcendence, and of the Only-begotten Son who "hath revealed Him" as God immanent in the universe, not in any pantheistic sense, but as its free creator and upholder, the controller of all its movement and life. "He is in creation," says Athanasius, "and yet He does not partake of its nature in the least degree, but rather all things partake of His power." And in the same way, as being the creator and sustainer of universal nature, He is the creator and sustainer of mankind, and the light which lighteth every man coming into the world, not as being identified or identifiable with every man, but as freely endowing every man with life and reason and will and love. But in creating man He created a being capable of knowing God, and desirous of communion with God. Hence as the natural sequence of this creation, in the order of time, though its presupposition in the order of divine thought "before the foundation of the world" He became incarnate[1] to enable and assist this

---

[1] See Note 6.

knowledge and communion : " till we all attain unto the unity of the faith, and of the knowledge of the Son of God, unto a full-grown man, unto the measure of the stature of the fulness of Christ : that we may . . . grow up in all things into Him which is the head, even Christ : from whom all the body fitly framed and knit together through that which every joint supplieth, according to the working in due measure of every part, maketh the increase of the body unto the building up of itself in love."

The Incarnation thus regarded is no exceptional intervention in human affairs, but the natural continuation of God's original purpose in creating man, a being capable of such development that eventually Christ may be " formed in " him, and he may be able to say, " I live, yet not I, Christ liveth in me," and who does not really come to be himself till by the completion of this development he is " made in the image of God."

It is important to bear in mind that this view of the Incarnation was that of the great philosophical thinkers of the early Church, especially of the Alexandrian theologians and Athanasius, because at a later date it came to be obscured in the popular mind by a narrower conception, which saw in the Incarnation only the Atonement or Redemption of man from sin. Many causes contributed to this. The western Church was essentially practical, and therefore naturally gave prominence to that element in Christian teaching which bore most immediately upon the reformation and restoration of moral and spiritual life. Moreover, the western Church was profoundly influenced by Augustine; and Augustine partly from his bent of character and personal history, partly from the nature of the controversies to which his age gave rise, was led to lay especial stress upon the problems of free-will and grace and sin. These problems were again accentuated in the ascetic life of the cloister, and in the fierce conflict of the Church through the dark ages with a lawless world. And when the Reformation came it was no less preoccupied with sin, and therefore no less affected by Augustine.

Hence during a long period the atoning aspect of the Incarnation assumed exclusive prominence in men's minds, as being that of which they immediately had need. And as a consequence the Incarnation itself came to be regarded as contingent upon or indirectly due to human sin. But with the revival of more philosophic thought the grave speculative difficulties that such a theory involved could not but become apparent. And this led Duns Scotus to revive the older view, which he cast into hypothetical form by saying that the Incarnation would have taken place even if man had never sinned. And this Scotist view of the Incarnation, as it came after him to be called, has, as is now well known, gained increasing recognition in the Church, being in fact a republication of what was substantially the Alexandrian theology. This does not, of course, mean that we abandon any of the valuable elements in the Augustinian teaching, or go back to anything which that teaching superseded, but merely that we restore to its due place another important element of Christian thought which had fallen into comparative abeyance during a period when it was not practically needed, because men's minds were not exercised about the relation of Christianity to our general philosophy of the world, as once they had been, and now are again. We thus regard the Incarnation, including its redemptive efficacy and sanctifying power, as the continuance of God's creative operation in the world. This means that it is no mere stage in human evolution, but a divine revelation, the

upcrop through the strata of history of that
spiritual world-ground which evolution, as we
have seen, must presuppose: not, that is to say,
the final discovery by man of his own essential
unity with God, but the gift to man of a com-
municated union with One who is transcendently
Other than himself, and therefore the God whom
his spirit naturally seeks.   In the words of St.
Hilary, "This sonship to God is not a compul-
sion, but a possibility; for while the divine gift is
offered to all, it is no heredity inevitably imprinted,
but a prize awarded to willing choice."[1]

"As many as received Him, to them gave He
power to become the sons of God, even to them
that believe on His name."   What degree of
union this sonship may imply, when "we shall be
like Him, for we shall see Him as He is," must
for ever pass our present powers of comprehension.   But it must be a union, as we have seen
above, based on personal distinction, in which the
outlines between God and man, the creator and
the creature, are not confused; but the one
remains always the giver, and the other the re-
cipient of His gift.   "What hast thou that thou
didst not receive?" must remain for ever true.

----

[1] *De Trin.* i. 11.

Thus the doctrine of the Trinity and the Incarnation combines the truth of God's transcendence, with the truth of His immanence or indwelling presence in the world, in a way which while giving the fullest emphasis to both thoughts prevents either from being isolated in one-sided exaggeration. It does not, of course, explain what, under our present limitations, can never be explained; but it points to the direction in which explanation lies. It assures us that the two deliverances of our religious consciousness are equally trustworthy and essentially harmonious, and imparts greater vividness to our apprehension of what we cannot comprehend.

But this would not be the case, we must once more recall to mind, if the doctrine in question were merely a speculative creation of the human intellect, either an hypothesis or a deduction. It is simply and solely because we believe God the Son to have become incarnate, and to have revealed the existence of Father, Son, and Spirit in terms which, again under divine guidance as we further believe, led to the subsequent creed of the Church that we can find intellectual satisfaction in that creed.

That is to say, we understand the language of

its technical formulation, in accordance with the express and reiterated intention of those who framed it, as intended to do no more than interpret the meaning of Scripture.   And within the bounds of Scripture itself we believe St. Paul and St. John to do no more than explain with inspired insight the meaning of what Jesus Christ had Himself revealed through His personality and in His teaching, by His words and work.   And the creed so regarded assists our thought as divine grace assists our life, precisely because it comes from our Other, and not ourselves; it is a gift, not a result of our thought, but a fresh *datum* on which our thought may work.   And though it does not explain or profess to explain the whole of "the burden and the mystery of all this unintelligible world," it does supply us with a few illuminating truths, which we can hold as fixed, amid the fluctuations of human speculation; a few steady stars to guide us as we drift on the dark waters of thought and wait with wonder for the dawn of intellectual day.

CHAPTER XI

REVELATION THE CONTINUANCE OF CREATION

THE revelation of which we have been speaking, and which the Christian Church has always taught—a revelation made through the medium of historic events, and thus coming to us, so to speak, from without as well as from above—is often unfavourably contrasted in the present day with an interior revelation in the mind. The latter is supposed to be a more spiritual conception, as well as more in harmony with all our experience; while the element of externality in the former is deprecated, as allied to a mechanical and magical view of religion, natural enough in unenlightened ages, but incompatible with our worthier notions of God. And as a revelation which takes place entirely within the mind is practically indistinguishable from the proper action of the mind, it may equally well be described in terms of that action as quickened insight, or heightened religious consciousness; and as a natural consequence the whole process may be viewed from the human side as the evolution of religion. Revelation, therefore, thus regarded comes to be synonymous with the gradual growth of spiritual insight in the human race. This is all, it is maintained, that has ever really taken place; and the notion of an historic revelation is due to the tendency of uncritical ages to project their inner experience upon the outer world, and see miracles when in reality they only feel wonders.

This position is common enough at the present time to need serious consideration, and it may be met, of course, by a direct appeal to the evidence of the historic incarnation; but we may also ask the previous question, whether it is in itself defensible, and whether its claim to philosophical superiority is really philosophical at all?

In the first place, there is the tacit assumption that a process which takes place entirely within the mind is more spiritual than one which is mediated by external or material facts. But is this true? Is it philosophical? Is the divorce which it makes between spirit and matter, as they are called, anything better than a vague popular prejudice, an idol of the market-place, as Bacon would say? For consider the facts. To begin with, whatsoever takes place within the mind must be mediated through the action of the brain, and can therefore only be realised by material agency. Without the brain, and the food that feeds the brain, with our present constitution, we can neither think, nor will, nor love, nor pray. And then what is the course of all our conscious life? It begins, the psychologists tell us, in the reactive response of our organism to external stimulation, and it retains this initial character to the end. Our education begins by reaction of one kind or another on the influence of those around us, exercised through their bodily presence. We enlarge our ideas through the material instrumentality of books, and experience of what happens in the world without us. We are inspired with ideals by the recorded history of what other men have been and done. Our love, our crowning grace, is elicited by the character and conduct of other persons which can only be made known to us by their bodily behaviour. While, finally, our religious consciousness, for all its inwardness, is developed by external means. For the Christian Church stands over against us as a society in the outer world, which admits us to its membership by sensible sacraments, and teaches and exhorts and guides us through the ministry of men. In a word, our whole internal spiritual development is mediated by external material machinery. So far, there fore, from being mutually exclusive, what we call spirit and matter mingle and blend in our experience, as two aspects or elements of one process, and their relation may perhaps best be described by saying that spirit includes and utilises matter in its own larger life. Witness the expression of an eye, the meaning of a voice, the magnetism of a hand, the influence which radiates from the bodily presence of a saint. There can be no necessary antithesis, therefore, between a revelation in the heart or mind and a revelation through the instrumentality of historical events, nor any superior spirituality in the former. On the contrary, universal analogy, as we see, would lead us to expect that, in the event of a revelation being made to us, it would include both these elements, and reach the inner through the outer life, precisely as Christianity has always claimed to do.

Indeed, this is only another way of stating the familiar fact that the spread of religion is always due to individuals. All great religious movements have been the work of one or more individuals, the contagion of whose enthusiasm has infected their disciples, thus passing into the hearts of the multitude from an historically external person or persons. We should naturally, therefore, expect the supreme religion to be a supreme instance of the same spiritual law. We do not say this, it should be noticed, in proof of the Incarnation, but merely in disproof of the objection to it raised upon the specific ground of its externality considered as a mode of revelation.

To this, again, some would reply that it is not the external or historic element in Christianity, as such, that is matter of objection, but the unusual form of its supposed occurrence. The appearance of a religious teacher in the line of other human teachers, and acting upon his followers as other such have acted—Confucius, Zarathustra, Moses, Buddha, or Mahomet—would be credible enough, because it would be a normal event, in harmony with our usual experience. But a personal intervention of God in history is contrary to our experience of the way in which God habitually works. It is not a normal use of the external order, but an abnormal interference with its course, and therefore inconceivable. Upon this we may recall the weighty remark of Butler that " upon supposition of a revelation, it is highly credible beforehand, we should be incompetent judges of it to a great degree, and that it would contain many things appearing to us liable to great objection." The very notion of a revelation implies some kind of intervention or interference with the ordinary course of our experience; to object to it, therefore, upon this ground is to deny that it is a revelation, simply because it has the characteristic appearance of a revelation. And if this means anything, it can only mean that instead of making " the supposition of a revelation," we already presuppose its impossibility.

But the Christian who does make this supposition takes a wider view of things than is presented by our ordinary experience. For he regards the Incarnation as in a line, so to speak, with creation, as in the succession of creative acts. And every creative act transcends the ordinary course of the past, the previous condition of things, and introduces a new era of being. This is equally true whether we regard the creative act as realised by an evolutionary process or no, so long as we recognise that evolution presupposes a creator, or, in its other mode of expression, that relative change presupposes an absolute being. Thus, to quote a few broadly obvious instances, the reduction of our planet to a habitable condition, the emergence thereon of vegetable life, and then of animal life, and then of man, are events which lie wholly outside our ordinary experience, and yet which we know for certain must have occurred in time past, and at the moment of their occurrence been new, and unexampled in the previous order of things. And however numerous and subtle the gradations by which these salient events may have been effected, the case is the same. We can see plainly, for instance, that the animal kingdom is a new order, when compared with the vegetable; that the lion and the eagle mark a creative advance upon the lily or the oak. But if we think that there is sufficient ground for believing that the higher order has been evolved from the lower through an infinite series of infinitesimal modifications, then each of these modifications must have been new and original when compared with what went before it. We merely multiply our novelties, and substitute a myriad for a few stages in creation. Indeed, strictly speaking, every individual is a novelty, and vital variety, rather than mechanical uniformity, the characteristic of the universe.

> The old order changeth, giving place to new,
> And God fulfils Himself in many ways.

In a word, if we believe in a creator and sustainer of the universe, every fresh moment of its existence must be as much a creative act as the last. Evolution is merely the phenomenon, the appearance to a spectator in place and time, of what is essentially creation. And, viewing the world in this way, we regard the Incarnation as a new creative act, whose object was to lead man forward in the direction destined from his original creation, and, in so far as he had marred his nature by sin, to re-create him.

There can be no doubt that this was the way in which the Incarnation was interpreted by St. Paul and St. John. And the truth of the interpretation is assured to us by the fact that the Christian Church has been continuing this work of man's re-creation ever since, and is continuing it before our eyes to-day.   The Christian saint surpasses the natural man as the natural man surpasses the "ape and tiger," and thus reveals to us a new level of creation.   "If any man is in Christ, he is a new creature : the old things are passed away ; behold, they are become new." And through all the twenty centuries of its hampered and hindered history the Christian Church has never lost the power of creating saints—saints who, beneath all the phenomenal conditions that have shaped their lives, plainly recognise the act of their creator.

"Thou hadst pierced our heart," says one of them, "with Thy love, and we carried Thy words fixed like arrows in our inmost being ; and the examples of Thy servants whom from black Thou hadst made white, and from dead, alive, crowded together in the storehouse of our memory, kindled and consumed our sloth." [1]

In other words, the Incarnation was no isolated interference with an otherwise uniform course of human nature, which subsequently closed over it and continued to flow as before.   It was an event which permanently changed the course of human nature, in the case of its believers, by lifting them

[1] Augustine's *Confessions*.

to a new level of life and experience, and so divided history for ever into the times before and after Christ. Thenceforward there has always existed a higher type of humanity, that of the real and sincere followers of Christ. These are the only competent critics of their own experience. For, in St. Paul's language, " the natural man receiveth not the things of the Spirit of God : for they are foolishness unto him : and he cannot know them, because they are spiritually judged. But He that is spiritual judgeth all things, and He himself is judged of no man. . . . But we have the mind of Christ." And the verdict of such men is that they have been regenerated, recreated from above ; by an act which, however wonderful, lessens the sum of the world's wonder, by the light which it throws on the original meaning of creation.

For, after all, the greatest wonder of the world is its existence. We have, as we noticed above, grown so accustomed to ourselves and our fellows and the ordinary course of our daily affairs, that we are apt to forget this, and to take our human nature for granted, as if it were a thing that we fully understood. Hence when any abnormal occurrence, like that of the gospel story, takes us by surprise, we endeavour at once to reduce it to terms of ordinary humanity, as if by so doing we should explain it. But when we pause to philosophise, that is, to wonder, our own existence is our greatest mystery ; and the crux of that mystery is not "how" but "why" we exist. It may be well enough for science to ignore all final causes, as interfering with its own proper study of efficient causation. But when we have gained all the knowledge that science can afford us, and all the additional appliances with which it can supply us, we are no nearer to the solution of the only question that is of primary and permanent interest,—Why do we exist ? Human nature, as it pursues what we call its ordinary course from generation to generation has always this question at heart. It so essentially and inevitably arises within us, from the very make and constitution of our minds, that we may reasonably say that we were created to ask it. And if, in a rationally ordered world, we were created to ask it, we must conclude that we were created to be answered. And that answer, by its very character, must come from outside ourselves. Since, therefore, it is natural for us to ask this question, and natural to expect its answer, we cannot call the answer unnatural, merely because it comes in what we think an unusual way. On the contrary, if the Incarnation is the answer, as Christians believe it to be, it may be every whit as natural, to a wider view, as the natural question which it meets; both alike being parts of one ordered whole.

The fact is, that the legitimate elimination of teleological considerations from scientific inquiry has more or less unconsciously discredited their use in general. But this, of course, is a total mistake; for in the moral and spiritual region they are all-important. This is practically illustrated in our daily life.

"Est aliquid quo tendis et in quod dirigis arcum?"

asks the heathen moralist. Success of any ordinary kind depends on our having an aim, a purpose, an end in view; and the aimless man is a failure. In the same way if we would understand our moral and spiritual life, we must ask not the scientific question, "What is the composition of our faculties?" "What are they made of?" but the philosophical question, "What is their significance?" "To what end do they point?" And when we find, as we do find, that in the last analysis, they point Godward, this teleological consideration should have great weight in our estimate of the probability of a revelation, claiming, like the Christian, to be the complement and completion of man's nature.

Indeed, the rational arguments in favour of the Incarnation are so strong as to suggest that the rejection of them is not purely or even mainly rational, but imaginative and emotional. If we try to conceive such an event happening at the present day the shock of the conception is too great for us. It seems too improbable; too impossible : but it is not our reason so much as our feelings that say so. When Peter said, "Depart from me, for I am a sinful man, O Lord," and when the Gadarenes besought Christ that He would depart out of their coasts, they were, no doubt, spiritually poles asunder. But they were both expressing the same human instinct which shrinks from any startling spiritual manifestation—

> "Before which our mortal nature
> Did tremble like a guilty thing surprised."

And a kindred feeling arises when we attempt to picture to ourselves the occurrence of the Incar-

nation. The more vividly it is realised the more
incredible does it often seem. But only because
it is so strange, so surprising, so stupendous; all
of which are terms expressive of emotional shock.
This feeling may perhaps be more closely connected with the sinful taint in our nature than
we suppose; but on the surface it seems more
emotional than moral, and akin to the discomfort
that we experience at the violation of a customary habit; the habit in this case being our
ordinary way of looking at the world. At any
rate, it is not an intellectual judgment; and its
negative influence must be detected and dis-
counted, before we can reach a judgment that is
properly intellectual, an impartial view of the
facts.

And when we try to face the facts, without
this influence, we must notice that our ability to
interpret human history by the light of present
experience is far inferior to our power of similarly
interpreting physical phenomena. In the latter
case, we understand the laws of the physical
universe better than did our ancestors, and feel
justified in asserting that under similar conditions
they must have operated in the past as they do
now. Even so we labour under two limitations.

For in the first place, our knowledge is after all only relative and partial, and may be seriously modified therefore by future discoveries, as has recently been the case in physics. And, secondly, the similarity of the conditions may often be difficult to determine; as witness the old controversy between the uniformitarians and the advocates of cataclysmic changes in geology, a case that is typical of many more. But these limitations are trifling compared with those that confront us when we turn to human history; and endeavour there to make our present experience a criterion of what is likely to have happened in the past. For then free-will and individuality have to be taken into account. Different generations have lived on very different psychological levels, and with very different degrees of psychological intensity. Great epochs when great deeds were possible, and men "flared out in the flaring of mankind" have been followed by days of small things, without obvious reason for the change. All history is full of surprises. When therefore we attempt to reconstruct the past as it appeared to contemporary eyes—the past as it actually was—we move on very uncertain ground. This is true of all ordinary history; but it is true in a far greater degree of our present subject, God's revelation of Himself to men, in time past. For if we believe in a revelation at all, we must believe that it would be made in the way best fitted to be understood by its recipients. And as the modes and conditions of thought in bygone times have been very materially different from our own, we should expect that a revelation made to any given age in the past, would take the form best suited to that age, and not to the present day; a form therefore of whose probability or improbability our present experience is no criterion. And this is precisely what, in our Christian reading of history did in fact take place. We feel the supreme difficulty, before mentioned, of conceiving such a thing as an Incarnation happening at the present day. But then neither are we called upon to conceive it. Whereas at the period of its historic occurrence there were conditions in the world of thought which made the acceptance of such a conception easier, and did, in fact, enable it rapidly to win its way among men. For there was the remarkable Messianic expectation of the Jews, preparing the members of that particular race for the appearance of an unique personality.

And we can see how Jesus Christ claimed and gradually established His claim to fulfil this expectation in a way which the spirit of the age made perfectly possible. He was recognised by His followers as the very person for whom their race had long been confidently waiting, — the Messiah. And this point being once definitely reached, it was again perfectly possible to lead men on to a larger and deeper conception of who and what Messiah was, when once His resurrection had invested Him with more than human dignity. That conception would doubtless have been too intolerable to be comprehended or sustained by His human followers, while He walked the earth among them ; but could be borne as soon as the awe of His personal presence was removed, as He had said. " I have many things to say unto you, but ye cannot bear them now. . . . Howbeit when He, the Spirit of truth, is come, He shall guide you into all truth. . . . He shall take of Mine, and shall shew it unto you."

Again, in the impression produced by Christ upon His contemporaries signs and wonders bore an important part. And this too was in accordance with the spirit of the age. We whose imaginations are impressed, if not even oppressed,

Q

by the vast scale of the physical universe which science has disclosed, have come, in consequence, to think more of the uniformity than of the spontaneity of nature. And our presuppositions have been formed accordingly. We expect to see Divine action manifested through the operation of general laws, and not through their occasional transcendence. We do not, as a generation, look for miracles; and, as a generation, we do not find them. But it was obviously otherwise with the Jews of the first century. Their view of the world was religious rather than scientific; they saw spiritual operations behind what would nowadays be called natural phenomena. They had God's wondrous works of old time recorded in their history; and they expected miracle to be the credential of a divine message. Miracle was a natural language to them; how natural indeed we may gather from the simple way in which St. Paul takes it for granted, as a thing familiar to his hearers, while laying comparatively slight stress upon the importance of its use. Miracle was a natural language; and accordingly Christ used it. He used it indeed with such reserve and dignity and significance as to separate His "signs" from all vulgar wonder-working, and

constitute them, for all time, a fitting expression
of His unique personality. He rebuked them
that sought after a sign, while remaining in moral
and spiritual blindness. But, we read, "this
beginning of signs did Jesus . . . and His disciples
believed on Him." He arrested interest and
bespoke attention to His character and claim by
their use. And nowhere do we see this more
emphasised than amid all the profound spirituality
of the Fourth Gospel.

Such has always been the common Christian
belief. But the same tendency that we have
noticed above to prefer a revelation made
subjectively or through the mind shows itself
again in a desire to bring the miracles of the
gospels into a line with ordinary events as they
happen in the present day. And notably is this
the case, as we have already had occasion to
point out, with the crowning miracle of the
Resurrection. This is resolved into a subjective
conviction that Jesus Christ was spiritually alive,
and that spiritual intercourse with Him was
therefore possible. "St. Paul," says one writer,
"knew nothing of the empty tomb," forgetting
that by Easter evening the empty tomb had
done its work, and ceased to have any further

significance for those who had already seen the Lord.

Now all that we have said above on the relation of matter to spirit in general applies also to this case; but here in particular with exceptional importance. For the early Christian conviction of the Resurrection was conspicuously different from the faith with which we believe in the continual existence of a martyr, and trust that he lives unto God and there finds his reward. For the whole point of the conviction was that Christ lived again "unto man." God had not only accepted the sinless life and obedient death, but he had proclaimed that acceptance to men. "This is My beloved Son, in whom I am well pleased." He had vindicated and justified and glorified Christ in the eyes of those who loved and trusted Him. In this light the Resurrection was the completion of the Incarnation, the climax of the creation of man, the advent of the "new creature." Spiritual facts are not complete, as we have seen, till they have expressed themselves; and matter, as we call it, is their language, the medium of their expression. And the risen body of Christ was to His disciples this expression; the exhibition, the manifestation, and therefore the assurance of the spiritual triumph which it revealed. The cross had indeed completed the spiritual conflict; but the Resurrection exhibited to men God's recognition of the victor; it was the proclamation of His victory. All our moral instincts demand that, if the world should indeed be rational, virtue in the end shall triumph openly; and here was the beginning of that open triumph; the earnest of the ultimate fulfilment of our instinctive demand. " He is the head of the body, the Church : who is the beginning, the first - born from the dead "; " the first - born among many brethren "; " the first - fruits of them that slept."

There can be no question that this is the way in which the early Church viewed the Resurrection; and no other view would conceivably explain the moral miracle of the change in the disciples, from cowardice and diffidence to confidence and strength. Thus the externality or objective character of the Resurrection was of its very essence; and carried its message home, like the other miracles, to minds prepared for their reception.

Then there came the time for Christianity to break from the limitations of Judaism, and pro-

claim itself an universal religion. Consequently
the Person who had been brought home to the
Jewish mind as the Messiah, must be described
in terms that the world at large could understand. And so, under the promised guidance,
as Christians believe, of the Holy Spirit, a new
category from the thought of the age was adopted,
that of the Word, or Divine Reason; a conception
implicit in St. Paul, and explicit in St. John,
which at once gave the Incarnation its place in
general thought, and enabled its proclamation
to all nations. "The Word became flesh, and
dwelt among us." "Who, being in the form of
God, counted it not a prize to be on an equality
with God: but emptied Himself, taking the form
of a servant, being made in the likeness of men."
Here again we have a mode of speech, which we
indeed have inherited as a part of our Christianity,
but which belongs to the philosophical phraseology
of another age than ours. We could never have
employed it for the first time to-day. Yet it was
precisely the term adapted to give expression to
the Church's belief that Jesus Christ was very
God of very God; and so to enable the transmission of that belief along the ages.

Thus the Messianic expectation, the acceptance

of miracle, and the conception of the Logos or Word were among the mental conditions which enabled men first to realise and transmit the doctrine of the Incarnation. And this does not mean that the doctrine resulted from modes of thought which we have outgrown and superseded; but simply that the Incarnation took place at the precise period in history when the current modes of thought were most appropriate for its reception. There was a fulness of time, a particular conjuncture, a right moment for its occurrence ; and it thereupon occurred. Historians have often pointed out how remarkably this was the case with the material conditions of the contemporary world ; how the universal empire, the universal language, the Roman peace (*pax Romana*) and the Roman roads, with all that they involved, were adapted, as never before, for the spread of a universal religion. And the same was the case in the intellectual world. It was at the right stage for the entry of the new creation.

But for us the day of "origins" is long since passed. The morning stars no more sing together. "Custom lies upon us with a weight." We live in a routine that has become a second nature. And so the Church appeals to us in customary ways; through the usages of a society that has been so long in the world as to seem a part of it, and the ministry of men that are of like passions with ourselves. But this must not mislead us into thinking that we have evolved our own religion. Its appeal still comes to us from outside ourselves. The Church still confronts the world; still proclaims a revelation; still bids us come and see. And, once within its precincts, we forget the fleeting fashions of the ages, in presence of the Eternal—" the Eternal not ourselves "—Jesus Christ the same, yesterday, and to-day, and for ever; and realise that now, as of old, though John did no miracle, all things whatsoever John spake of this man were true.

CHAPTER XII

RECAPITULATION AND CONCLUSION

As we have had occasion in the course of the previous pages to make various digressions, it may be well in conclusion to recapitulate the chief points of our main contention.

In the first place, we must revert to the two ways of looking at the world, which are often somewhat miscalled the scientific and the theological. But as these terms are apt to carry with them prepossessions of one kind or another, it may be more satisfactory, as well as more accurate, to say mechanical or dynamical and teleological : the mechanical or dynamical view being that which considers how the world works, or its efficient causes ; and the teleological view that which considers why it exists, or its final causes. The distinction may perhaps be illustrated by what happens in an ocean voyage. The engineers of the vessel must be thoroughly acquainted with every detail of their machinery, and perfectly capable, in consequence, to control its action ; and upon this knowledge the possibility of the voyage depends. But they need know nothing of the passengers, or the various purposes which have brought them on their journey, nor indeed need they even know their port of destination. On the other hand, the passengers probably know nothing of machinery, and could never work the engines. But they all have their different reasons for embarking ; purposes of business or of pleasure, errands of sorrow or of joy. And it is to enable the fulfilment of these objects that the voyage takes place. Here therefore we have the two kinds of knowledge in sharp contrast, side by side ; the dynamical knowledge of the engineers, without which the passengers could not achieve their purposes ; and the purposes without which there would be no use for the engineers. And however complementary they may be in practice, the two things are fundamentally distinct.

Now the earliest Greek thinkers, the pioneers of European thought, were mainly occupied with speculations about the constitution of the universe, which, however crude, would have to be placed

in the dynamical or scientific class. And it was
not till the Socratic age, and chiefly through
Socrates and his influence upon Plato and Aristotle, that the interests of philosophy came to be
centred upon man and the meaning of his life,
and therefore became teleological. And, roughly
speaking, we may say that teleological considerations remained predominant in thought from that
day till the dawn of modern science at the
Renaissance; that is to say, during the ages of
Plato and Aristotle, the Stoics and Neoplatonists,
the Christian fathers and the schoolmen. Then
with the gradual growth of science and multi-
plication of discoveries, attention shifted increasingly to the mechanical and dynamical aspect of
things, the nature and constitution and processes
and history of man and the world; while teleology
fell into comparative abeyance, and in some
quarters into complete disrepute. We have to
bear in mind, therefore, that this is but a temporary
accident, which does not really affect the importance of final causes. For the question, "Why
was man created?" "What is the end of man?"
must always remain the problem of supreme
interest for man, since it is the question upon
whose answer the practical conduct of his life

depends. And this is essentially a teleological question, that can only be answered, if at all, by examining our personality to see whither it points; to what end our wants and aspirations ultimately tend; what would give us real and adequate satisfaction if attained. No future advance of science can ever have more than the most indirect effect upon this problem; for such advance can only mean increased knowledge of what and how things are, not why they are; it would merely be like the introduction of abler engineers and improved machinery into our ocean steamer. And for the same reason, our present advance upon the science of the past, and consequently wider knowledge of the histories of things, does not materially avail us in the matter. Whereas the long line of thinkers who in bygone ages have dealt with this especial problem, though unacquainted with our later discoveries in science or our historical method, were as well acquainted as ourselves, and often more profoundly acquainted, with the only region of experience that is germane to the question, that is, the moral and spiritual nature of man. And they have argued from it again and again, as we argue after them to-day, that the constitution of our human nature points to communion with God as its only adequate object and end ; and consequently that, in a world which we believe to be rationally ordered, this end must in the ultimate event be realised. This great teleological consideration therefore affects our whole view of the probabilities of things, and leads us not only to desire, but to expect, a revelation as the natural consequence and complement of our original creation.

This presupposition, therefore, is all-important in estimating the evidence of the Incarnation ; and read in the light of it we find that evidence to be irresistibly strong ; and because we believe that Jesus Christ was God Incarnate, and Incarnate in order to reveal Himself to men, we are prepared to find Him teaching more about the Divine Nature than we knew before, namely, that there are a Father, a Son, and a Spirit, in the Godhead, as the gospels represent Him to have done. The Church subsequently formulated this teaching for the purpose of transmission through the ages in terms which were as far as possible negative ; exclusive, that is to say, rather than inclusive of new thoughts upon the subject ; and, moreover, did so in the firm conviction of being guided by the Holy Ghost. And we can still accept the terms in which the doctrine of the Trinity was thus formulated, not as committing us to the adoption of bygone modes of thought, but as symbols selected out of bygone thoughts for Christian use, and thereby invested with the permanence and vitality of the tradition that they were employed to symbolise; which tradition, in the Christian belief, was no more than the authorised interpretation of what Jesus Christ had revealed. Moreover, though transmitted in technical formulæ, the doctrine of the Trinity has been retranslated out of those formulæ by each successive generation for its daily use. And as the belief, the simple belief in Father, Son, and Spirit, it has been the most practically efficient conception of God that has appeared in the world; since it has brought the reality of the divine personality home to men in an unique degree; while, as the theological background of the Incarnation, it has been the presupposition of all that the Christian Church has ever accomplished for mankind. And this practical efficiency of the conception, in an otherwise rationally ordered world, affords the strongest presumption of its truth. Furthermore, though primarily practical, the doctrine has possessed a distinct speculative value for thinkers, as throwing light upon the metaphysical difficulties that attend our conception of God. For by exhibiting relations analogous to those which we call social, within the Godhead, it has enabled us to comprehend, however dimly, that personality, and goodness and love ; and, in a word, all those characteristics which imply reference to another, may exist within the unity of the Godhead without detracting from its absolute and eternal nature. And, finally, this doctrine fulfils the purpose for which we desire a revelation, the only purpose for which we can conceive a revelation to be made, by providing for the possibility of communion with God in a greater degree than any alternative creed. For the only possible alternatives are Deism and Pantheism in one or another of their various forms. And of these, Deism, the belief in a God who is only transcendent and remote, obviously does not satisfy the human desire, and can only appear to do so when qualified by thoughts which are really borrowed from Christianity, as in some of the modern unitarian creeds. While Pantheism can only satisfy our desires at the cost of our personality, by so absorbing man into God that he loses his individual identity, his personal distinction, and ceases, in fact, to be man; in other words, it substitutes annihilation for communion.

This is the central position that we have been endeavouring to emphasise—the time-honoured tradition of the Christian Church. But we must remember that, in thus discussing its intellectual justification, we may easily make the doctrine of the Trinity seem too exclusively intellectual a thing; as if it were some metaphysical theory to be defended. Whereas, of course, the very opposite is the case. For how is it that we really come into immediate contact with the Christian creed in our own experience at the present day? Not primarily as a doctrine at all, but as a living and breathing and organised society of men and women all around us, whose creed is only the intellectual explanation of their actual life. And that actual life consists in the conviction of those who are sincerely living it, in progressive communion with the Father, through fellowship in the mystical body of His Son, effected by the operation of the Holy Spirit within them. First we meet the living Christians (they are the Aristotelian πρότερον ἡμῖν), and then we learn the principle (πρότερον ἁπλῶς) that underlies their life. And so the doctrine first reaches us commended by the whole weight of the life which it visibly and palpably enables. To test the nature of this life we must not look at the multitude of its merely nominal or conventional professors, but at its noblest exemplars, those who have proved what its latent capabilities really are—the recognised saints of old, or the hidden saints of our own day. And, so tested, we recognise a life in which sin is progressively overcome, and the true energies of the soul thereby set free to find their full development; and consequently a life in which personal individuality is not lost, but emphasised, every "diversity of gifts" finding its appropriate realisation. Further, the sole animating motive of this life is love—active, practical, self-sacrificing love of God and man; fruitful, therefore, in good works for others, or, in modern language, essentially altruistic. And it is all this because it is founded on the faith that "God is love; and that whoso dwelleth in love dwelleth in God, and He in him."

We can estimate this life best, as we have said, in its typical examples; but at the same time we must remember that every eminent saint is surrounded by countless approximations to sanc-

R

tity, men and women who move more slowly, but
still surely, in the same direction.　And when
these too are taken into account, the result is
a vast aggregate of Christian characters.　Now,
these characters are facts; there is no disputing
the reality of their existence; we can handle
them, so to speak, and see that they are genuine.
And they are facts whose supreme value is as
obvious as the beauty of the lily or the rose;
things worthy to exist for their own sake, as ends
in themselves.　Merely to see them is at once
to recognise this.　They show, moreover, what
human nature is capable of becoming, by showing
what individual human beings have actually become, and thus illuminate the purpose of man's
original creation.　He was created capable of
becoming, and therefore in order to become this;
this character that we instinctively recognise as
worthy to exist, and therefore as prophetic of its
own continued existence in the world beyond the
grave.　Man, that is to say, has already exhibited
a character, under his present conditions of existence, which, if it only survive in a world of
ampler scope and opportunity, will fully justify
at the bar of reason his original creation; and a
factor in the formation of that character has been

the confident conviction that such is in reality his predestined end.

Thus the doctrine of the Trinity first comes to us by way of personal experience; our personal experience, that is, of the characters which it has created and is creating. It is a force as obviously operating around us as any physical force, and as plainly to be recognised by these results that we can see and test and verify. These results, moreover—Christian characters— are the best, the worthiest, the loveliest things within the range of our experience. Their cause, therefore, must be deemed the most important, the most valuable force in the world; a force, too, whose operation, if we return to our teleological view, must have been included within the purpose of man's original creation, since it renders him what reason recognises that he ought to be, or, in other words, was intended to be; what he must therefore become before ever the rationality of the moral world can be completely established.

Now this force is a spiritual force. It does not compel man blindly, but appeals to his heart and will through his consciousness; through the meaning which it has for him; through his belief

about it. His belief is thus an essential condition
of its operation. And this belief, as it has acted
through nineteen centuries, has not been a mere
general belief in God, but a specific belief in
God's love as revealed in and through the Incarnation. " This is the victory that hath overcome
the world, even our faith. And who is he that
overcometh the world, but he that believeth that
Jesus is the Son of God?" We are confronted,
therefore, with the old alternative that has been
oftener put than ever adequately parried. Either
the most valuable and rational result in the world
has issued from a false belief—the effect has been
a fact, and its cause a fiction; or the force in
question is nothing less than the action of the
Holy Trinity; God in Christ reconciling the world
to Himself. " My Father worketh hitherto, and
I work." And if this be so, that part of the
picture which we cannot as yet see must be as
real as the part which we can see, and the
Christian destiny complete and justify the Christian history—" the building up of the body of
Christ: till we all attain unto the unity of the
faith, and of the knowledge of the Son of God,
unto a full-grown man, unto the measure of the
stature of the fulness of Christ: . . . which is

the head, even Christ; from whom all the body fitly framed and knit together through that which every joint supplieth, according to the working in due measure of each several part, maketh the increase of the body unto the building up of itself in love."

This would be a society of realised personalities, a society in which the personal ideals of every member would be fulfilled; while the will of each, being identified with God's will, would be equally the will of all, and corporate communion would thus be completely attained. And in this statement we recognise the goal which philosophy, as well as religion, has ever sought. For though thinkers have had different conceptions of what constituted reality, their aim has always been the real; to reach reality, to attain realisation, to become real.[1]   Even pessimism bears negative witness to the same effect; for it exhibits the despair that comes of thinking that there is nothing ultimately real.

Finally, this realisation for which the Christian looks, while it is the realisation of himself, is not self-realisation.   For though it requires, as a matter of course, the active co-operation of his

[1] See Note 7.

will, it is not in the last resort his own achievement, but the gift of God, the continuance of
that gift of life to which he owes his original
creation; the fulfilment of the divine purpose in
that creation to make man "in the image of
God," by enabling him to have "Christ formed
in" him—Christ who "came that they may have
life, and may have it abundantly."

If, therefore, we speak in modern language
of the evolution of the Christian religion, we do
not mean by the phrase a process of human discovery, but a process of which, from first to last,
the initiative is divine; the gradual appearance
in history of a divine operation, the gradual unfolding of a divine purpose and plan. God first
created man, as we believe, with religious instincts, that is to say, with an implicit desire for
communion with Himself, and therefore with the
intention of granting that communion. He inspired the Jewish prophets to educate the religion
of their nation, in a way which they unquestionably
believed to be divine, and described by saying
"the word of the Lord came unto me." He
aroused in the Jewish race, through the teaching
of their prophets, a growing expectation of a
greater One to come. Jesus Christ, "in the

fulness of time," came claiming to be that greater
One sent by the Father into the world, and was
subsequently recognised by His Church as the
personal Word of God. He founded His Church
with the words, "As the Father hath sent Me,
even so send I you." And the Christian Church
from that day to this has claimed to be divinely
commissioned, sent with a mission from God.
The ordering of its ministry, the administration
of its sacraments, the nature of its message, all
alike exhibit its claim to be a divine and not a
human institution. While, finally, its profession
of hope for the future is that " He which raised
up the Lord Jesus shall raise up us also by
Jesus." "God hath both raised up the Lord,
and will also raise up us by His own power."
Thus from beginning to end it is God's action,
God's increasing revelation of Himself to the
being whom He created with the desire for that
revelation. And an integral element in this revelation, interwoven with its very texture, is the
doctrine of the Trinity in Unity, which enables
us to see more clearly than otherwise, if still
"through a glass darkly," how God is Love, how
His incarnation is conceivable, and how men
may thereby be raised, without loss of personal

identity, into conscious communion with the fulness of the divine life, "the fulness of Him who filleth all in all."

Now behind all the specific evidence, the weighty and cumulative evidence of the truth of this Christian revelation, there lies the fact of its congruity with the great teleological question which, as we have seen, mankind is for ever impelled to ask,—what is the end of man? what is the true purpose of life's voyage? We never can be satisfied while that question remains unanswered; and if it cannot be answered, we never can be satisfied at all. But the very importunity of the question, as well as its importance to our conduct, lead us to believe that it was meant to be answered "from the foundation of the world." And when as a fact of present experience we are confronted by a society which claims a divine authority to give the answer, and a divine commission to carry it home to all the nations of the earth, and that an answer which adequately satisfies the highest human aspirations, we feel a strong teleological presumption that its message must be true. Such a presumption does not of course act independently of all the other arguments which authenticate the message; but it invests them all with additional significance, as pointing to a conclusion that we antecedently expect to be true. We have described this expectation or presumption in intellectual terms, as being a rational argument from final causes; and such it essentially is, as rational as reason can make it. But it is at the same time much more than this; for it comes to us weighted with all the unsatisfied emotion of the world; all the love that here has found no outlet; all the tears of mourners for their dear ones in the grave; all the righteous efforts that here have not succeeded; all the prayers that here have seemed to meet with no response; all the courage of the martyrs; all the patience of the saints; all the yearning of the human heart for God. It is the conviction— the confident conviction—of our whole personality, our reason, our feelings, and our will together that these things will not, cannot be in vain. With this conviction we approach the history of Him who said, "Come unto Me all ye that labour and are heavy laden, and I will give you rest"; and in that history, so approached, we find the answer to the world's great need.

This then is the region wherein our doctrine lies—the region of the purpose of the passengers through life, not that of the machinery whereby life is carried on; the region not of life's how, but of life's why; a region which, in the words that we quoted at starting, remains "relatively stable, through the flux of change in which development works out its results."

On the other hand, it is in this latter region that both scientific research and historical criticism move and have their being. Consequently they cannot directly affect the teleological question of man's destiny, or his present consciousness of relation to God, Christian belief, or Christian experience. They could only do so indirectly by inducing a modification of our whole philosophy of life; and this they cannot legitimately effect, since that philosophy mainly depends, as we have seen, upon other than scientific or critical considerations. This has now come to be generally recognised in the case of physical science. A generation or more ago there was a notorious tendency on the part of many, though not all, scientific thinkers towards materialism. They had "swept the heavens with their telescopes and found no God"; they had scrutinised the brain with their microscopes and seen no soul. But the extravagance of the position provoked

its own refutation. For it obviously resulted
from the illegitimate importation of philosophical
or rather unphilosophical assumptions into the
scientific facts — assumptions about spiritual
existence, with which scientific methods of inquiry have nothing to do. Hence the result has
been a more general recognition of the limits
within which true science works, and to the
observation of which it owes its intellectual progress and practical utility.

And a similar process has taken place with
regard to the criticism of the New Testament.
About the time when the above-mentioned wave
of materialism was rising to its height, the extremely negative critics of the New Testament
were proclaiming that they found in it no Incarnation, and no revelation of the Trinity. And
many searchings of hearts were the result. But
this again has led to counter-criticism, in the
course of which we have come to distinguish,
with increasing clearness, between criticism
proper and the negative assumptions of particular critics—assumptions that the doctrines in
question were antecedently incredible, and must
therefore be explained away. These assumptions
do not arise out of the documents criticised by

any logical process of deduction ; but, as in the parallel case of science, they are imported into the facts ; they are presuppositions in the minds of the individual critics formed on other than strictly critical grounds. And when once this distinction has become clear, negative criticism need no longer be so disconcerting as it formerly was to many minds. For when we ask on what grounds the assumptions in question ultimately rest, we are brought back at once to the region of our general philosophy of life. And there our teleological considerations immediately reassume their sway; there the profound adaptation of Christianity to human need reappears ; there, above all, the fact has to be reckoned with, that the doctrines in question supposed to be incredible, have been for nigh twenty centuries, and still are at the present day, through the living agency of the Christian society, the foremost force in the spiritual world.

ILLUSTRATIVE NOTES

NOTE 1

THIS is of course the traditional Christian position; but since I have been criticised for maintaining it in a previous book, on the ground that it implies an undue distrust of reason, I am glad to quote the following passage from so thoroughly philosophical a modern theologian to the same effect :—

"It is not pretended for one moment that the doctrine of the Trinity can be proved by philosophy. That doctrine in its Christian form could never have existed except for the revelation of the Divine which took place in the person, life, teaching, death, and resurrection of Jesus Christ. The Son revealed the Father, and only through the Son can God be known as the Father. In knowing the Son we know the Father, and in knowing the Father we know the Son. The revelation which took place in Christ was the joint revelation of both. So is it also with the revelation of the Spirit. It is only on the basis of the Christian revelation that we can found a doctrine of the Holy Ghost as the Spirit of Truth who guides the thoughts of the Christian ages, who teaches and imparts the mind of Christ, who takes of Christ and declares it to Christ's people. It is only the thoughts which move within the circuit of the Christian revelation which find themselves compelled to fall back upon the Christian doctrine of the Trinity. Or, in other words, it is only within the sphere of the Holy Ghost's influence that Father and Son in their mutual relations are revealed. 'In that day,' said Christ, speaking of the coming of the Paraclete, 'ye shall know that I am in My Father, and ye in Me, and I in you.' The Spirit makes the knowledge of the Father and the Son in their relation to one another and to men possible. And in this fact the Spirit's own existence and relation to both are implied. Thus Christianity itself may be regarded as the revelation of the Trinity, and apart from that revelation it is vain to seek for any proof of the doctrine.

"This seems to be undoubtedly the Christian position as explained by our Lord Himself, and as understood by all the profounder minds among Christian theologians from the beginning.

"The proof of the doctrine of the Trinity remains then, for us, where it has always been. It depends upon the Christian revelation. The doctrine comes to light whenever men accept the facts of the life of Christ, and honestly and intelligently attempt to discover the theory of the Divine Nature which is implied in them. Or, in other words, the doctrine of the Trinity is the theoretical presupposition of the Christian religion."—D'ARCY, *Idealism and Theology*, Lect. vi.

NOTE 2

The essentially social nature of personality is admirably analysed in W. Richmond's *Essay on Personality*, of which the following two passages are to our point :—

"It is the individuality of personal life which marks the characteristically modern idea of a person, as, *e.g.*, when we speak of personal sympathy, of personal antipathy, of personal affection, of personal religion. All these emotions are eminently personal in the sense that they are eminently individual. They intensify the sense of individual life. They are keen, vivid, emphatically accented moments of individual existence. But on a moment's consideration it is plain that in such cases as these, what evokes and intensifies the personal life of the individual person is some relation to a person other than himself. Personal religion is perhaps the most suggestive instance. There is no stronger case of the use of the word 'personal' to indicate what is genuinely and thoroughly spontaneous, inward, individual. Personal religion emphatically means the religion which is one's own. There is, in fact, no religion in which men have claimed so decidedly to call their souls their own. And yet it is just in regard to their own relation to a person other than themselves that they make the claim. It is in regard to faith, the dependence of the soul on God; to believe, the formulation of the soul's own knowledge of God; to love, the devotion of the soul to God. The only quarrel of the champions of personal religion with the ecclesiastical system from which they wished to make good their escape, has been that by these systems the spiritual relationship and communion between the soul and God had been obscured and clogged. Religion is here conceived as a relation between the personal being of God and the personal being of man; and the complaint is that, God being shut off, the personal life of man is impoverished and starved. The closer consideration, indeed, of this and similar uses of the word would suggest the hypothesis that the word 'personal' is only rightly applied to any feeling of the individual, when the feeling is a consciousness of relation to another person."— WILFRED RICHMOND, *An Essay on Personality*, ii. 18.

"When Christian theology conceives God as a Personal Being, it does not conceive God as *a* Person. Personality attaches to God not as one Person, but as Three. God is One, individual, in the sense that He is whole, complete in Himself, but, as it has been said, ' whereas each human individual being has one personality, the Divine Being has Three.'[1] His unity is a unity of Persons, and it is as a unity of Persons, and as a unity of Persons only, that Personality is conceived to be the supreme Reality. Personality, in the form in which it is supposed to be most intensely and unmistakably real, is a communion, a fellowship of Persons, a communion of will and character, a communion of intelligence and mind, a communion of love, implying that each Person is, in these various phases or aspects of personal life, capable of complete communion with others.

"And it is further to be observed that the person thus conceived is definitely conceived as an object of knowledge. The purpose of theology in this region was to define the personality of God as *known*; not to describe His operations on the will, or to shadow forth the meaning of religious emotion, but definitely to answer the question what God *is*. The personality, that is, which we have described, had the definiteness of conception which belongs to an idea of what is conceived actually to exist. The question of theology was: What *is* God? And the answer was: God *is* a fellowship, a communion of Persons."—*Ibid.* ii. 17.

NOTE 3

For a philosophical analysis of this class of arguments see Ormond's *Foundations of Knowledge*. His conclusion is as follows:—

"Nothing is more common than for men to assert the truth of things on the ground of their practical value. They

---

[1] Newman, *Arians*, Appendix, p. 439.

begin by wishing that they were true, and end by affirming that they must be true. This is the natural history of a large proportion of the most cherished beliefs of the race, and there is no disposition here to challenge the validity of many of the beliefs so favoured. But the question here is not whether the will to believe may or may not lead to true beliefs, but rather whether the will to believe, the determination to assent to the truth of a thing because of its practical relation to good, is a sufficient ground for any belief. . . . In the discussion of the epistomological value of motives of practical worth we found that it was necessary to apply the general test of rationality, and we found in general that it is possible for what Kant calls a postulate of the practical reason to take such a form that the denial of it would be tantamount to a denial of the objective rationality of our world. In this case we saw that our postulate acquires the force of knowledge. Again, we have found that a practical postulate may assume such a form that the denial of it would be tantamount to the denial of the subjective rationality of our world; that is to an overthrowal of all standards of value. In this case the belief takes on the form of necessity. . . . Now, the conclusion which I wish to draw from these considerations is just this : that while the fact that the will to believe is a generator of beliefs is not in dispute, yet when the question of the legitimacy of beliefs thus generated comes up it cannot be answered by simply claiming the right to believe a proposition because its affirmation carries with it a practical good. This would inevitably throw wide open the floodgates of credulity and superstition. But what is needed is such a criticism of the grounds of belief as will enable us to determine the relation of the good involved to our world as a whole. If the good is of such a nature that it is involved in the rationality of our world, and its denial would be tantamount to a wreck of that rationality, then we have the strongest reason for believing it to be true, and the same is true in regard to beliefs that may be asserted as necessary or as only probable. *The final ground of their affirmation is not the fact that they are good, but rather our conviction that they are implicated either necessarily or in a lesser degree, in the rationality of the world, and that their denial would leave the world, so far forth, irrational and absurd.* And this conviction rests in the last analysis *on our intuition of the truth that the ultimate harmony of the good and the true, so that the good shall be true and the true good, is involved in the essence of that idea of rationality the denial of which means the wreck of all knowledge."*—ORMOND, *Foundations of Knowledge,* iii. 3.

NOTE 4.—BUDDHISM

" The motive which Buddhist morality recognises, if it can be said to recognise any, is wholly selfish and individual. It is not for the love of truth or goodness, nor for the benefit of others,—to instance the two principal motives recognised by other merely human systems,—it is solely for the individual's own advantage that he is incited to cultivate virtue. Nor is it a very brave or noble selfishness. It seeks, not to make the best of self, like the Greek selfishness, but to escape from pain and from the burdens of life. It is not ennobling.

"And the idea of duty is utterly absent. From first to last, the sacred books are terribly consistent in failing to recognise any sort of 'obligation.' . . . Much as we read of effort, it is always effort for self, effort to attain independence and quiet; never work for the sake of work, or work for the sake of others, or work for the sake of duty. This system is unsocial. If it recognises the propriety of mutual kindness, it recognises—except in certain family relationships—no duty of mutual service or action.

"For with all its proud claims and assertions of attainment, Buddhism does in effect deny the high capacities of man. The Brahmin ideal of absorption into the One Supreme Being was nobler and nearer truth. That Buddhism knows nothing of such absorption, if only because it admits no such Supreme Being, is now at last beginning to be understood. The Buddhist theory makes the fatal mistake of supposing that it is grand to have nothing and no one to look up to. The monk, if he has attained the further stages of his course, can look down, it is pretended, on deities and all that is divine. Sakra, prince of the gods, and the great Brahma himself, are supposed to pay homage to a monk. But this does not exalt the monk ; it takes away from him the opportunity of being great. There is no reality about it; if it is a kind of greatness, it is one not compatible with humanity. Buddhism degrades man by denying that there is any being above him. A similar complaint may justly be made against that which Buddhism does propose as man's final goal and aim, extinction or Nirvana. No language could be too strong to express the indignation with which a true sense of human dignity rouses us to protest against this dreary calumny.

"In view of such defects . . . I cannot, for my part, rank this system, regarded as a theory of human life and action, with the best of those which, apart from divine revelation, men have found."—COPLESTONE, *Buddhism*, c. 15.

NOTE 5.—MAHOMETANISM

"The writer of the Koran does indeed, if any discerner of hearts ever did, take the measure of mankind ; and his measure is the same that Satire has taken, only expressed with the majestic brevity of one who had once lived in the realm of silence. 'Man is weak,' says Mahomet. And upon that maxim he legislates. 'God is minded to make His religion light unto you, for man was created weak.' 'God would make his religion an ease unto you' — a suitable foundation of the code which followed, and fit parent of that numerous offspring of accommodations, neutralising qualifications, and thinly-disguised loopholes to the fraud and rapacity of the Oriental, which appear in the Koran, and show, where they do appear, the author's deep acquaintance with the besetting sins of his devoted followers. The keenness of Mahomet's insight into human nature ; a wide knowledge of its temptations, persuasives, influences under which it acts ; a vast immense capacity of forbearance for it, half grave half genial, half sympathy half scorn, issue in a somewhat Horatian model, the character of the man of experience who despairs of any change in man, and lays down the maxim that we must take him as we find him. . . . The breadth and flexibility of mind that could negotiate with every motive of interest, passion, and pride in man is surprising ; there is boundless sagacity ; what is wanting is hope, a belief in the capabilities of human nature. There is no upward flight in the teacher's idea of man. Instead of which, the notion of the power of earth, and the impossibility of resisting it, depresses his whole aim, and the shadow of the tomb falls upon the work of the great false Prophet.

"The idea of God is akin to the idea of man. 'He knows us,' says Mahomet. God's *knowledge*, the vast *experience*, so to speak, of the Divine Being, his infinite acquaintance with man's frailties and temptations, is appealed to as the ground of confidence. 'He is the Wise, the Knowing One,' 'He is the Knowing, the Wise,' 'He is easy to be reconciled.' Thus is raised a notion of the Supreme Being which is rather an extension of the character of the large-minded and sagacious man of the world, than an extension of man's virtue and holiness. He forgives because he knows too much to be rigid, because sin universal ceases to be sin, and must be given way to. Take a man who has had large opportunity of studying mankind, and has come into contact with every form of human weakness and corruption; such a man is indulgent as a simple consequence of his knowledge, because nothing surprises him. So the God of Mahomet forgives by reason of His vast knowledge. The absence of the doctrine of the Atonement makes itself felt in the character of that Being who forgives without a Sacrifice for sin; showing that without that doctrine there cannot even be high Deism. So knit together is the whole fabric of truth; without a sacrifice, a pardoning God becomes an easy God: and an easy God makes a low human nature. No longer awful in His justice, the Wise, 'the Knowing one,' degrades His own act of forgiveness by converting it into connivance; and man takes full advantage of so tolerant and convenient a master. 'Man is weak,' and 'God knows him,'—these two maxims taken together constitute an ample charter of freedom for human conduct. 'God knows us,' says man; He knows that we are not adapted to a very rigid rule, He does not look upon us in that light, He does not expect any great things from us; not an inflexible justice, not a searching self-denial, not a punctilious love of our neighbour; He is considerate, He is wise, He knows what we can do, and what we cannot do; He does not condemn us, He makes allowance for us, 'He knows us.' So true is the saying of Pascal that 'without the knowledge of Jesus Christ we see nothing but confusion in the nature of God and in our own nature.' "—MOZLEY, *Bampton Lectures*, vii.

NOTE 6

As the doctrine of the Divine immanence is now sometimes proclaimed as a substitute for that of the Incarnation, it may be as well to point out that this is the exact converse of the Patristic view; which regarded the former doctrine as the necessary ground and presupposition of the latter, and the latter as the natural consequence of the former. Compare the following passages :—

" The philosophers of the Greeks say that the universe is a great body; and rightly so. For we see it and its parts as objects of our senses. If, then, the Word of God is in the Universe, which is a body, and has united Himself with the whole and with all its parts, what is there surprising or absurd, if we say that He has united Himself with man also. For if it were absurd for Him to have been in a body at all, it would be absurd for Him to be united with the whole either, and to be giving light and movement to all things by His providence. For the whole also is a body. But if it become Him to unite Himself with the universe, and to be made known in the whole, it must beseem Him also to appear in a human body, and that by Him it should be illumined and worked. For mankind is part of the whole, as well as the rest, and if it be unseemly for a part to have been adopted as His instrument to teach men of his Godhead, it must be most absurd that He should be made known even by the whole universe.

" For just as, while the whole body is quickened and illumined by man, supposing one said it were absurd that man's power should also be in the toe, he would be thought foolish; because, while granting that he pervades and works in the whole, he demurs to his being in the part also; thus he who grants and believes that the Word of God is in the whole universe, and that the whole is illumined and moved by Him, should not think it absurd that a single human body also should receive movement and light from Him. But if it is because the human race is a thing created and has been made out of nothing, that they regard that manifestation of

the Saviour in man, which we speak of, as not seemly, it is
high time for them to eject Him from creation also; for it
too has been brought into existence by the Word out of
nothing. But if, even though creation be a thing made, it is
not absurd that the Word should be in it, then neither is it
absurd that He should be in man. For whatever idea they
form of the whole, they must necessarily apply the like idea
to the part. For man also, as I said before, is a part of the
whole. Thus it is not at all unseemly that the Word should
be in man, while all things are deriving from Him their light
and movement and light, as also their authors say, 'In him
we live and move and have our being.' So, then, what is
there to scoff at in what we say, if the Word has used that,
wherein He is, as an instrument to manifest Himself? For
were He not in it, neither could he have used it; but if we
have previously allowed that He is in the whole and in its
parts, what is there incredible in His manifesting Himself in
that wherein He is? For by His own power He is united
wholly with each and all, and orders all things without stint,
so that no one could have called it out of place for Him to
speak, and make known Himself and His Father, by means of
sun, if He so willed, or moon, or heaven, or earth, or waters,
or fire; inasmuch as He holds in one all things at once, and
is in fact not only in all, but also in the part in question, and
there invisibly manifests Himself. In like manner, it cannot
be absurd if, ordering as He does the whole, and giving life
to all things, and having willed to make Himself known
through men, He has used as His instrument a human body
to manifest the truth and knowledge of the Father. For
humanity, too, is an actual part of the whole, and as mind,
pervading man all through, is interpreted by a part of the
body, I mean the tongue, without any one saying, I suppose,
that the essence of the mind is on that account lowered, so
if the Word, pervading all things, has used a human instru-

ment, this cannot appear unseemly. For, as I have said previously, if it be unseemly to have used a body as an instrument, it is unseemly also for Him to be in the whole."— ATHANASIUS, *De In.* §§ 41, 42.

"That Deity should be born in our nature ought not reasonably to present any strangeness to the minds of those who do not take too narrow a view of things. For who, when he takes a survey of the universe, is so simple as not to believe that there is Deity in everything, penetrating it, embracing it, and seated in it? For all things depend on Him who is, nor can there be anything which has not its being in Him who is. If, therefore, all things are in Him, and He in all things, why are they scandalised at the plan of revelation, when it teaches that God was born among men, that same God whom we are convinced is even now not outside mankind? For although this last form of God's presence amongst us is not the same as that former presence, still His existence amongst us equally both then and now is evidenced; only now He who holds together Nature in existence is transfused in *us*; while at that other time He was transfused throughout *our nature*, in order that our nature might by this transfusion of the Divine become itself divine. —GREG. NYS. *Great Cat.* 25.

"'But the nature of man,' it is said 'is narrow and circumscribed, whereas the Deity is infinite. How could the infinite be included in the atom?' But who is it that says the infinitude of the Deity is comprehended in the envelopment of the flesh as if it were in a vessel? Not even in the case of our own life is the intellectual nature shut up within the boundary of the flesh. On the contrary . . . the soul by the movements of its thinking faculty can coincide at will with the whole of creation. . . . If, then, the soul of man although by the necessity of its nature it is transfused through the body, yet presents itself everywhere at will, what necessity is there for saying that the Deity is hampered by an environment of fleshly nature ?"—*Id. ib.* 10.

An interesting statement of the immanence of Christ in the universe seems probably to be contained in the Oxyrhynchus "Saying of Jesus":

"Wherever there are two, they are not without God's presence, and if anywhere one is alone, I say I am with him. Raise the stone, and there thou shalt find me; cleave the wood, and I am there."—LOCK and SANDAY, *Sayings of Jesus.*

NOTE 7

Compare the text with the following definition of reality by one of our most recent philosophers :—

"Being is something Other than themselves which finite ideas seek. They seek Being as that which, if at present known, would end their doubts. Now Being is not something independent of finite ideas, nor yet a merely immediate fact that quenches them. . . . Being involves the validity of ideas. . . . Yet mere validity, mere truths of ideas cannot be conceived as a bare universal fact. We wanted to find its concreter content, its finally determinate form. . . . No finite idea can have or conform to any object, save what its own meaning determines, or seek any meaning or truth but its own meaning and truth. Furthermore, a finite idea is as much an instance of will as it is a knowing process. In seeking its own meaning, it seeks then simply the fuller expression of its own will. Its only Other is an Other that would more completely express it. Its object proves therefore to be, as proximate finite object, any fuller determination whatever of its own will and meaning. But as final object, the idea can have only its final embodiment in a complete and individual form. This final form of the idea, this final object sought when we seek Being is (1) a complete expression of the internal meaning of the finite idea with which, in any case, we start our quest ; (2) a complete fulfilment of the will or purpose partially embodied in this idea ; (3) an individual life for which no other can be substituted.

"Now in defining this complete life, in which alone the finite idea, as a passing thrill of conscious meaning, can find the genuine object that it means fully embodied, we have so far still used many expressions derived from the conception of mere validity. We have spoken of what this life would be *if it were* completely present. But having used these forms of expression as mere scaffolding, at the close we must indeed observe afresh that all validity, as an incomplete universal conception, needs another to give it final meaning. If there is validity, there is then an object more than merely valid which gives the very conception of validity its own meaning. . . . We have now defined what this object is. It is an individual life, present as a whole, *totum simul,* as the scholastics would have said. This life is at once a system of facts, and the fulfilment of whatever purpose any finite idea, in so far as it is true to its own meaning, already fragmentarily embodies. This life is the completed will, as well as the completed experience, corresponding to the will and experience of any one finite idea.

"In its wholeness the world of Being is the world of individually expressed meanings—an individual life, consisting of the individual embodiments of the wills represented by all finite ideas. Now *to be,* in the final sense, means to be just such a life, complete, present to experience, and conclusive of the search for perfection which every finite idea in its own measure undertakes whenever it seeks for any object. We may therefore lay aside altogether our *ifs* and *thens,* our *validity* and our other such terms, when we speak of the final concept of Being. What is, is for us no longer a mere Form, but a Life ; and in our world of what was before mere truth the light of individuality and of will have finally began to shine.   The sun of true Being has arisen before our eyes.

"In finding this world have we not been already led to the very definition of the divine life?"—J. ROYCE, *The World and the Individual*, Lect. vii. p. 341.

THE END

Printed by R. & R. CLARK, LIMITED, *Edinburgh*

MACMILLAN AND CO.'S NEW BOOKS.

FREDERICK TEMPLE. An Appreciation. By E. G. SANDFORD, Archdeacon of Exeter. With a Biographical Introduction by WILLIAM TEMPLE, Fellow of Queen's College, Oxford; son of the Archbishop. With Portraits, etc. 8vo. 4s. net.

INTRODUCTION AND NOTES ON THE APOCALYPSE. Ch. I.—III. By the late Rev. F. J. A. HORT, D.D. Crown 8vo.

A HISTORY OF THE CHRISTIAN CHURCH FROM THE REFORMATION TO THE PRESENT TIME. By S. CHEETHAM, D.D., F.S.A., Archdeacon and Canon of Rochester. Crown 8vo.

ST. PAUL'S EPISTLE TO THE THESSALONIANS. Greek Text, with Commentary by the Rev. WILLIAM MILLIGAN, D.D. 8vo.

CRITICAL NOTES ON OLD TESTAMENT HISTORY. THE TRADITIONS OF SAUL AND DAVID. By STANLEY A. COOK, M.A., Fellow and Lecturer in Hebrew and Syriac, Gonville and Caius College, Cambridge; Member of the Editorial Staff of the "Encyclopædia Biblica." 8vo. 2s. 6d. net.

CHRISTUS FUTURUS. By the Author of "Pro Christo et Ecclesia." Crown 8vo. 5s. net.

LETTERS OF MARTIN LUTHER. Translated by MARGARET ANDERSON CURRIE. 8vo.

SPIRITUAL TRUTHS. A Volume of Sermons. By the late Prebendary WHITWORTH. Crown 8vo.

SERMONS. By the late Rev. J. W. SHEPARD. With a Portrait of the Author, and Prefatory Memoir by the Ven. Archdeacon BEVAN, Rector of Chelsea. Crown 8vo.

ALL SAINTS' SERMONS, 1905-1907. By the Rev. W. R. INGE, M.A., D.D., Vicar of All Saints', Ennismore Gardens, and Lady Margaret Professor of Divinity in the University of Cambridge. Crown 8vo.

THE ISLES AND THE GOSPEL, AND OTHER BIBLE STUDIES. By the late HUGH MACMILLAN, D.D., Author of "Bible Teachings in Nature," "Gleanings in Holy Fields," etc. With Portrait and Prefatory Memoir. Crown 8vo.

THE EMPIRE OF CHRIST. Being a Study of the Missionary Enterprise in the light of Modern Religious Thought. By Rev. BERNARD LUCAS, London Missionary Society, Author of "The Faith of a Christian," "The Fifth Gospel," etc. Crown 8vo.

MACMILLAN AND CO., LTD., LONDON.

WORKS BY BISHOP WESTCOTT, D.D.

VILLAGE SERMONS. Crown 8vo. 6s.

PETERBOROUGH SERMONS. Crown 8vo. 6s.

WORDS OF FAITH AND HOPE. Crown 8vo. 4s. 6d.

LESSONS FROM WORK. Second Impression. Crown 8vo. 6s.

A GENERAL SURVEY OF THE HISTORY OF THE CANON OF THE NEW TESTAMENT DURING THE FIRST FOUR CENTURIES. Sixth Edition. Crown 8vo. 10s. 6d.

GENERAL VIEW OF THE HISTORY OF THE ENGLISH BIBLE. Third Edition. Revised by WILLIAM ALDIS WRIGHT. 8vo. 12s. 6d.

THE BIBLE IN THE CHURCH. A Popular Account of the Collection and Reception of the Holy Scriptures in the Christian Churches. Tenth Edition. Pott 8vo. 4s. 6d.

INTRODUCTION TO THE STUDY OF THE FOUR GOSPELS. Eighth Edition. Crown 8vo. 10s. 6d.

THE GOSPEL OF THE RESURRECTION. Thoughts on its Relation to Reason and History. Sixth Edition. Crown 8vo. 6s.

THE REVELATION OF THE RISEN LORD. Fourth Edition. Crown 8vo. 6s.

THE HISTORIC FAITH. Short Lectures on the Apostles' Creed. Third Edition. Crown 8vo. 6s. Also 8vo. Sewed. 6d.

THE REVELATION OF THE FATHER. Short Lectures on the Titles of the Lord in the Gospel of St. John. Second Edition. Crown 8vo. 6s.

CHRISTUS CONSUMMATOR, and other Sermons. Second Edition. Crown 8vo. 6s.

SOCIAL ASPECTS OF CHRISTIANITY. Second Edition. Crown 8vo. 6s.

GIFTS FOR MINISTRY. Addresses to Candidates for Ordination. Crown 8vo. 1s. 6d.

SAINT PAUL'S EPISTLE TO THE EPHESIANS. The Greek Text, with Notes and Addenda. 8vo. 10s. 6d.

THE EPISTLE TO THE HEBREWS. The Greek Text, with Notes and Essays. Third Edition. 8vo. 14s.

THE EPISTLES OF ST. JOHN. The Greek Text, with Notes and Essays. Fourth Edition. 8vo. 12s. 6d.

THE INCARNATION AND COMMON LIFE. Crown 8vo. 9s.

CHRISTIAN ASPECTS OF LIFE. Crown 8vo. 7s. 6d.

THE GOSPEL OF LIFE : Thoughts Introductory to the Study of Christian Doctrine. Crown 8vo. 6s. Also 8vo. Sewed. 6d.

ESSAYS—THE HISTORY OF RELIGIOUS THOUGHT IN THE WEST. Globe 8vo. 4s. net. [Eversley Series.

ON SOME POINTS IN THE RELIGIOUS OFFICE OF THE UNIVERSITIES. Crown 8vo. 4s. 6d.

SOME THOUGHTS FROM THE ORDINAL. Globe 8vo. 1s. 6d.

THOUGHTS ON REVELATION AND LIFE. Being Selections from the Writings of Bishop WESTCOTT. Arranged and Edited by Rev. STEPHEN PHILLIPS. Crown 8vo. 6s.

THE OBLIGATIONS OF EMPIRE. A Sermon. Crown 8vo. Sewed. 3d. net.

CHRISTIAN SOCIAL UNION ADDRESSES. Crown 8vo. 1s. net.

COMMON PRAYERS FOR FAMILY USE. Crown 8vo. 1s. net.

ADDRESS TO MINERS, July 1901. Crown 8vo. Sewed. 6d.

LIFE AND LETTERS OF THE RIGHT REV. BISHOP WESTCOTT. By his Son, the Rev. ARTHUR WESTCOTT. Two Vols. Extra Crown 8vo. 17s. net. Abridged Edition, in One Volume. Extra Crown 8vo. 8s. 6d. net.

By Bishop WESTCOTT and Dr. F. J. A. HORT.

THE NEW TESTAMENT IN THE ORIGINAL GREEK. 8vo. 10s. net.

THE NEW TESTAMENT IN THE ORIGINAL GREEK. Vol. I. Text. Vol. II. Introduction and Appendix. Crown 8vo. 10s. 6d. each. Pott 8vo Edition, 4s. 6d. Roan, 5s. 6d. Morocco, 6s. 6d. India Paper Edition, limp calf, 7s. 6d. net.

MACMILLAN AND CO., LTD., LONDON.

A Catalogue

of

Theological Works

published by

Macmillan & Co., Ltd.

St. Martin's Street
London, W.C.

CONTENTS

THE BIBLE——   PAGE

     History of the Bible   3

     Biblical History   3

     The Old Testament   5

     The New Testament   7

HISTORY OF THE CHRISTIAN CHURCH .   .   .   14

THE CHURCH OF ENGLAND   15

DEVOTIONAL BOOKS   19

THE FATHERS   20

HYMNOLOGY   21

RELIGIOUS TEACHING   22

SERMONS, LECTURES, ADDRESSES, AND THEOLOGICAL
     ESSAYS   22

THEOLOGICAL CATALOGUE

Ube Bible

HISTORY OF THE BIBLE

THE BIBLE IN THE CHURCH. By Right Rev. Bishop WEST-
COTT. 10th Edition. Pott 8vo. 4s. 6d.

A GENERAL VIEW OF THE HISTORY OF THE ENGLISH
BIBLE. By the Right Rev. Bishop WESTCOTT. Revised by
W. ALDIS WRIGHT, Litt.D. 8vo. 12s. 6d.

BIBLICAL HISTORY

THE HOLY BIBLE. (Eversley Edition.) Arranged in Paragraphs,
with an Introduction. By J. W. MACKAIL, M.A. Vols. 2 to 8.
Globe 8vo. 4s. net each.

  Vol. II. Deuteronomy—2 Samuel. III. 1 Kings—Esther. IV.
  Job—Song of Solomon. V. Isaiah—Lamentations. VI. Ezekiel
  —Malachi. VII. Matthew—John. VIII. Acts—Revelation.

THE MODERN READER'S BIBLE. A Series of Books from the
Sacred Scriptures presented in Modern Literary Form. The Text
is that of the Revised Version. It is used by special permission
of the University Presses of Oxford and Cambridge. Edited by
R. G. MOULTON, M.A. Pott 8vo. 2s. 6d. each volume.

HISTORY SERIES, 6 volumes.—Genesis, The Exodus, Deuteronomy,
The Judges, The Kings, The Chronicles.

POETRY SERIES, 3 volumes.—The Psalms and Lamentations, 2 vols.
Biblical Idylls—Solomon's Song, Ruth, Esther, Tobit.

WISDOM SERIES, 4 volumes.—The Proverbs, Ecclesiasticus, Ecclesiastes
and the Wisdom of Solomon, The Book of Job.

PROPHECY SERIES, 4 volumes.—Isaiah, Jeremiah, Ezekiel, Daniel.

NEW TESTAMENT SERIES, 4 volumes.—St. Matthew and St. Mark and
the General Epistles; The Gospel, Epistles, and Revelation of St.
John. St. Luke and St. Paul, 2 vols.

INTRODUCTORY SERIES, 3 volumes.—Bible Stories (Old Testament),
Bible Stories (New Testament), Select Masterpieces of Biblical
Literature.

INTRODUCTORY SERIES. *Cheap Editions.* 1s. 6d. each. Bible Stories
(Old Testament), Bible Stories (New Testament).

ST. JAMES'S GAZETTE.—"While the sacred text has in no way been tampered
with, the books are presented in modern literary form, and are furnished with an introduction and notes by Professor Richard G. Moulton. The notes are scholarly, and of
real help to the student."

BIBLE LESSONS. By Rev. E. A. ABBOTT, D.D. Crown 8vo. 4s. 6d.

SIDE-LIGHTS UPON BIBLE HISTORY. By Mrs. SYDNEY BUXTON.
Illustrated. Crown 8vo. 5s.

STORIES FROM THE BIBLE. First Series. By Rev. A. J. CHURCH.
Illustrated. Crown 8vo. 3s. 6d.

BIBLE READINGS SELECTED FROM THE PENTATEUCH
AND THE BOOK OF JOSHUA. By Rev. J. A. CROSS.
2nd Edition. Globe 8vo. 2s. 6d.

Biblical History—*continued.*

CHILDREN'S TREASURY OF BIBLE STORIES. By Mrs. H. GASKOIN. Pott 8vo. 1s. each. Part I. Old Testament ; II. New Testament ; III. Three Apostles.

THE NATIONS AROUND ISRAEL. By A. KEARY. Cr. 8vo. 3s. 6d.

VILLAGE SERMONS. By Rev. F. J. A. HORT, D.D. 8vo. 6s.
> This Volume contains a Series of Sermons dealing in a popular way with the successive Books of which the Bible is made up. They form an admirable introduction to the subject.

SERMONS ON THE BOOKS OF THE BIBLE. (Selected from *Village Sermons.*) Crown 8vo. 3s. 6d.

POLITICS AND RELIGION IN ANCIENT ISRAEL. An Introduction to the Study of the Old Testament. By the Rev. J. C. TODD, M.A. Cantab., Canon of St. Saviour's Cathedral, Natal. Crown 8vo. 6s.
> The author writes from the standpoint of a frank acceptance of the results of Biblical criticism, and the necessity of restating the history in the light of modern research. His chief aim is to assist those who have been placed in a condition of uncertainty by the results of criticism, and to bring back the attention of intelligent men and women to the Scriptures as a source of spiritual instruction. Canon Todd in his work has assumed the main results of criticism, and while, for the most part, he has avoided the discussion of disputed points, he has in some details advanced views which have not hitherto been suggested.

CRITICAL NOTES ON OLD TESTAMENT HISTORY. The Traditions of Saul and David. By STANLEY A. COOK, M.A. 8vo. 2s. 6d. net.

HISTORY, PROPHECY, AND THE MONUMENTS ; OR, ISRAEL AND THE NATIONS. By Prof. J. F. M'CURDY. 3 Vols. 8vo. Vol. I. To the Downfall of Samaria. Vol. II. To the Fall of Nineveh. Vol. III. To the end of Exile (completing the work). 14s. net each.
> *TIMES.*—"A learned treatise on the ancient history of the Semitic peoples as interpreted by the new light obtained from the modern study of their monuments."

A CLASS-BOOK OF OLD TESTAMENT HISTORY. By Rev. Canon MACLEAR. With Four Maps. Pott 8vo. 4s. 6d.

A CLASS-BOOK OF NEW TESTAMENT HISTORY. Including the connection of the Old and New Testaments. By the same. Pott 8vo. 5s. 6d.

A SHILLING BOOK OF OLD TESTAMENT HISTORY. By the same. Pott 8vo. 1s.

A SHILLING BOOK OF NEW TESTAMENT HISTORY. By the same. Pott 8vo. 1s.

THE BIBLE FOR HOME READING. Edited, with Comments and Reflections for the use of Jewish Parents and Children, by C. G. MONTEFIORE. Part I. TO THE SECOND VISIT OF NEHEMIAH TO JERUSALEM. 2nd Edition. Extra Crown 8vo. 4s. 6d. net. Part II. Containing Selections from the Wisdom Literature, the Prophets, and the Psalter, together with extracts from the Apocrypha. Extra Crown 8vo. 5s. 6d. net.

Biblical History—*continued.*

VOCAL AND LITERARY INTERPRETATION OF THE BIBLE.
By S. S. CURRY, Ph.D. Introduction by FRANCIS G. PEABODY,
D.D. Crown 8vo. 6s. 6d. net.

SCOTSMAN.—"The book, itself a cultured and erudite treatise upon a matter too
often left to teachers of mere physical accomplishments, is further recommended by an
introduction from the pen of an eminent American divine, Dr. Francis G. Peabody. It
deserves the attention of every one interested in its subject."

THE OLD TESTAMENT

SCRIPTURE READINGS FOR SCHOOLS AND FAMILIES.
By C. M. YONGE. Globe 8vo. 1s. 6d. each ; also with comments,
3s. 6d. each.—First Series : GENESIS TO DEUTERONOMY.—Second
Series : JOSHUA TO SOLOMON.—Third Series: KINGS AND THE
PROPHETS.—Fourth Series : THE GOSPEL TIMES.—Fifth Series :
APOSTOLIC TIMES.

THE DIVINE LIBRARY OF THE OLD TESTAMENT. Its
Origin, Preservation, Inspiration, and Permanent Value. By the
Very Rev. Dean KIRKPATRICK, D.D. Crown 8vo. 3s. net.

TIMES.—"An eloquent and temperate plea for the critical study of the Scriptures.
MANCHESTER GUARDIAN.—"An excellent introduction to the modern view
of the Old Testament. . . . The learned author is a genuine critic. . . . He expounds
clearly what has been recently called the 'Analytic' treatment of the books of the Old
Testament, and generally adopts its results. . . . The volume is admirably suited to
fulfil its purpose of familiarising the minds of earnest Bible readers with the work which
Biblical criticism is now doing."

THE DOCTRINE OF THE PROPHETS. Warburtonian Lectures
1886-1890. By the Very Rev. Dean KIRKPATRICK, B.D. 3rd
Edition. Crown 8vo. 6s.

SCOTSMAN.—"This volume gives us the result of ripe scholarship and competent
learning in a very attractive form. It is written simply, clearly, and eloquently ; and it
invests the subject of which it treats with a vivid and vital interest which will commend
it to the reader of general intelligence, as well as to those who are more especially
occupied with such studies."
GLASGOW HERALD.—"Professor Kirkpatrick's book will be found of great value
for purposes of study."
BOOKMAN.—"As a summary of the main results of recent investigation, and as a
thoughtful appreciation of both the human and divine sides of the prophets' work and
message, it is worth the attention of all Bible students."

THE PATRIARCHS AND LAWGIVERS OF THE OLD
TESTAMENT. By FREDERICK DENISON MAURICE. New
Edition. Crown 8vo. 3s. 6d.

THE PROPHETS AND KINGS OF THE OLD TESTAMENT.
By the same. New Edition. Crown 8vo. 3s. 6d.

THE CANON OF THE OLD TESTAMENT. An Essay on the
Growth and Formation of the Hebrew Canon of Scripture. By the
Right Rev. H. E. RYLE, Bishop of Winchester. 2nd Ed. Cr. 8vo. 6s.

EXPOSITOR.—"Scholars are indebted to Professor Ryle for having given them for
the first time a complete and trustworthy history of the Old Testament Canon."
EXPOSITORY TIMES.—"He rightly claims that his book possesses that most
English of virtues—it may be read throughout. . . . An extensive and minute research
lies concealed under a most fresh and flexible English style."

The Old Testament—*continued.*

THE MYTHS OF ISRAEL. THE ANCIENT BOOK OF GENESIS. WITH ANALYSIS AND EXPLANATION OF ITS COMPOSITION. By Amos Kidder Fiske, Author of "The Jewish Scriptures," etc. Crown 8vo. 6s.

THE EARLY NARRATIVES OF GENESIS. By the Right Rev. H. E. Ryle, Bishop of Winchester. Cr. 8vo. 3s. net.

PHILO AND HOLY SCRIPTURE; OR, THE QUOTATIONS OF PHILO FROM THE BOOKS OF THE OLD TESTAMENT. With Introduction and Notes by the Right Rev. H. E. Ryle, Bishop of Winchester. Cr. 8vo. 10s. net.

In the present work the attempt has been made to collect, arrange in order, and for the first time print in full all the actual quotations from the books of the Old Testament to be found in Philo's writings, and a few of his paraphrases. For the purpose of giving general assistance to students Dr. Ryle has added footnotes, dealing principally with the text of Philo's quotations compared with that of the Septuagint; and in the introduction he has endeavoured to explain Philo's attitude towards Holy Scripture, and the character of the variations of his text from that of the Septuagint.

TIMES.—"This book will be found by students to be a very useful supplement and companion to the learned Dr. Drummond's important work, *Philo Judæus.*"

The Pentateuch—

AN HISTORICO-CRITICAL INQUIRY INTO THE ORIGIN AND COMPOSITION OF THE HEXATEUCH (PENTATEUCH AND BOOK OF JOSHUA). By Prof. A. Kuenen. Translated by Philip H. Wicksteed, M.A. 8vo. 14s.

The Psalms—

GOLDEN TREASURY PSALTER. The Student's Edition. Being an Edition with briefer Notes of "The Psalms Chronologically Arranged by Four Friends." Pott 8vo. 2s. 6d. net.

THE PSALMS. With Introductions and Critical Notes. By A. C. Jennings, M.A., and W. H. Lowe, M.A. In 2 vols. 2nd Edition. Crown 8vo. 10s. 6d. each.

THE BOOK OF PSALMS. Edited with Comments and Reflections for the Use of Jewish Parents and Children. By C. G. Montefiore. Crown 8vo. 1s. net.

THE PRAYER-BOOK PSALMS. Relieved of Obscurities, and made smoother for Chanting, with scarcely noticeable alteration. By the Rev. E. D. Cree, M.A. Fcap. 8vo. 2s. net.

Isaiah—

ISAIAH XL.—LXVI. With the Shorter Prophecies allied to it. By Matthew Arnold. With Notes. Crown 8vo. 5s.

A BIBLE-READING FOR SCHOOLS. The Great Prophecy of Israel's Restoration (Isaiah xl.-lxvi.) Arranged and Edited for Young Learners. By the same. 4th Edition. Pott 8vo. 1s.

Zechariah—

THE HEBREW STUDENT'S COMMENTARY ON ZECHARIAH, Hebrew and LXX. By W. H. Lowe, M.A. 8vo. 10s. 6d.

THE NEW TESTAMENT

THE AKHMIM FRAGMENT OF THE APOCRYPHAL GOSPEL OF ST. PETER. By H. B. Swete, D.D. 8vo. 5s. net.

THE PROGRESS OF DOCTRINE IN THE NEW TESTAMENT: The Bampton Lectures, 1864. By Canon Thomas Dehany Bernard, M.A. Fifth Edition. Crown 8vo. 6s.

HANDBOOK TO THE TEXTUAL CRITICISM OF NEW TESTAMENT. By F. G. Kenyon, D.Litt., Assistant Keeper of Manuscripts in the British Museum. 8vo. 10s. net.

THE NEW TESTAMENT IN THE CHRISTIAN CHURCH. Eight Lectures. By Professor E. C. Moore of Harvard University. Crown 8vo. 6s. 6d. net.

THE SOTERIOLOGY OF THE NEW TESTAMENT. By W. P. Du Bose, M.A. Crown 8vo. 7s. 6d.

THE MESSAGES OF THE BOOKS. Being Discourses and Notes on the Books of the New Testament. By Dean Farrar. 8vo. 14s.

ON A FRESH REVISION OF THE ENGLISH NEW TESTAMENT. With an Appendix on the last Petition of the Lord's Prayer. By Bishop Lightfoot. Crown 8vo. 7s. 6d.

DISSERTATIONS ON THE APOSTOLIC AGE. By Bishop Lightfoot. 8vo. 14s.

BIBLICAL ESSAYS. By Bishop Lightfoot. 8vo. 12s.

THE UNITY OF THE NEW TESTAMENT. By F. D. Maurice. 2nd Edition. 2 vols. Crown 8vo. 12s.

A GENERAL SURVEY OF THE HISTORY OF THE CANON OF THE NEW TESTAMENT DURING THE FIRST FOUR CENTURIES. By Right Rev. Bishop Westcott. 7th Edition. Crown 8vo. 10s. 6d.

THE STUDENT'S LIFE OF JESUS. By G. H. Gilbert, Ph.D. Crown 8vo. 5s. net.

THE STUDENT'S LIFE OF PAUL. By G. H. Gilbert, Ph.D. Crown 8vo. 5s. net.

THE REVELATION OF JESUS: A Study of the Primary Sources of Christianity. By G. H. Gilbert, Ph.D. Crown 8vo. 5s. net.

THE FIRST INTERPRETERS OF JESUS. By G. H. Gilbert, Ph.D. Crown 8vo. 5s. net.

NEW TESTAMENT HANDBOOKS. Edited by Shailer Mathews, Professor of New Test. Hist. at the University of Chicago.

A HISTORY OF NEW TESTAMENT TIMES IN PALESTINE (175 B.C.–70 A.D.). By Shailer Mathews, A.M. Crown 8vo. 3s. 6d. net.

A HISTORY OF THE TEXTUAL CRITICISM OF THE NEW TESTAMENT. By Marvin R. Vincent, D.D. Crown 8vo. 3s. 6d. net.

THE BIBLICAL THEOLOGY OF THE NEW TESTAMENT. By Ezra P. Gould, D.D. Crown 8vo. 3s. 6d. net.

The New Testament—*continued.*

A HISTORY OF THE HIGHER CRITICISM OF THE NEW TESTAMENT. By Prof. H. S. NASH. 3s. 6d. net.

AN INTRODUCTION TO THE NEW TESTAMENT. By B. W. BACON, D.D. Crown 8vo. 3s. 6d. net.

THE TEACHING OF JESUS. By G. B. STEVENS, D.D. Crown 8vo. 3s. 6d. net.

THE NEW TESTAMENT IN THE ORIGINAL GREEK. The Text revised by Bishop WESTCOTT, D.D., and Prof. F. J. A. HORT, D.D. 2 vols. Crown 8vo. 10s. 6d. each.—Vol. I. Text; II. Introduction and Appendix.

Library Edition. 8vo. 10s. net. [*Text in Macmillan Greek Type.* School Edition. 12mo, cloth, 4s. 6d.; roan, 5s. 6d.; morocco, 6s. 6d.; India Paper Edition, limp calf, 7s. 6d. net.

GREEK-ENGLISH LEXICON TO THE NEW TESTAMENT. By W. J. HICKIE, M.A. Pott 8vo. 3s.

ACADEMY.—"We can cordially recommend this as a very handy little volume compiled on sound principles."

GRAMMAR OF NEW TESTAMENT GREEK. By Prof. F. BLASS, University of Halle. Auth. English Trans. 8vo. 14s. net.

TIMES.—"Will probably become the standard book of reference for those students who enter upon minute grammatical study of the language of the New Testament."

THE GOSPELS—

PHILOLOGY OF THE GOSPELS. By Prof. F. BLASS. Crown 8vo. 4s. 6d. net.

GUARDIAN.—"On the whole, Professor Blass's new book seems to us an important contribution to criticism. . . . It will stimulate inquiry, and will open up fresh lines of thought to any serious student."

THE SYRO-LATIN TEXT OF THE GOSPELS. By the Rev. FREDERIC HENRY CHASE, D.D. 8vo. 7s. 6d. net.

The sequel of an essay by Dr. Chase on the old Syriac element in the text of Codex Bezae.

TIMES.—"An important and scholarly contribution to New Testament criticism."

SYNOPTICON: An Exposition of the Common Matter of the Synoptic Gospels. By W. G. RUSHBROOKE. Printed in Colours. 4to. 35s. net. Indispensable to a Theological Student.

A SYNOPSIS OF THE GOSPELS IN GREEK. With various Readings and Critical Notes. By the Rev. ARTHUR WRIGHT, B.D., Vice-President of Queens' College, Cambridge Third Edition, Revised. Demy 4to. 10s. net.

THE COMPOSITION OF THE FOUR GOSPELS. By Rev. ARTHUR WRIGHT. Crown 8vo. 5s.

CAMBRIDGE REVIEW.—"The wonderful force and freshness which we find on every page of the book. There is no sign of hastiness. All seems to be the outcome of years of reverent thought, now brought to light in the clearest, most telling way. . . . The book will hardly go unchallenged by the different schools of thought, but all will agree in gratitude at least for its vigour and reality."

INTRODUCTION TO THE STUDY OF THE FOUR GOSPELS. By Right Rev. Bishop WESTCOTT. 8th Ed. Cr. 8vo. 10s. 6d.

FOUR LECTURES ON THE EARLY HISTORY OF THE GOSPELS. By the Rev. J. H. WILKINSON, M.A., Rector of Stock Gaylard, Dorset. Crown 8vo. 3s. net.

The Gospels—*continued.*

THE LEADING IDEAS OF THE GOSPELS. By W. ALEXANDER, D.D. Oxon., LL.D. Dublin, D.C.L. Oxon., Archbishop of Armagh, and Lord Primate of All Ireland. New Edition, Revised and Enlarged. Crown 8vo. 6s.

TWO LECTURES ON THE GOSPELS. By F. CRAWFORD BURKITT, M.A. Crown 8vo. 2s. 6d. net.

Gospel of St. Matthew—

THE GOSPEL ACCORDING TO ST. MATTHEW. Greek Text as Revised by Bishop WESTCOTT and Dr. HORT. With Introduction and Notes by Rev. A. SLOMAN, M.A. Fcap. 8vo. 2s. 6d.

MANCHESTER GUARDIAN.—"It is sound and helpful, and the brief introduction on Hellenistic Greek is particularly good."

Gospel of St. Mark—

THE GREEK TEXT. With Introduction, Notes, and Indices. By Rev. H. B. SWETE, D.D., Regius Professor of Divinity in the University of Cambridge. 2nd Edition. 8vo. 15s.

TIMES.—"A learned and scholarly performance, up to date with the most recent advances in New Testament criticism."

THE EARLIEST GOSPEL. A Historico-Critical Commentary on the Gospel according to St. Mark, with Text, Translation, and Introduction. By ALLAN MENZIES, Professor of Divinity and Biblical Criticism, St. Mary's College, St. Andrews. 8vo. 8s. 6d. net.

SCHOOL READINGS IN THE GREEK TESTAMENT. Being the Outlines of the Life of our Lord as given by St. Mark, with additions from the Text of the other Evangelists. Edited, with Notes and Vocabulary, by Rev. A. CALVERT, M.A. Fcap. 8vo. 2s. 6d.

Gospel of St. Luke—

THE GOSPEL ACCORDING TO ST. LUKE. The Greek Text as Revised by Bishop WESTCOTT and Dr. HORT. With Introduction and Notes by Rev. J. BOND, M.A. Fcap. 8vo. 2s. 6d.

GLASGOW HERALD.—"The notes are short and crisp—suggestive rather than exhaustive."

THE GOSPEL OF THE KINGDOM OF HEAVEN. A Course of Lectures on the Gospel of St. Luke. By F. D. MAURICE. Crown 8vo. 3s. 6d.

THE GOSPEL ACCORDING TO ST. LUKE IN GREEK, AFTER THE WESTCOTT AND HORT TEXT. Edited, with Parallels, Illustrations, Various Readings, and Notes, by the Rev. ARTHUR WRIGHT, M.A. Demy 4to. 7s. 6d. net.

ST. LUKE THE PROPHET. By EDWARD CARUS SELWYN, D.D.
[Crown 8vo. 8s. 6d. net.

Gospel of St. John—

THE CENTRAL TEACHING OF CHRIST. Being a Study and Exposition of St. John, Chapters XIII. to XVII. By Rev. CANON BERNARD, M.A. Crown 8vo. 7s. 6d.

EXPOSITORY TIMES.—"Quite recently we have had an exposition by him whom many call the greatest expositor living. But Canon Bernard's work is still the work that will help the preacher most."

THE GOSPEL OF ST. JOHN. By F. D. MAURICE. Cr. 8vo. 3s. 6d.

THE ACTS OF THE APOSTLES.

ADDRESSES ON THE ACTS OF THE APOSTLES. By the late ARCHBISHOP BENSON. With an Introduction by ADELINE, DUCHESS OF BEDFORD. Super Royal 8vo. 21s. net.

THE CREDIBILITY OF THE BOOK OF THE ACTS OF THE APOSTLES. Being the Hulsean Lectures for 1900-1. By the Rev. Dr. CHASE, President of Queens' College, Cambridge. Crown 8vo. 6s.

THE OLD SYRIAC ELEMENT IN THE TEXT OF THE CODEX BEZAE. By the Rev. F. H. CHASE, D.D. 8vo. 7s. 6d. net.

THE ACTS OF THE APOSTLES IN GREEK AND ENGLISH. With Notes by Rev. F. RENDALL, M.A. Cr. 8vo. 6s.

SATURDAY REVIEW.—"Mr. Rendall has given us a very useful as well as a very scholarly book."

MANCHESTER GUARDIAN.—"Mr. Rendall is a careful scholar and a thoughtful writer, and the student may learn a good deal from his commentary."

THE ACTS OF THE APOSTLES. By F. D. MAURICE. Cr. 8vo. 3s. 6d.

THE ACTS OF THE APOSTLES. Being the Greek Text as Revised by Bishop WESTCOTT and Dr. HORT. With Explanatory Notes by T. E. PAGE, M.A. Fcap. 8vo. 3s. 6d.

ACTS OF THE APOSTLES. The Authorised Version, with Introduction and Notes, by T. E. PAGE, M.A., and Rev. A. S. WALPOLE, M.A. Fcap. 8vo. 2s. 6d.

BRITISH WEEKLY.—"Mr. Page's Notes on the Greek Text of the Acts are very well known, and are decidedly scholarly and individual. . . . Mr. Page has written an introduction which is brief, scholarly and suggestive."

THE CHURCH OF THE FIRST DAYS. THE CHURCH OF JERUSALEM. THE CHURCH OF THE GENTILES. THE CHURCH OF THE WORLD. Lectures on the Acts of the Apostles. By Very Rev. C. J. VAUGHAN. Crown 8vo. 10s. 6d.

THE EPISTLES—The Epistles of St. Paul—

ST. PAUL'S EPISTLE TO THE ROMANS. The Greek Text, with English Notes. By Very Rev. C. J. VAUGHAN. 7th Edition. Crown 8vo. 7s. 6d.

ST. PAUL'S EPISTLE TO THE ROMANS. A New Translation by Rev. W. G. RUTHERFORD. 8vo. 3s. 6d. net.

PILOT.—"Small as the volume is, it has very much to say, not only to professed students of the New Testament, but also to the ordinary reader of the Bible. . . . The layman who buys the book will be grateful to one who helps him to realise that this perplexing Epistle 'was once a plain letter concerned with a theme which plain men might understand.'"

PROLEGOMENA TO ST. PAUL'S EPISTLES TO THE ROMANS AND THE EPHESIANS. By Rev. F. J. A. HORT. Crown 8vo. 6s.

TIMES.—"Will be welcomed by all theologians as 'an invaluable contribution to the study of those Epistles' as the editor of the volume justly calls it."

DAILY CHRONICLE.—"The lectures are an important contribution to the study of the famous Epistles of which they treat."

ST. PAUL'S EPISTLE TO THE GALATIANS. An Essay on its Destination and Date. By E. H. ASKWITH, D.D. Crown 8vo. 3s. 6d. net.

The Epistles of St. Paul—*continued*.

ST. PAUL'S EPISTLE TO THE GALATIANS. A Revised Text, with Introduction, Notes, and Dissertations. By Bishop LIGHTFOOT. 10th Edition. 8vo. 12s.

SAINT PAUL'S EPISTLE TO THE EPHESIANS. The Greek Text with Notes and Addenda. By the late BROOKE FOSS WEST-COTT, D.D., D.C.L., Lord Bishop of Durham. 8vo. 10s. 6d.

ST. PAUL'S EPISTLE TO THE EPHESIANS. A Revised Text and Translation, with Exposition and Notes. By J. ARMITAGE ROBINSON, D.D., Dean of Westminster. 2nd Edition. 8vo. 12s.

GUARDIAN.—"Although we have some good commentaries on Ephesians, . . . no one who has studied this Epistle would say that there was no need for further light and leading ; and the present volume covers a good deal of ground which has not been covered, or not nearly so well covered, before."

CHURCH TIMES. "We have no hesitation in saying that this volume will at once take its place as the standard commentary upon the Epistle to the Ephesians. . . . We earnestly beg the clergy and intelligent laity to read and ponder over this most inspiring volume."

PILOT.—"We can scarcely give higher praise to Dr. Robinson's 'Ephesians' than that which is implied in the expression of our opinion that it is worthy of a place beside the commentaries of Lightfoot, Westcott, and Swete. And an exposition of this Epistle on the scale of their writings was much needed. . . . For soberness of judgment, accuracy of scholarship, largeness of view, and completeness of sympathy with the teaching of St. Paul, the work which is now in our hands leaves nothing to be desired. . . . A work which is in every way so excellent, and which in every page gives us a fresh insight into the meaning and purpose of what is, from at least one point of view, the greatest of St. Paul's Epistles."

ST. PAUL'S EPISTLE TO THE PHILIPPIANS. A Revised Text, with Introduction, Notes, and Dissertations. By Bishop LIGHTFOOT. 9th Edition. 8vo. 12s.

ST. PAUL'S EPISTLE TO THE PHILIPPIANS. With translation, Paraphrase, and Notes for English Readers. By Very Rev. C. J. VAUGHAN. Crown 8vo. 5s.

ST. PAUL'S EPISTLES TO THE COLOSSIANS AND TO PHILEMON. A Revised Text, with Introductions, etc. By Bishop LIGHTFOOT. 9th Edition. 8vo. 12s.

THE EPISTLE TO THE COLOSSIANS. Analysis and Examination Notes. By Rev. G. W. GARROD. Crown 8vo. 3s. net.

AN INTRODUCTION TO THE THESSALONIAN EPISTLES. By E. H. ASKWITH, D.D., Chaplain of Trinity College, Cambridge. Crown 8vo. 4s. net.

ST. PAUL'S EPISTLE TO THE THESSALONIANS. Greek Text, with Commentary by the Rev. GEORGE MILLIGAN, D.D. 8vo.

THE FIRST EPISTLE TO THE THESSALONIANS. With Analysis and Notes by the Rev. G. W. GARROD, B.A. Crown 8vo. 2s. 6d. net.

THE SECOND EPISTLE TO THE THESSALONIANS. With Analysis and Notes by Rev. G. W. GARROD. Cr. 8vo. 2s. 6d. net.

THE EPISTLES OF ST. PAUL TO THE EPHESIANS, THE COLOSSIANS, AND PHILEMON. With Introductions and Notes. By Rev. J. LL. DAVIES. 2nd Edition. 8vo. 7s. 6d.

The Epistles of St. Paul—*continued.*

THE EPISTLES OF ST. PAUL. For English Readers. Part I. containing the First Epistle to the Thessalonians. By Very Rev. C. J. VAUGHAN. 2nd Edition. 8vo. Sewed. 1s. 6d.

NOTES ON EPISTLES OF ST. PAUL FROM UNPUBLISHED COMMENTARIES. By Bishop LIGHTFOOT, D.D. Second Edition. 8vo. 12s.

THE LETTERS OF ST. PAUL TO SEVEN CHURCHES AND THREE FRIENDS. With the Letter to the Hebrews. Translated by ARTHUR S. WAY, D.Litt. Second Edition. Crown 8vo. 5s. net.

ANALYSIS OF CERTAIN OF ST. PAUL'S EPISTLES. Reprinted from Bishop LIGHTFOOT's Commentaries. With Preface by the LORD BISHOP OF DURHAM. Fcap. 8vo. 1s. net.

The Epistles of St. Peter—

THE FIRST EPISTLE OF ST. PETER, I. 1 to II. 17. The Greek Text, with Introductory Lecture, Commentary, and additional Notes. By the late F. J. A. HORT, D.D., D.C.L., LL.D. 8vo. 6s.

THE FIRST EPISTLE OF ST. PETER (Greek Text). By J. HOWARD B. MASTERMAN, Principal of the Midland Clergy College, Edgbaston, Birmingham. Crown 8vo. 3s. 6d. net.

The Epistle of St. Jude and the Second Epistle of St. Peter—

THE EPISTLE OF ST. JUDE AND THE SECOND EPISTLE OF ST. PETER. Greek Text, with Introduction, Notes, and Comments. By JOSEPH B. MAYOR, M.A., Litt.D. 8vo. 14s. net.

NATION.—" An edition which will rank for many years as the most generous and probably the most competent in existence . . . For its excellence the scholar will seek in vain elsewhere."

The Epistle of St. James—

THE EPISTLE OF ST. JAMES. The Greek Text, with Introduction and Notes. By Rev. JOSEPH B. MAYOR, M.A. 2nd Edition. 8vo. 14s. net.

The Epistles of St. John—

THE EPISTLES OF ST. JOHN. By F. D. MAURICE. Crown 8vo. 3s. 6d.

THE EPISTLES OF ST. JOHN. The Greek Text, with Notes. By Right Rev. Bishop WESTCOTT. 4th Edition. 8vo. 12s. 6d.

GUARDIAN.—" It contains a new or rather revised text, with careful critical remarks and helps ; very copious footnotes on the text ; and after each of the chapters, longer and more elaborate notes in treatment of leading or difficult questions, whether in respect of reading or theology. . . . Dr. Westcott has accumulated round them so much matter that, if not new, was forgotten, or generally unobserved, and has thrown so much light upon their language, theology, and characteristics. . . . The notes, critical, illustrative, and exegetical, which are given beneath the text, are extraordinarily full and careful. . . . They exhibit the same minute analysis of every phrase and word, the same scrupulous weighing of every inflection and variation that characterised Dr. Westcott's

The Epistles of St. John—*continued.*

commentary on the Gospel. . . . There is scarcely a syllable throughout the Epistles which is dismissed without having undergone the most anxious interrogation."

SATURDAY REVIEW.—" The more we examine this precious volume the more its exceeding richness in spiritual as well as in literary material grows upon the mind."

The Epistle to the Hebrews—

THE EPISTLE TO THE HEBREWS IN GREEK AND ENGLISH. With Notes. By Rev. F. RENDALL. Cr. 8vo. 6s.

THE EPISTLE TO THE HEBREWS. English Text, with Commentary. By the same. Crown 8vo. 7s. 6d.

THE EPISTLE TO THE HEBREWS. With Notes. By Very Rev. C. J. VAUGHAN. Crown 8vo. 7s. 6d.

TIMES.—" The name and reputation of the Dean of Llandaff are a better recommendation than we can give of the *Epistle to the Hebrews*, the Greek text, with notes ; an edition which represents the results of more than thirty years' experience in the training of students for ordination."

THE EPISTLE TO THE HEBREWS. The Greek Text, with Notes and Essays. By Right Rev. Bishop WESTCOTT. 8vo. 14s.

GUARDIAN.—" In form this is a companion volume to that upon the Epistles of St. John. The type is excellent, the printing careful, the index thorough ; and the volume contains a full introduction, followed by the Greek text, with a running commentary, and a number of additional notes on verbal and doctrinal points which needed fuller discussion. . . . His conception of inspiration is further illustrated by the treatment of the Old Testament in the Epistle, and the additional notes that bear on this point deserve very careful study. The spirit in which the student should approach the perplexing questions of Old Testament criticism could not be better described than it is in the last essay."

The Book of Revelations—

THE APOCALYPSE OF ST. JOHN. The Greek Text, with Introduction, Notes, and Indices. By the Rev. Professor H. B. SWETE, D.D. Second Edition. 8vo. 15s.

CHURCH TIMES.—" We may at once say that no student of the Apocalypse will in the future be able to do without it. Dr. Swete's treatment is exhaustive and impartial, his personal modesty with regard to expressions of opinion is great, while his knowledge is wide and varied, and his method is characterised by intense reverence. . . . The commentary is a model of painstaking care and thought, and particularly strong on its linguistic side."

INTRODUCTION AND NOTES ON THE APOCALYPSE. Ch. I.-III. By the late Rev. F. J. A. HORT, D.D. Crown 8vo.

THE APOCALYPSE. A Study. By ARCHBISHOP BENSON. 8vo. 8s. 6d. net.

LECTURES ON THE APOCALYPSE. By Rev. Prof. W. MILLIGAN. Crown 8vo. 5s.

DISCUSSIONS ON THE APOCALYPSE. By the same. Crown 8vo. 5s.

LECTURES ON THE REVELATION OF ST. JOHN. By Very Rev. C. J. VAUGHAN. 5th Edition. Crown 8vo. 10s. 6d.

THE CHRISTIAN PROPHETS AND THE PROPHETIC APOCALYPSE. By EDWARD CARUS SELWYN, D.D. Crown 8vo. 6s. net.

THE BIBLE WORD-BOOK. By W. ALDIS WRIGHT, Litt.D., LL.D. 2nd Edition. Crown 8vo. 7s. 6d.

C

Christian Church, History of the

Bury (Professor J. B.)—THE LIFE OF ST. PATRICK, AND HIS PLACE IN HISTORY. 8vo. 12s. net.

Cheetham (Archdeacon).—A HISTORY OF THE CHRISTIAN CHURCH DURING THE FIRST SIX CENTURIES. Cr. 8vo. 10s. 6d.

> *TIMES.*—" A brief but authoritative summary of early ecclesiastical history."
> *GLASGOW HERALD.*—" Particularly clear in its exposition, systematic in its disposition and development, and as light and attractive in style as could reasonably be expected from the nature of the subject."

A HISTORY OF THE CHRISTIAN CHURCH FROM THE REFORMATION TO THE PRESENT TIME. Cr. 8vo. [*In the Press.*

Gwatkin (H. M.)—SELECTIONS FROM EARLY WRITERS Illustrative of Church History to the Time of Constantine. 2nd Edition. Revised and Enlarged. Cr. 8vo. 4s. 6d. net.
> To this edition have been prefixed short accounts of the writers from whom the passages are selected.

Hardwick (Archdeacon).—A HISTORY OF THE CHRISTIAN CHURCH. Middle Age. Ed. by Bishop STUBBS. Cr. 8vo. 10s. 6d.
A HISTORY OF THE CHRISTIAN CHURCH DURING THE REFORMATION. Revised by Bishop STUBBS. Cr. 8vo. 10s. 6d.

Hort (Dr. F. J. A.)—TWO DISSERTATIONS. I. On ΜΟΝΟΓΕΝΗΣ ΘΕΟΣ in Scripture and Tradition. II. On the "Constantinopolitan" Creed and other Eastern Creeds of the Fourth Century. 8vo. 7s. 6d.
JUDAISTIC CHRISTIANITY. Crown 8vo. 6s.
THE CHRISTIAN ECCLESIA. A Course of Lectures on the Early History and Early Conceptions of the Ecclesia, and Four Sermons. Crown 8vo. 6s.

Krüger (Dr. G.)—HISTORY OF EARLY CHRISTIAN LITERATURE IN THE FIRST THREE CENTURIES. Cr. 8vo. 8s. 6d. net.

Lowrie (W.)—CHRISTIAN ART AND ARCHÆOLOGY: A HANDBOOK TO THE MONUMENTS OF THE EARLY CHURCH. Crown 8vo. 10s. 6d. [8vo. 21s. net.

Oliphant (T. L. Kington).—ROME AND REFORM. 2 vols.

Simpson (W.)—AN EPITOME OF THE HISTORY OF THE CHRISTIAN CHURCH. Fcap. 8vo. 3s. 6d.

Sohm (Prof.) — OUTLINES OF CHURCH HISTORY. Translated by Miss MAY SINCLAIR. With a Preface by Prof. H. M. GWATKIN, M.A. Crown 8vo. 3s. 6d.

> *MANCHESTER GUARDIAN.*—" It fully deserves the praise given to it by Professor Gwatkin (who contributes a preface to this translation) of being ' neither a meagre sketch nor a confused mass of facts, but a masterly outline,' and it really ' supplies a want,' as affording to the intelligent reader who has no time or interest in details, a connected general view of the whole vast field of ecclesiastical history."

Vaughan (Very Rev. C. J.)—THE CHURCH OF THE FIRST DAYS. THE CHURCH OF JERUSALEM. THE CHURCH OF THE GENTILES. THE CHURCH OF THE WORLD. Crown 8vo. 10s. 6d.

The Church of England

Catechism of—

CATECHISM AND CONFIRMATION. By Rev. J. C. P. ALDOUS. Pott 8vo. 1s. net.

THOSE HOLY MYSTERIES. By Rev. J. C. P. ALDOUS. Pott 8vo. 1s. net.

A CLASS-BOOK OF THE CATECHISM OF THE CHURCH OF ENGLAND. By Rev. Canon MACLEAR. Pott 8vo. 1s. 6d.

A FIRST CLASS-BOOK OF THE CATECHISM OF THE CHURCH OF ENGLAND, with Scripture Proofs for Junior Classes and Schools. By the same. Pott 8vo. 6d.

THE ORDER OF CONFIRMATION, with Prayers and Devotions. By the Rev. Canon MACLEAR. 32mo. 6d.

NOTES FOR LECTURES ON CONFIRMATION. By the Rev. C. J. VAUGHAN, D.D. Pott 8vo. 1s. 6d.

THE BAPTISMAL OFFICE AND THE ORDER OF CONFIRMATION. By the Rev. F. PROCTER and the Rev. CANON MACLEAR. Pott 8vo. 6d.

Disestablishment—

DISESTABLISHMENT AND DISENDOWMENT. What are they? By E. A. FREEMAN. Crown 8vo. Sewed, 6d.

A DEFENCE OF THE CHURCH OF ENGLAND AGAINST DISESTABLISHMENT. By ROUNDELL, EARL OF SELBORNE. Crown 8vo. 2s. 6d.

ANCIENT FACTS & FICTIONS CONCERNING CHURCHES AND TITHES. By the same. 2nd Edition. Crown 8vo. 7s. 6d.

A HANDBOOK ON WELSH CHURCH DEFENCE. By the Bishop of ST. ASAPH. 3rd Edition. Fcap. 8vo. Sewed, 6d.

Dissent in its Relation to—

DISSENT IN ITS RELATION TO THE CHURCH OF ENGLAND. By Rev. G. H. CURTEIS. Bampton Lectures for 1871. Crown 8vo. 7s. 6d.

History of—

HISTORY OF THE ENGLISH CHURCH. Edited by the late DEAN STEPHENS and the Rev. W. HUNT, D.Litt. In Eight Volumes. Crown 8vo.

Vol. I. HISTORY OF THE CHURCH OF ENGLAND FROM ITS FOUNDATION TO THE NORMAN CONQUEST (597-1066). By the Rev. W. HUNT. 7s. 6d.

Vol. II. THE ENGLISH CHURCH FROM THE NORMAN CONQUEST TO THE ACCESSION OF EDWARD I. (1066-1272). By DEAN STEPHENS. 7s. 6d.

Vol. III. THE ENGLISH CHURCH IN THE FOURTEENTH AND FIFTEENTH CENTURIES (1272-1486). By the Rev. CANON CAPES, sometime Reader of Ancient History in the University of Oxford. 7s. 6d.

History—*continued.*

Vol. IV. THE ENGLISH CHURCH IN THE SIX-TEENTH CENTURY, FROM THE ACCESSION OF HENRY VIII. TO THE DEATH OF MARY (1509-1558). By JAMES GAIRDNER, C.B., LL.D. 7s. 6d.

Vol. V. THE ENGLISH CHURCH IN THE REIGNS OF ELIZABETH AND JAMES I. (1558-1625). By the Rev. W. H. FRERE. 7s. 6d.

Vol. VI. THE ENGLISH CHURCH FROM THE ACCESSION OF CHARLES I. TO THE DEATH OF ANNE (1625-1714). By the Rev. W. H. HUTTON, B.D., Fellow of St. John's College, Oxford. 7s. 6d.

Vol. VII. THE ENGLISH CHURCH FROM THE ACCESSION OF GEORGE I. TO THE END OF THE EIGHTEENTH CENTURY (1714-1800). By the late Rev. Canon OVERTON, D.D., and the Rev. F. RELTON, A.K.C. 7s. 6d.

In Preparation.

Vol. VIII. THE ENGLISH CHURCH IN THE NINE-TEENTH CENTURY. By F. W. CORNISH, M.A., Vice-Provost of Eton College.

THE STATE AND THE CHURCH. By the Hon. ARTHUR ELLIOT. New Edition. Crown 8vo. 2s. 6d.

DOCUMENTS ILLUSTRATIVE OF ENGLISH CHURCH HISTORY. Compiled from Original Sources by HENRY GEE, B.D., F.S.A., and W. J. HARDY, F.S.A. Cr. 8vo. 10s. 6d.

ENGLISH HISTORICAL REVIEW.—" Will be welcomed alike by students and by a much wider circle of readers interested in the history of the Church of England. For the benefit of the latter all the Latin pieces have been translated into English. . . . It fully deserves the hearty imprimatur of the Bishop of Oxford prefixed to it."

DAILY CHRONICLE.—" Students of the English Constitution as well as students of Church History will find this volume a valuable aid to their researches."

SCOTTISH GUARDIAN.—" There is no book in existence that contains so much original material likely to prove valuable to those who wish to investigate ritual or historical questions affecting the English Church."

Holy Communion—

THE COMMUNION SERVICE FROM THE BOOK OF COMMON PRAYER, with Select Readings from the Writings of the Rev. F. D. MAURICE. Edited by Bishop COLENSO. 6th Edition. 16mo. 2s. 6d.

FIRST COMMUNION, with Prayers and Devotions for the newly Confirmed. By Rev. Canon MACLEAR. 32mo. 6d.

A MANUAL OF INSTRUCTION FOR CONFIRMATION AND FIRST COMMUNION, with Prayers and Devotions. By the

Liturgy— [same. 32mo. 2s.

A COMPANION TO THE LECTIONARY. By Rev. W. BENHAM, B.D. Crown 8vo. 4s. 6d.

AN INTRODUCTION TO THE CREEDS. By Rev. Canon MACLEAR. Pott 8vo. 3s. 6d.

CHURCH QUARTERLY REVIEW.—" Mr. Maclear's text-books of Bible history are so well known that to praise them is unnecessary. He has now added to them *An Introduction to the Creeds*, which we do not hesitate to call admirable. The book consists, first, of an historical introduction, occupying 53 pages, then an exposition of the twelve articles of the Creed extending to page 299, an appendix containing the texts

Liturgy—*continued.*

of a considerable number of Creeds, and lastly, three indices which, as far as we have tested them, we must pronounce very good. . . . We may add that we know already that the book has been used with great advantage in ordinary parochial work."

AN INTRODUCTION TO THE ARTICLES OF THE CHURCH OF ENGLAND. By Rev. G. F. MACLEAR, D.D., and Rev. W. W. WILLIAMS. Crown 8vo. 10s. 6d.

The BISHOP OF SALISBURY at the Church Congress spoke of this as "a book which will doubtless have, as it deserves, large circulation."

ST. JAMES'S GAZETTE.—"Theological students and others will find this comprehensive yet concise volume most valuable."

GLASGOW HERALD.—"A valuable addition to the well-known series of Theological Manuals published by Messrs. Macmillan."

CHURCH TIMES.—"Those who are in any way responsible for the training of candidates for Holy Orders must often have felt the want of such a book as Dr. Maclear, with the assistance of his colleague, Mr. Williams, has just published."

NEW HISTORY OF THE BOOK OF COMMON PRAYER. With a rationale of its Offices on the basis of the former Work by FRANCIS PROCTER, M.A. Revised and re-written by WALTER HOWARD FRERE, M.A., Priest of the Community of the Resurrection. Second Impression. Crown 8vo. 12s. 6d.

AN ELEMENTARY INTRODUCTION TO THE BOOK OF COMMON PRAYER. By Rev. F. PROCTER and Rev. Canon MACLEAR. Pott 8vo. 2s. 6d.

THE ELIZABETHAN PRAYER-BOOK AND ORNAMENTS. With an Appendix of Documents. By HENRY GEE, D.D. Crown 8vo. 5s.

TWELVE DISCOURSES ON SUBJECTS CONNECTED WITH THE LITURGY AND WORSHIP OF THE CHURCH OF ENGLAND. By Very Rev. C. J. VAUGHAN. 4th Edition. Fcap. 8vo. 6s.

Historical and Biographical—

THE ECCLESIASTICAL EXPANSION OF ENGLAND IN THE GROWTH OF THE ANGLICAN COMMUNION. Hulsean Lectures, 1894-95. By ALFRED BARRY, D.D., D.C.L., formerly Bishop of Sydney and Primate of Australia and Tasmania. Crown 8vo. 6s.

The author's preface says : "The one object of these lectures—delivered on the Hulsean Foundation in 1894-95—is to make some slight contribution to that awakening of interest in the extraordinary religious mission of England which seems happily characteristic of the present time."

DAILY NEWS.—"These lectures are particularly interesting as containing the case for the Christian missions at a time when there is a disposition to attack them in some quarters."

LIVES OF THE ARCHBISHOPS OF CANTERBURY. From St. Augustine to Juxon. By the Very Rev. WALTER FARQUHAR HOOK, D.D., Dean of Chichester. Demy 8vo. The volumes sold separately as follows :—Vol. I., 15s. ; Vol. II., 15s. ; Vol. V., 15s. ; Vols. VI. and VII., 30s. ; Vol. VIII., 15s. ; Vol. X., 15s. ; Vol. XI., 15s. ; Vol. XII., 15s.

ATHENÆUM.—"The most impartial, the most instructive, and the most interesting of histories."

Historical and Biographical—*continued.*

THE LIFE OF THE RIGHT REVEREND BROOKE FOSS
WESTCOTT, D.D., Late Lord Bishop of Durham. By his Son,
the Rev. ARTHUR WESTCOTT. With Photogravure Portraits.
2 vols. Extra Crown 8vo. 17s. net. Abridged edition in One
Vol. Extra Crown 8vo. 8s. 6d. net.

MEMOIRS OF ARCHBISHOP TEMPLE. By SEVEN FRIENDS.
Edited by E. G. SANDFORD. With Photogravure and other
Illustrations. 2 vols. 8vo. 36s. net.

RUGBY MEMOIR OF ARCHBISHOP TEMPLE, 1857-1869.
By F. E. KITCHENER, Assistant Master at Rugby School, 1862-
1875. With Portrait. 8vo. Sewed, 1s. 6d. net.

THE EXETER EPISCOPATE OF ARCHBISHOP TEMPLE,
1869-1885. By E. G. SANDFORD, his sometime Chaplain, Archdeacon of Exeter. With Photogravure and other Illustrations.
8vo. 3s. 6d. net.

FREDERICK TEMPLE. An Appreciation. By E. G. SANDFORD,
Archdeacon of Exeter. With a Biographical Introduction by
WILLIAM TEMPLE, Fellow of Queen's College, Oxford ; son of
the Archbishop. With Frontispiece. 8vo. 4s. net.

LIFE AND LETTERS OF ARCHBISHOP BENSON. By his
SON.
Abridged Edition. In one Vol. 8s. 6d. net.

CHARLOTTE MARY YONGE : HER LIFE AND LETTERS.
By CHRISTABEL COLERIDGE. With Portraits. 8vo. 12s. 6d. net.

LIFE AND LETTERS OF AMBROSE PHILLIPPS DE LISLE.
By E. S. PURCELL. Two Vols. 8vo. 25s. net.

THE OXFORD MOVEMENT. Twelve Years, 1833-45. By
DEAN CHURCH. Globe 8vo. 4s. net.

THE LIFE AND LETTERS OF R. W. CHURCH, late Dean
of St. Paul's. Globe 8vo. 4s. net.

LIFE AND LETTERS OF FENTON JOHN ANTHONY
HORT, D.D., D.C.L., LL.D., sometime Hulsean Professor and
Lady Margaret's Reader in Divinity in the University of Cambridge.
By his Son, ARTHUR FENTON HORT, late Fellow of Trinity College,
Cambridge. In two Vols. With Portrait. Ex. Cr. 8vo. 17s. net.

THE LIFE OF FREDERICK DENISON MAURICE. Chiefly
told in his own letters. Edited by his Son, FREDERICK MAURICE.
With Portraits. Two Vols. Crown 8vo. 16s.

MEMORIALS. (PART I.) FAMILY AND PERSONAL, 1766-
1865. By ROUNDELL, EARL OF SELBORNE. With Portraits and
Illustrations. Two Vols. 8vo. 25s. net. (PART II.) PERSONAL
AND POLITICAL, 1865-1895. Two Vols. 25s. net.

LIFE AND LETTERS OF WILLIAM JOHN BUTLER, late
Dean of Lincoln, sometime Vicar of Wantage. 8vo. 12s. 6d. net.

Historical and Biographical—*continued.*

IN THE COURT OF THE ARCHBISHOP OF CANTER-
BURY. Read and others *v.* The Lord Bishop of Lincoln.
Judgment, Nov. 21, 1890. 2nd Edition. 8vo. 2s. net.

THE ARCHBISHOP OF CANTERBURY ON RESERVATION
OF THE SACRAMENT. Lambeth Palace, May 1, 1900.
8vo. Sewed. 1s. net.

THE ARCHBISHOP OF YORK ON RESERVATION OF
SACRAMENT. Lambeth Palace, May 1, 1900. 8vo. Sewed.
1s. net.

CANTERBURY DIOCESAN GAZETTE. Monthly. 8vo. 2d.

JEWISH QUARTERLY REVIEW. Edited by I. ABRAHAMS and
C. G. MONTEFIORE. Demy 8vo. 3s. 6d. Vols. 1-7, 12s. 6d.
each. Vol. 8 onwards, 15s. each. (Annual Subscription, 11s.)

Devotional Books

Cornish (J. F.)—WEEK BY WEEK. Fcap. 8vo. 3s. 6d.

Eastlake (Lady).—FELLOWSHIP: LETTERS ADDRESSED
TO MY SISTER-MOURNERS. Crown 8vo. 2s. 6d.

ATHENÆUM.—"Tender and unobtrusive, and the author thoroughly realises the
sorrow of those she addresses ; it may soothe mourning readers, and can by no means
aggravate or jar upon their feelings."

CONTEMPORARY REVIEW.—"A very touching and at the same time a very
sensible book. It breathes throughout the truest Christian spirit."

NONCONFORMIST.—"A beautiful little volume, written with genuine feeling,
good taste, and a right appreciation of the teaching of Scripture relative to sorrow and
suffering."

IMITATIO CHRISTI, LIBRI IV. Printed in Borders after Holbein,
Dürer, and other old Masters, containing Dances of Death, Acts of
Mercy, Emblems, etc. Crown 8vo. 7s. 6d.

Keble (J.)—THE CHRISTIAN YEAR. Edited by C. M.
YONGE. Pott 8vo. 2s. 6d. net.

Kingsley (Charles).—OUT OF THE DEEP: WORDS
FOR THE SORROWFUL. From the writings of CHARLES
KINGSLEY. Extra Fcap. 8vo. 3s. 6d.

DAILY THOUGHTS. Selected from the Writings of CHARLES
KINGSLEY. By his Wife. Crown 8vo. 6s.

FROM DEATH TO LIFE. Fragments of Teaching to a Village
Congregation. With Letters on the "Life after Death." Edited
by his Wife. Fcap. 8vo. 2s. 6d.

Maclear (Rev. Canon).—A MANUAL OF INSTRUCTION
FOR CONFIRMATION AND FIRST COMMUNION, WITH
PRAYERS AND DEVOTIONS. 32mo. 2s.

Maurice (Frederick Denison).—LESSONS OF HOPE. Readings from the Works of F. D. MAURICE. Selected by Rev. J. LL. DAVIES, M.A. Crown 8vo. 5s.

THE COMMUNION SERVICE. From the Book of Common Prayer, with select readings from the writings of the Rev. F. D. MAURICE, M.A. Edited by the Rev. JOHN WILLIAM COLENSO, D.D., Lord Bishop of Natal. 16mo. 2s. 6d.

THE WORSHIP OF GOD, AND FELLOWSHIP AMONG MEN. By FREDERICK DENISON MAURICE and others. Fcap. 8vo. 3s. 6d.

RAYS OF SUNLIGHT FOR DARK DAYS. With a Preface by Very Rev. C. J. VAUGHAN, D.D. New Edition. Pott 8vo. 3s. 6d.

Welby-Gregory (The Hon. Lady).—LINKS AND CLUES. 2nd Edition. Crown 8vo. 6s.

Westcott (Bishop).—THOUGHTS ON REVELATION AND LIFE. Selections from the Writings of Bishop WESTCOTT. Edited by Rev. S. PHILLIPS. Crown 8vo. 6s.

The Fathers

INDEX OF NOTEWORTHY WORDS AND PHRASES FOUND IN THE CLEMENTINE WRITINGS, COMMONLY CALLED THE HOMILIES OF CLEMENT. 8vo. 5s.

Benson (Archbishop).—CYPRIAN : HIS LIFE, HIS TIMES, HIS WORK. By the late EDWARD WHITE BENSON, Archbishop of Canterbury. 8vo. 21s. net.

TIMES.—"In all essential respects, in sobriety of judgment and temper, in sympathetic insight into character, in firm grasp of historical and ecclesiastical issues, in scholarship and erudition, the finished work is worthy of its subject and worthy of its author. . . . In its main outlines full of dramatic insight and force, and in its details full of the fruits of ripe learning, sound judgment, a lofty Christian temper, and a mature ecclesiastical wisdom."

SATURDAY REVIEW.—"On the whole, and with all reservations which can possibly be made, this weighty volume is a contribution to criticism and learning on which we can but congratulate the Anglican Church. We wish more of her bishops were capable or desirous of descending into that arena of pure intellect from which Dr. Benson returns with these posthumous laurels."

Gwatkin (H. M.)—SELECTIONS FROM EARLY WRITERS ILLUSTRATIVE OF CHURCH HISTORY TO THE TIME OF CONSTANTINE. 2nd Edition. Crown 8vo. 4s. 6d. net.

Hort (Dr. F. J. A.)—SIX LECTURES ON THE ANTE-NICENE FATHERS. Crown 8vo. 3s. 6d.

TIMES.—"Though certainly popular in form and treatment they are so in the best sense of the words, and they bear throughout the impress of the ripe scholarship, the rare critical acumen, and the lofty ethical temper which marked all Dr. Hort's work."

NOTES ON CLEMENTINE RECOGNITIONS. Crown 8vo. 4s. 6d.

Hort (Dr. F. J. A.) and **Mayor** (J. B.)—CLEMENT OF ALEX-ANDRIA: MISCELLANIES (STROMATEIS). Book VII. The Greek Text, with Introduction, Translation, Notes, Dissertations, and Indices. 8vo. 15s. net.

Krüger (G.)—HISTORY OF EARLY CHRISTIAN LITERA-TURE IN THE FIRST THREE CENTURIES. Crown 8vo. 8s. 6d. net.

Lightfoot (Bishop).—THE APOSTOLIC FATHERS. Part I. ST. CLEMENT OF ROME. Revised Texts, with Introductions, Notes, Dissertations, and Translations. 2 vols. 8vo. 32s.

THE APOSTOLIC FATHERS. Part II. ST. IGNATIUS to ST. POLY-CARP. Revised Texts, with Introductions, Notes, Dissertations, and Translations. 3 vols. 2nd Edition. Demy 8vo. 48s.

THE APOSTOLIC FATHERS. Abridged Edition. With Short Introductions, Greek Text, and English Translation. 8vo. 16s.

MANCHESTER GUARDIAN.—"A conspectus of these early and intensely interesting Christian 'Documents' such as had not hitherto been attainable, and thereby renders a priceless service to all serious students of Christian theology, and even of Roman history."

NATIONAL OBSERVER.—"From the account of its contents, the student may appreciate the value of this last work of a great scholar, and its helpfulness as an aid to an intelligent examination of the earliest post-Apostolic writers. The texts are constructed on the most careful collation of all the existing sources. The introductions are brief, lucid, and thoroughly explanatory of the historical and critical questions related to the texts. The introduction to the *Didache*, and the translation of the 'Church Manual of Early Christianity,' are peculiarly interesting, as giving at once an admirable version of it, and the opinion of the first of English biblical critics on the latest discovery in patristic literature."

Hymnology

Bernard (Canon T. D.)—THE SONGS OF THE HOLY NATIVITY. Being Studies of the Benedictus, Magnificat, Gloria in Excelsis, and Nunc Dimittis. Crown 8vo. 5s.

Brooke (Stopford A.)—CHRISTIAN HYMNS. Edited and arranged. Fcap. 8vo. 2s. 6d. net.

Selborne (Roundell, Earl of)—

THE BOOK OF PRAISE. From the best English Hymn Writers. Pott 8vo. 2s. 6d. net.

A HYMNAL. Chiefly from *The Book of Praise.* In various sizes. B. Pott 8vo, larger type. 1s.—C. Same Edition, fine paper. 1s. 6d.—An Edition with Music, Selected, Harmonised, and Composed by JOHN HULLAH. Pott 8vo. 3s. 6d.

Smith (Horace).—HYMNS AND PSALMS. Ex. Crown 8vo. 2s. 6d.

Woods (M. A.)—HYMNS FOR SCHOOL WORSHIP. Compiled by M. A. WOODS. Pott 8vo. 1s. 6d.

Religious Teaching

Bell (Rev. G. C.)—RELIGIOUS TEACHING IN SECOND-ARY SCHOOLS. For Teachers and Parents. Suggestions as to Lessons on the Bible, Early Church History, Christian Evidences, etc. By the Rev. G. C. BELL, M.A., Master of Marlborough College. 2nd Edition. With new chapter on Christian Ethic. Crown 8vo. 3s. 6d.

> *GUARDIAN.*—"The hints and suggestions given are admirable, and, as far as Bible teaching or instruction in 'Christian Evidences' is concerned, leave nothing to be desired. Much time and thought has evidently been devoted by the writer to the difficulties which confront the teacher of the Old Testament, and a large portion of the volume is taken up with the consideration of this branch of his subject."
>
> *EDUCATIONAL REVIEW.*—"For those teachers who are dissatisfied with the existing state of things, and who are striving after something better, this little handbook is invaluable. Its aim is 'to map out a course of instruction on practical lines, and to suggest methods and books which may point the way to a higher standpoint and a wider horizon.' For the carrying out of this, and also for his criticism of prevailing methods, all teachers owe Mr. Bell a debt of gratitude; and if any are roused to a due sense of their responsibility in this matter, he will feel that his book has not been written in vain."

Gilbert (Dr. G. H.)—A PRIMER OF THE CHRISTIAN RELIGION. Based on the Teaching of Jesus, its Founder and Living Lord. Crown 8vo. 4s. 6d. net.

Joseph (N. S.)—RELIGION, NATURAL AND REVEALED. A Series of Progressive Lessons for Jewish Youth. Revised Edition. Crown 8vo. 1s. net. Leather, gilt edges, 3s. 6d. net.

Knox (E. M.)—BIBLE LESSONS FOR SCHOOLS. GENESIS. Globe 8vo. 1s. 6d.

Lawson (H. N.)—THE BIBLE STORY. For Children of all Ages. Revised by FREDERICK P. LAWSON, M.A., Hon. Canon of Peterborough. The Beginnings of the Jewish Church. Illustrated. Extra Crown 8vo. 3s. 6d.

Sermons, Lectures, Addresses, and Theological Essays

(See also 'Bible,' 'Church of England,' 'Fathers')

Abrahams (Israel).—FESTIVAL STUDIES. Being Thoughts on the Jewish Year. Crown 8vo. 2s. 6d.

Abrahams (I.)—**Montefiore** (C. G.)—ASPECTS OF JUDAISM. Being Eighteen Sermons. 2nd Edition. Fcap. 8vo. 3s. 6d. net.

> *TIMES.*—"There is a great deal in them that does not appeal to Jews alone, for, especially in Mr. Montefiore's addresses, the doctrines advocated, with much charm of style, are often not by any means exclusively Jewish, but such as are shared and honoured by all who care for religion and morality as those terms are commonly under-stood in the western world."
>
> *GLASGOW HERALD.*—"Both from the homiletic and what may be called the big-world point of view, this little volume is one of considerable interest."

Ainger (Rev. Alfred).—THE GOSPEL AND HUMAN LIFE. Edited, with Preface, by Canon BEECHING.   Cr. 8vo.   6s.

DAILY NEWS.—" We think we can safely say that no one commencing to read this volume will leave any single sermon unread.   Canon Ainger was a careful and conscientious writer, and composed his sermons with a fidelity to literary form and exactness of expression that will please the most imperious critic.   If we were to single out any one quality of these discourses, it would be the close, searching analysis of human nature. He was a close observer of human life in all its strange inconsistencies and varying moods, a shrewd judge of motive and disposition."

Allen (V. G.)—FREEDOM IN THE CHURCH, OR THE DOCTRINE OF CHRIST AS THE LORD HATH COMMANDED, AND AS THIS CHURCH HATH RECEIVED THE SAME ACCORDING TO THE COMMANDMENTS OF GOD.   Crown 8vo.   6s. 6d. net.

Askwith (E. H.)—THE CHRISTIAN CONCEPTION OF HOLINESS.   Crown 8vo.   6s.

THE SPECTATOR.—" A well-reasoned and really noble view of the essential purpose of the Christian revelation. . . . We hope that Mr. Askwith's work will be widely read."

Bather (Archdeacon).—ON SOME MINISTERIAL DUTIES, CATECHISING, PREACHING, ETC.   Edited, with a Preface, by Very Rev. C. J. VAUGHAN, D.D.   Fcap. 8vo.   4s. 6d.

Benson (Archbishop)—
    ARCHBISHOP BENSON IN IRELAND.   A record of his Irish Sermons and Addresses.   Edited by J. H. BERNARD.   Crown 8vo.   3s. 6d.

PALL MALL GAZETTE.—" No words of mine could appreciate, or do justice to, the stately language and lofty thoughts of the late Primate ; they will appeal to every Churchman."

Bernard (Canon Ed. Russell).—GREAT MORAL TEACHERS. Eight Lectures on Confucius, Buddha, Socrates, and Epictetus delivered in Salisbury Cathedral.   Crown 8vo.   3s. 6d. net.

Bernard (Canon T.D.)—THE SONGS OF THE HOLY NATIVITY CONSIDERED (1) AS RECORDED IN SCRIPTURE, (2) AS IN USE IN THE CHURCH.   Crown 8vo.   5s.

Brastow (Prof. L. O.)—REPRESENTATIVE MODERN PREACHERS.   Crown 8vo.   6s. 6d. net.
    THE MODERN PULPIT.   A Study of Homiletic Sources and Characteristics.   Crown 8vo.   6s. 6d. net.

Brooke (Rev. Stopford A.)—SHORT SERMONS.   Cr. 8vo.   6s.

Brooks (Phillips, late Bishop of Massachusetts)—
    THE CANDLE OF THE LORD, and other Sermons.   Cr. 8vo.   6s.
    SERMONS PREACHED IN ENGLISH CHURCHES.   Crown 8vo.   6s.
    TWENTY SERMONS.   Crown 8vo.   6s.
    THE LIGHT OF THE WORLD.   Crown 8vo.   3s. 6d.
    THE MYSTERY OF INIQUITY.   Crown 8vo.   6s.
    ESSAYS AND ADDRESSES, RELIGIOUS, LITERARY, AND SOCIAL.   Edited by the Rev. JOHN COTTON BROOKS.   Crown 8vo.   8s. 6d. net.

Brooks (Phillips, late Bishop of Massachusetts)—*continued.*
> NEW STARTS IN LIFE, AND OTHER SERMONS. Crown
> 8vo. 6s.
> THE MORE ABUNDANT LIFE. Lenten Readings. Royal
> 16mo. 5s.
> THE LAW OF GROWTH, and other Sermons. Crown 8vo. 6s.
>
> *SCOTSMAN.*—"All instinct with the piety, breadth of mind, and eloquence which
> have given Phillips Brooks' pulpit prolocutions their rare distinction among productions
> of this kind, that of being really and truly suitable for more Sundays than one."
> *GLOBE.*—"So manly in outlook and so fresh and suggestive in treatment."
>
> SEEKING LIFE, AND OTHER SERMONS. Crown 8vo. 6s.
>
> *CHRISTIAN WORLD.*—"It will, we think, be generally agreed that the twenty-
> one sermons in this concluding volume are worthy to rank with the other volumes of a
> notable series. There is the wonted felicity in the choice of subjects, and the wonted
> combination of spiritual insight and practical force in their treatment."
>
> THE INFLUENCE OF JESUS. The Bohlen Lectures, 1879.
> Crown 8vo. 6s.
> LECTURES ON PREACHING DELIVERED AT YALE COL-
> LEGE. Crown 8vo. 6s.
> THE PHILLIPS BROOKS YEAR BOOK. Selections from the
> Writings of Bishop Phillips Brooks. By H. L. S. and L. H. S.
> Globe 8vo. 3s. 6d. net.
> CHRIST THE LIFE AND LIGHT. Lenten Readings selected
> from the Writings of the Rt. Rev. PHILLIPS BROOKS, D.D.
> By W. M. L. JAY. Crown 8vo. 6s.

Campbell (Dr. John M'Leod)—
> THE NATURE OF THE ATONEMENT. 6th Ed. Cr. 8vo. 6s.
> THOUGHTS ON REVELATION. 2nd Edition. Crown 8vo. 5s.
> RESPONSIBILITY FOR THE GIFT OF ETERNAL LIFE.
> Compiled from Sermons preached at Row, in the years 1829-31.
> Crown 8vo. 5s.

Carpenter (W. Boyd, Bishop of Ripon)—
> TRUTH IN TALE. Addresses, chiefly to Children. Crown 8vo.
> 4s. 6d.
> THE PERMANENT ELEMENTS OF RELIGION: Bampton
> Lectures, 1887. 2nd Edition. Crown 8vo. 6s.
> TWILIGHT DREAMS. Crown 8vo. 4s. 6d.
> LECTURES ON PREACHING. Crown 8vo. 3s. 6d. net.
> SOME THOUGHTS ON CHRISTIAN REUNION. Being a
> Charge to the Clergy. Crown 8vo. 3s. 6d. net.
>
> *TIMES.*—"Dr. Boyd Carpenter treats this very difficult subject with moderation
> and good sense, and with a clear-headed perception of the limits which inexorably cir-
> cumscribe the natural aspirations of Christians of different churches and nationalities for
> a more intimate communion and fellowship."
> *LEEDS MERCURY.*—"He discusses with characteristic vigour and felicity the
> claims which hinder reunion, and the true idea and scope of catholicity."

Charteris (Prof. A. H.)—THE CHURCH OF CHRIST, ITS
> LIFE AND WORK. An Attempt to trace the work of the
> Church in some of its Departments from the Earliest Times to the
> Present Day. Crown 8vo. 6s.

CHRISTIANITY AND THE WORKING CLASSES. Edited by
GEORGE HAW. Crown 8vo. 3s. 6d. net.

Church (Dean)—

HUMAN LIFE AND ITS CONDITIONS. Crown 8vo. 6s.

THE GIFTS OF CIVILISATION, and other Sermons and Lectures.
2nd Edition. Crown 8vo. 7s. 6d.

DISCIPLINE OF THE CHRISTIAN CHARACTER, and other
Sermons. Crown 8vo. 4s. 6d.

ADVENT SERMONS. 1885. Crown 8vo. 4s. 6d.

VILLAGE SERMONS. Crown 8vo. 6s.

VILLAGE SERMONS. Second Series. Crown 8vo. 6s.

VILLAGE SERMONS. Third Series. Crown 8vo. 6s.

TIMES.—"In these sermons we see how a singularly gifted and cultivated mind was
able to communicate its thoughts on the highest subjects to those with whom it might
be supposed to have little in common. . . . His village sermons are not the by-work of
one whose interests were elsewhere in higher matters. They are the outcome of his
deepest interests and of the life of his choice. . . . These sermons are worth perusal if
only to show what preaching, even to the humble and unlearned hearers, may be made
in really competent hands."

CATHEDRAL AND UNIVERSITY SERMONS. Crown 8vo. 6s.

PASCAL AND OTHER SERMONS. Crown 8vo. 6s.

CLERGYMAN'S SELF-EXAMINATION CONCERNING THE
APOSTLES' CREED. Extra Fcap. 8vo. 1s. 6d.

Congreve (Rev. John).—HIGH HOPES AND PLEADINGS
FOR A REASONABLE FAITH, NOBLER THOUGHTS,
LARGER CHARITY. Crown 8vo. 5s.

Davidson (Archbishop)—

A CHARGE DELIVERED TO THE CLERGY OF THE
DIOCESE OF ROCHESTER, October 29, 30, 31, 1894.
8vo. Sewed. 2s. net.

A CHARGE DELIVERED TO THE CLERGY OF THE
DIOCESE OF WINCHESTER, Sept. 28, 30, Oct. 2, 3, 4,
and 5, 1899. 8vo. Sewed. 2s. 6d. net.

THE CHRISTIAN OPPORTUNITY. Being Sermons and
Speeches delivered in America. Crown 8vo. 3s. 6d. net.

SPECTATOR.—"To all who hope for and long to help our age, to the true Christian
and the true patriot on both sides of the seas, in the new home where the speaker spent
so happy and fruitful a sojourn, in the old to which he has returned, as we hope, refreshed
and encouraged, we commend these hopeful, prayerful, suggestive words as in a very real
sense the best of Christmastide reading."

Davies (Rev. J. Llewelyn)—

THE GOSPEL AND MODERN LIFE. 2nd Edition, to which is
added Morality according to the Sacrament of the Lord's Supper.
Extra fcap. 8vo. 6s.

SOCIAL QUESTIONS FROM THE POINT OF VIEW OF
CHRISTIAN THEOLOGY. 2nd Edition. Crown 8vo. 6s.

Davies (Rev. J. Llewelyn)—*continued.*

WARNINGS AGAINST SUPERSTITION. Extra Fcap.8vo. 2s.6d.

THE CHRISTIAN CALLING. Extra Fcap. 8vo. 6s.

BAPTISM, CONFIRMATION, AND THE LORD'S SUPPER, as interpreted by their Outward Signs. Three Addresses. New Edition. Pott 8vo. 1s.

ORDER AND GROWTH AS INVOLVED IN THE SPIRITUAL CONSTITUTION OF HUMAN SOCIETY. Crown 8vo. 3s.6d.

SPIRITUAL APPREHENSION : Sermons and Papers. Crown 8vo. 6s.

Day (E. E.)—SEEKING THE KINGDOM. A Study. Crown 8vo. 6s. 6d. net.

THE DIARY OF A CHURCH-GOER. Second Impression. Crown 8vo. Gilt top. 3s. 6d. net.

Canon BEECHING in a letter to the Editor of the *SPECTATOR.*—"I should like to draw the attention of your readers to a book recently published, *The Diary of a Church-Goer.* . . . What in my judgment, gives the book its value, and makes it worth the attention of thoughtful people, is the glimpse it affords of a cultivated mind worshipping and reflecting upon its religious experiences. . . . It is this positive side of the book with which I feel myself most in sympathy ; but its critical side also is worth serious attention, especially from the clergy, because it will show them where at least one thoughtful man finds difficulties."

Donehoo (J. de Quincey).—THE APOCRYPHAL AND LE-GENDARY LIFE OF CHRIST. Being the Whole Body of the Apocryphal Gospels and other Extra Canonical Literature which pretends to tell of the Life and Words of Jesus Christ, including much Matter which has not before appeared in English. In continuous Narrative Form, with Notes, Scriptural References, Prolegomena, and Indices. 8vo. 10s. 6d. net.

Edghill (Rev. E. A.)—AN ENQUIRY INTO THE EVIDENTIAL VALUE OF PROPHECY. Being the Hulsean Prize Essay for 1904. Crown 8vo. 7s. 6d.

Edwards (Jonathan), SELECTED SERMONS OF. Edited by Prof. H. N. GARDINER. 16mo. 1s. net.

Ellerton (Rev. John).—THE HOLIEST MANHOOD, AND ITS LESSONS FOR BUSY LIVES. Crown 8vo. 6s.

English Theological Library. Edited by Rev. FREDERIC RELTON. With General Introduction by the late BISHOP CREIGHTON. A Series of Texts Annotated for the Use of Students, Candidates for Ordination, etc. 8vo.

Re-issue at Reduced Prices.

I. HOOKER'S ECCLESIASTICAL POLITY, Book V., Edited by Rev. Ronald E. Bayne. 10s. 6d. net.

II. LAW'S SERIOUS CALL, Edited by Rev. Canon J. H. Overton. 4s. 6d. net.

English Theological Library—*continued.*

DAILY NEWS.—"A well-executed reprint. . . . Canon Overton's notes are not numerous, and are as a rule very interesting and useful."

III. WILSON'S MAXIMS, Edited by Rev. F. Relton.   3s. 6d. net.

GUARDIAN.—"Many readers will feel grateful to Mr. Relton for this edition of Bishop Wilson's 'Maxims.' . . . Mr. Relton's edition will be found well worth possessing: it is pleasant to the eye, and bears legible marks of industry and study."

IV. THE WORKS OF BISHOP BUTLER.   Vol. I. Sermons, Charges, Fragments, and Correspondence.   Vol. II. The Analogy of Religion, and two brief dissertations : I. Of Personal Identity. II. Of the Nature of Virtue.   Edited by the Very Rev. J. H. BERNARD, D.D., Dean of St. Patrick's, Dublin.   4s. 6d. net each.

THE PILOT.—"One could hardly desire a better working edition than this which Dr. Bernard has given us. . . . Sure to become the standard edition for students."
THE SPECTATOR.—"An excellent piece of work."

V. THE CONFERENCE BETWEEN WILLIAM LAUD AND MR. FISHER, THE JESUIT.   Edited by Rev. C. H. SIMPKINSON, M.A.   Author of *The Life of Archbishop Laud.*   4s. 6d. net.

ESSAYS ON SOME THEOLOGICAL QUESTIONS OF THE DAY.   By Members of the University of Cambridge.   Edited by H. B. SWETE, D.D.   8vo.   12s. net.

Everett (Dr. C. C.)—THE PSYCHOLOGICAL ELEMENTS OF RELIGIOUS FAITH.   Crown 8vo.   5s. net.

EVIL AND EVOLUTION.   An attempt to turn the Light of Modern Science on to the Ancient Mystery of Evil.   By the author of *The Social Horizon.*   Crown 8vo.   3s. 6d. net.

FAITH AND CONDUCT : An Essay on Verifiable Religion.   Crown 8vo.   7s. 6d.

FAITH OF A CHRISTIAN, THE.   By a Disciple.   8vo.   Sewed.   6d.

GUARDIAN.—"The general impression left upon our mind by this book is so good that we wish to recommend it to our readers' attention, for we believe that any one who reads it through will lay it down with a feeling of gratitude to its author."

CONVERSATIONS WITH CHRIST.   A Biographical Study.   By the Author of *The Faith of a Christian.*   Cr. 8vo.   3s. 6d. net.

FIFTH GOSPEL, THE : BEING THE PAULINE INTERPRETATION OF THE CHRIST.   By the Author of *The Faith of a Christian.*   Crown 8vo.   3s. 6d. net.

LAYMAN.—"Its characteristics are scholarliness in tone, care and lucidity in exposition, a vigorous literary style, earnest faith. . . . Unquestionably a noteworthy volume."

THE EMPIRE OF CHRIST : being a Study of the Missionary Enterprise in the Light of Modern Religious Thought.   By BERNARD LUCAS, Author of *The Faith of a Christian.*   Crown 8vo.   2s. 6d. net.

Farrar (Very Rev. F. W., late Dean of Canterbury)—
    Collected Edition of the Sermons, etc.   Cr. 8vo.   3s. 6d. each.
    SEEKERS AFTER GOD.
    ETERNAL HOPE.   Sermons Preached in Westminster Abbey.   Also
        8vo.   Sewed.   6d.
    THE FALL OF MAN, and other Sermons.
    THE WITNESS OF HISTORY TO CHRIST.   Hulsean Lectures.
    THE SILENCE AND VOICES OF GOD.
    IN THE DAYS OF THY YOUTH.   Sermons on Practical Subjects.
    SAINTLY WORKERS.   Five Lenten Lectures.
    EPHPHATHA : or, The Amelioration of the World.
    MERCY AND JUDGMENT.   A few words on Christian Eschatology.
    SERMONS AND ADDRESSES delivered in America.

Fiske (John).—MAN'S DESTINY VIEWED IN·THE LIGHT
    OF HIS ORIGIN.   Crown 8vo.   3s. 6d.
    · LIFE EVERLASTING.   Globe 8vo.   3s. 6d.

Foxell (W. J.)—GOD'S GARDEN : Sunday Talks with Boys.
    With an Introduction by Dean FARRAR.   Globe 8vo.   3s. 6d.
    IN A PLAIN PATH.   Addresses to Boys.   Globe 8vo.   3s. 6d.

Fraser (Bishop). — UNIVERSITY SERMONS.   Edited by
    Rev. JOHN W. DIGGLE.   Crown 8vo.   6s.

Grane (W. L.)—THE WORD AND THE WAY: or, The
    Light of the Ages on the Path of To-Day.   Crown 8vo.   6s.
    HARD SAYINGS OF JESUS CHRIST.   A Study in the Mind
    and Method of the Master.   Second Edition.   Crown 8vo.   5s.

GREATHEART.   Some Talks with Him.   By a Pilgrim.   Crown
    8vo.   3s. net.

Green (S. G.)—THE CHRISTIAN CREED AND THE
    CREEDS OF CHRISTENDOM.   Seven Lectures delivered
    in 1898 at Regent's Park College.   Crown 8vo.   6s.

Griffis (W. E.) — DUX CHRISTUS : An Outline Study of
    Japan.   Globe 8vo.   2s. net.   Sewed.   1s. 3d. net.

Harcourt (Sir W. V.)—LAWLESSNESS IN THE NATIONAL
    CHURCH.   8vo.   Sewed.   1s. net.

Hardwick (Archdeacon). — CHRIST AND OTHER MAS-
    TERS.   6th Edition.   Crown 8vo.   10s. 6d.

Hare (Julius Charles).—THE MISSION OF THE COM-
    FORTER.   New Edition.   Edited by Dean PLUMPTRE.   Crown
    8vo.   7s. 6d.

Harrison (F.)—THE CREED OF A LAYMAN ; APOLOGIA
    PRO FIDE MEA.   Extra Crown 8vo.   7s. 6d. net.
    TIMES.—" Mr. Harrison's history of his religious opinions will be followed with
  sustained interest by all unprejudiced students of philosophical and religious thought."

Headlam (Rev. A. C.)—THE SOURCES AND AUTHORITY OF DOGMATIC THEOLOGY. Being an Inaugural Lecture delivered by the Rev. ARTHUR C. HEADLAM, D.D. 8vo. Sewed. 1s. net.

GUARDIAN.—"A learned and valuable vindication of the place of dogmatic theology by a scholar trained in historical and critical methods."

Henson (Canon H. H.)—SERMON ON THE DEATH OF THE QUEEN. 8vo. Sewed. 1s. net.

SINCERITY AND SUBSCRIPTION. A Plea for Toleration in the Church of England. Globe 8vo. 1s. net.

THE VALUE OF THE BIBLE, AND OTHER SERMONS (1902-1904). With a letter to the Lord Bishop of London. Cr. 8vo. 6s.

CHURCH OF ENGLAND PULPIT.—"We can recommend this work to our readers with the conviction that if more preachers were as broad-minded and as outspoken as the Rector of St. Margaret's, Westminster, there would be no lack of large congregations in our London churches."

RELIGION IN THE SCHOOLS. Addresses on Fundamental Christianity. Crown 8vo. 2s. 6d. net.

Hicks (Rev. Canon E. L.)—ADDRESSES ON THE TEMPTATION OF OUR LORD. Crown 8vo. 3s. net.

Hillis (N. D.)— THE INFLUENCE OF CHRIST IN MODERN LIFE. A Study of the New Problems of the Church in American Society. Crown 8vo. 6s.

THE QUEST OF HAPPINESS. A Study of Victory over Life's Troubles. Extra Crown 8vo. 6s. net.

Hilty (Carl).—HAPPINESS: Essays on the Meaning of Life. Translated by Professor F. G. PEABODY. Crown 8vo. 5s. net.

THE STEPS OF LIFE. Further Essays on Happiness. Translated by MELVIN BRANDON. With an Introduction by Professor F. G. PEABODY. Crown 8vo. 5s. net.

Hodgkins (Louise M.)—VIA CHRISTI: An Introduction to the Study of Missions. Globe 8vo. 2s. net. Sewed. 1s. 3d. net.

Höffding (Prof. Harald.)— THE PHILOSOPHY OF RELIGION. Translated by Miss B. E. MEYER. 8vo. 12s. net.

Hort (Dr. F. J. A.)—THE WAY, THE TRUTH, THE LIFE. Hulsean Lectures, 1871. Crown 8vo. 6s.

JUDAISTIC CHRISTIANITY. Crown 8vo. 6s.

VILLAGE SERMONS. Crown 8vo. 6s.
Selected from the Sermons preached by Professor HORT to his village congregation at St. Ippolyt's, and including a series of Sermons dealing in a broad and suggestive way with the successive books of the Bible, from Genesis to Revelation.

SERMONS ON THE BOOKS OF THE BIBLE (selected from *Village Sermons*). Crown 8vo. 3s. 6d.

VILLAGE SERMONS. Second Series. Cr. 8vo. 6s.

Hort (Dr. F. J. A.)—*continued.*

VILLAGE SERMONS IN OUTLINE. Crown 8vo. 6s.
> CONTENTS : I. The Prayer Book, 16 Sermons. II. Baptism,
> 5 Sermons. III. Mutual Subjection the Rule of Life (Eph. v. 21),
> 6 Sermons. IV. The Sermon on the Mount (St. Matt. v. 1 ; vii.
> 29), 11 Sermons. V. Advent, 4 Sermons. VI. The Armour of
> the Cross. VII. The Resurrection, 7 Sermons.

CAMBRIDGE AND OTHER SERMONS. Crown 8vo. 6s.

Hoyt (Dr. Arthur S.)—THE WORK OF PREACHING.
A Book for the Class-room and Study. Crown 8vo. 6s. 6d. net.

Hughes (T.)—THE MANLINESS OF CHRIST. 2nd Ed.
Fcap. 8vo. 3s. 6d.   Also Medium 8vo, Sewed, 6d.
GLOBE.—" *The Manliness of Christ* is a species of lay sermon such as Judge Hughes
is well qualified to deliver, seeing that manliness of thought and feeling has been the
prevailing characteristic of all his literary products."
BRITISH WEEKLY.—" A new edition of a strong book."

Hutton (R. H.)—

ESSAYS ON SOME OF THE MODERN GUIDES OF ENG-
LISH THOUGHT IN MATTERS OF FAITH. Globe 8vo.
4s. net.

THEOLOGICAL ESSAYS. Globe 8vo. 4s. net.

ASPECTS OF RELIGIOUS AND SCIENTIFIC THOUGHT.
Selected from the *Spectator*, and edited by E. M. ROSCOE. Globe
8vo. 4s. net.

Hyde (W. De W.)—OUTLINES OF SOCIAL THEOLOGY
Crown 8vo. 6s.

Dr. Hyde thus describes the object of his book : " This little book aims
to point out the logical relations in which the doctrines of theology will
stand to each other when the time shall come again for seeing Christian
truth in the light of reason and Christian life as the embodiment of love."

PRACTICAL IDEALISM. Globe 8vo. 5s. net.

Illingworth (Rev. J. R.)—SERMONS PREACHED IN A
COLLEGE CHAPEL. Third Edition. Crown 8vo. 5s.

UNIVERSITY AND CATHEDRAL SERMONS. Crown 8vo. 5s.

PERSONALITY, HUMAN AND DIVINE. Bampton Lectures,
1894. Crown 8vo. 6s. Also 8vo. Sewed. 6d.
TIMES.—" Will take high rank among the rare theological masterpieces produced by
that celebrated foundation."
EXPOSITOR.—" It is difficult to convey an adequate impression of the freshness
and strength of the whole argument. . . . It is a book which no one can be satisfied with
reading once ; it is to be studied."

DIVINE IMMANENCE. An Essay on the Spiritual Significance of
Matter. New Edition. Cr. 8vo. 6s. Also 8vo. Sewed. 6d.
CHURCH QUARTERLY REVIEW.—" A very valuable book. . . . *Divine
Immanence* is likely to prove of great service to Christian truth. It combines, to a
remarkable extent, profound thought and clear expression. It is throughout written
in an interesting style."
GUARDIAN.—" Altogether, we have rarely read a book of such philosophical
earnestness in construing the Christian view of existence in terms of the thought and
knowledge of these days, nor one more likely to bring home the knowledge of a Saviour
to the modern man."

REASON AND REVELATION. An Essay in Christian Apology.
Third Edition. Crown 8vo. 6s.

Illingworth (Rev. J. R.)—*continued.*

CHRISTIAN CHARACTER. Being Some Lectures on the Elements of Christian Ethics. New and Cheaper Edition. Crown 8vo. 6s. Also 8vo, sewed, 6d.

TIMES.—" We should like to follow Dr. Illingworth further, but we have said enough to show that these studies are rooted in deep reading of things and men, and the best thoughts of men, and the fruit should be plentiful in proportion."

THE DOCTRINE OF THE TRINITY APOLOGETICALLY CONSIDERED. Crown 8vo. 6s.

Inge (Rev. Dr.)—ALL SAINTS' SERMONS, 1905-1907. Crown 8vo. 3s. 6d. net.

Inskip (Rev. J. T.)—THE PASTORAL IDEA. Lectures in Pastoral Theology delivered at the King's College, London, during the Lent term, 1905. Crown 8vo. 6s.

Jacob (Rev. J. A.) — BUILDING IN SILENCE, and other Sermons. Extra Fcap. 8vo. 6s.

Jacob (Rev. J. T.)—CHRIST THE INDWELLER. Cr. 8vo. 5s.

Jellett (Rev. Dr.)—

THE ELDER SON, and other Sermons. Crown 8vo. 6s.

Joceline (E.)—THE MOTHER'S LEGACIE TO HER UN-BORN CHILD. Cr. 16mo. 4s. 6d.

Jones (Jenkin Lloyd)—

JESS : BITS OF WAYSIDE GOSPEL. Crown 8vo. 6s.

Joseph (Rev. Morris).—JUDAISM AS CREED AND LIFE. Extra Crown 8vo. 5s. net.

The view of Judaism set forth in this work lies midway between the orthodoxy which regards the Shulchan Aruch, or at least the Talmud, as the final authority in Judaism, and the extreme liberalism which would lightly cut the religion loose from the bonds of tradition. The present volume, then, may fairly lay claim to novelty. Almost all the expositions of Judaism which have hitherto appeared in England have been written from the rigidly conservative standpoint, but thus far no attempt has been made to elucidate systematically the intermediate position, and to give a comprehensive account of Jewish belief and practice as they are conceived by men of moderate views.

Kellogg (Rev. S. H.)—

THE GENESIS AND GROWTH OF RELIGION. Cr. 8vo. 6s.

Kingsley (Charles)—

VILLAGE AND TOWN AND COUNTRY SERMONS. Crown 8vo. 3s. 6d.

THE WATER OF LIFE, and other Sermons. Crown 8vo. 3s. 6d.

SERMONS ON NATIONAL SUBJECTS, AND THE KING OF THE EARTH. Crown 8vo. 3s. 6d.

SERMONS FOR THE TIMES. Crown 8vo. 3s. 6d.

GOOD NEWS OF GOD. Crown 8vo. 3s. 6d.

THE GOSPEL OF THE PENTATEUCH, AND DAVID. Crown 8vo. 3s. 6d.

DISCIPLINE, and other Sermons. Crown 8vo. 3s. 6d.

WESTMINSTER SERMONS. Crown 8vo. 3s. 6d.

ALL SAINTS' DAY, and other Sermons. Crown 8vo. 3s. 6d.

Kirkpatrick (Dean).—THE DIVINE LIBRARY OF THE OLD TESTAMENT. Its Origin, Preservation, Inspiration, and Permanent Value. Crown 8vo. 3s. net.

THE DOCTRINE OF THE PROPHETS. Warburtonian Lectures 1886-1890. Third Edition. Crown 8vo. 6s.

Knight (W. A.)—ASPECTS OF THEISM. 8vo. 8s. 6d.

LETTERS FROM HELL. Newly translated from the Danish. With an Introduction by Dr. GEORGE MACDONALD. Twenty-eighth Thousand. Crown 8vo. 2s. 6d.

Leighton (Prof. J. A.)—JESUS CHRIST AND THE CIVIL-ISATION OF TO-DAY. The Ethical Teaching of Jesus considered in its Bearings on the Moral Foundations of Modern Culture. Crown 8vo. 6s. 6d. net.

Lightfoot (Bishop)—

THE CHRISTIAN MINISTRY. Reprinted from *Dissertations on the Apostolic Age.* Crown 8vo. 3s. net.

LEADERS IN THE NORTHERN CHURCH : Sermons Preached in the Diocese of Durham. 2nd Edition. Crown 8vo. 6s.

ORDINATION ADDRESSES AND COUNSELS TO CLERGY. Crown 8vo. 6s.

CAMBRIDGE SERMONS. Crown 8vo. 6s.

SERMONS PREACHED IN ST. PAUL'S CATHEDRAL. Crown 8vo. 6s.

SERMONS PREACHED ON SPECIAL OCCASIONS. Crown 8vo. 6s.

A CHARGE DELIVERED TO THE CLERGY OF THE DIOCESE OF DURHAM, 25th Nov. 1886. Demy 8vo. 2s.

ESSAYS ON THE WORK ENTITLED "Supernatural Religion." 8vo. Re-issue at 6s. net.

DISSERTATIONS ON THE APOSTOLIC AGE. 8vo. 14s.

BIBLICAL ESSAYS. 8vo. 12s.

Lillingston (Frank, M.A.)—THE BRAMO SAMAJ AND ARYA SAMAJ IN THEIR BEARING UPON CHRIS-TIANITY. A Study in Indian Theism. Cr. 8vo. 2s. 6d. net.

Lindsay (A. R. B.)—GLORIA CHRISTI. An Outline Study of Missions and Social Progress. Globe 8vo. 2s. net.

Luther.—LETTERS OF MARTIN LUTHER. Translated by Margaret Anderson Currie. 8vo.

M'Connell (Dr. S. D.)—CHRIST. Crown 8vo. 5s. net.

Macmillan (Rev. Hugh)—

THE ISLES AND THE GOSPEL, AND OTHER BIBLE STUDIES. With Portrait and Prefatory Memoir. Crown 8vo.

BIBLE TEACHINGS IN NATURE. 15th Ed. Globe 8vo. 6s.

THE TRUE VINE ; OR, THE ANALOGIES OF OUR LORD'S ALLEGORY. 5th Edition. Globe 8vo. 6s.

THE MINISTRY OF NATURE. 8th Edition. Globe 8vo. 6s.

THE SABBATH OF THE FIELDS. 6th Edition. Globe 8vo. 6s.

GLEANINGS IN HOLY FIELDS. Crown 8vo. 3s. 6d.

THE CORN OF HEAVEN. Crown 8vo. 6s.

Mahaffy (Rev. Prof.)—THE DECAY OF MODERN PREACH-
ING : AN ESSAY. Crown 8vo. 3s. 6d.

Marshall (H. Rutgers)—INSTINCT AND REASON : An
Essay with some Special Study of the Nature of Religion. 8vo.
12s. 6d. net.

Mason (Caroline A.)—LUX CHRISTI : An Outline Study of
India—A Twilight Land. Cr. 8vo. 2s. net. Sewed. 1s. 3d. net.

Mathews (S.)—THE SOCIAL TEACHING OF JESUS :
AN ESSAY IN CHRISTIAN SOCIOLOGY. Crown 8vo. 6s.
THE CHURCH AND THE CHANGING ORDER. Crown
8vo. 6s. 6d. net.

Maurice (Frederick Denison)—
THE KINGDOM OF CHRIST. 3rd Ed. 2 Vols. Cr. 8vo. 7s.
THE CONSCIENCE. Lectures on Casuistry. 3rd Ed. Cr. 8vo. 4s. 6d.
DIALOGUES ON FAMILY WORSHIP. Crown 8vo. 4s. 6d.
THE DOCTRINE OF SACRIFICE DEDUCED FROM THE
SCRIPTURES. 2nd Edition. Crown 8vo. 6s.
THE RELIGIONS OF THE WORLD. 6th Edition. Cr. 8vo. 4s. 6d.
ON THE SABBATH DAY ; THE CHARACTER OF THE
WARRIOR ; AND ON THE INTERPRETATION OF
HISTORY. Fcap. 8vo. 2s. 6d.
LEARNING AND WORKING. Crown 8vo. 4s. 6d.
THE LORD'S PRAYER, THE CREED, AND THE COM-
MANDMENTS. Pott 8vo. 1s.
Collected Works. Crown 8vo. 3s. 6d. each.
SERMONS PREACHED IN LINCOLN'S INN CHAPEL. In Six
Volumes. 3s. 6d. each.
SERMONS PREACHED IN COUNTRY CHURCHES.
CHRISTMAS DAY AND OTHER SERMONS.
THEOLOGICAL ESSAYS. (Also 8vo. Sewed. 6d.)
PROPHETS AND KINGS.
PATRIARCHS AND LAWGIVERS.
THE GOSPEL OF THE KINGDOM OF HEAVEN.
GOSPEL OF ST. JOHN.
EPISTLE OF ST. JOHN.
FRIENDSHIP OF BOOKS.
PRAYER BOOK AND LORD'S PRAYER.
THE DOCTRINE OF SACRIFICE.
THE ACTS OF THE APOSTLES.

Medley (Rev. W.)—CHRIST THE TRUTH. Being the
Angus Lectures for the year 1900. Crown 8vo. 6s.

Milligan (Rev. Prof. W.)—THE RESURRECTION OF OUR
LORD. Fourth Edition. Crown 8vo. 5s.

SPECTATOR.—" The argument is put with brevity and force by Dr. Milligan, and
every page bears witness that he has mastered the literature of the subject, and has made
a special study of the more recent discussions on this aspect of the question. . . . The
remaining lectures are more theological. They abound in striking views, in fresh and
vigorous exegesis, and manifest a keen apprehension of the bearing of the fact of the
Resurrection on many important questions of theology. The notes are able and
scholarly, and elucidate the teaching of the text."

Milligan (Rev. Prof. W.)—*continued.*

> THE ASCENSION AND HEAVENLY PRIESTHOOD OF OUR LORD. *Baird Lectures,* 1891. Crown 8vo. 7s. 6d.

MISSIONS—UNITED STUDY OF. *See under* GRIFFIS, HODGKINS, MASON, MONTGOMERY, PARSONS, SMITH, *and* LINDSAY.

Montefiore (Claude G.)—LIBERAL JUDAISM. An Essay. Crown 8vo. 3s. net.

> TRUTH IN RELIGION, AND OTHER SERMONS. Crown 8vo. 3s. 6d. net.

Montgomery (Helen Barrett).—CHRISTUS REDEMPTOR. An Outline Study of the Island World of the Pacific. Globe 8vo. 2s. net. Paper, 1s. 3d. net.

Moorhouse (Bishop)—

> JACOB : Three Sermons. Extra Fcap. 8vo. 3s. 6d.
>
> THE TEACHING OF CHRIST. Its Conditions, Secret, and Results. Crown 8vo. 3s. net.
>
> DANGERS OF THE APOSTOLIC AGE. Crown 8vo. 3s. net.
>
> CHURCH WORK : ITS MEANS AND METHODS. Crown 8vo. 3s. net.

Morrison (Rev. Dr.) — NEW IDEAS IN INDIA DURING THE NINETEENTH CENTURY. A Study of Social, Political, and Religious Developments. 8vo. 7s. 6d. net.

Myers (F. W. H.)—SCIENCE AND A FUTURE LIFE. Gl. 8vo. 4s. net.

Nash (H. S.)—GENESIS OF THE SOCIAL CONSCIENCE. THE RELATION BETWEEN THE ESTABLISHMENT OF CHRISTIANITY IN EUROPE AND THE SOCIAL QUESTION. Crown 8vo. 6s.

Parsons (E. C.)—CHRISTUS LIBERATOR : An Outline Study of Africa. With an Introduction by Sir HARRY H. JOHNSTON, K.C.B. With Coloured Map. Globe 8vo. 2s. net. Sewed. 1s. 3d. net.

Pattison (Mark).—SERMONS. Crown 8vo. 6s.

Peabody (Prof. F. G.)—JESUS CHRIST AND THE SOCIAL QUESTION. Crown 8vo. 6s.

> JESUS CHRIST AND THE CHRISTIAN CHARACTER. An Examination of the Teaching of Jesus in its relation to some of the Moral Problems of Personal Life. Crown 8vo. 6s. 6d. net.
>
> THE RELIGION OF AN EDUCATED MAN. Crown 8vo. Gilt top. 4s. 6d. net.

This little volume, by the well-known Harvard Professor, treats the subject under the following main heads :—Religion as Education ; The Message of Christ to the Scholar ; and Knowledge and Service.

Peabody (Prof. F. G.)—*continued.*

PEPLOGRAPHIA DVBLINENSIS. Memorial Discourses Preached in the Chapel of Trinity College, Dublin, 1895-1902. With Preface by the Very Rev. J. H. BERNARD, D.D., Dean of St. Patrick's. Crown 8vo. 3s. 6d. net.

Philipson (D.)—THE REFORM MOVEMENT IN JUDAISM. Extra Crown 8vo. 8s. 6d. net.

PHILOCHRISTUS. Memoirs of a Disciple of the Lord. 3rd Ed. 8vo. 12s.

Picton (J. Allanson).—THE RELIGION OF THE UNIVERSE. 8vo. 10s. net.

ACADEMY.—"The book is most seriously to be recommended to any one who desires a dignified and impressive statement of what is most obviously the religion of the coming time."

Pike (G. R.)—THE DIVINE DRAMA THE DIVINE MANIFESTATION OF GOD IN THE UNIVERSE. Crown 8vo. 6s.

Plumptre (Dean). — MOVEMENTS IN RELIGIOUS THOUGHT. Fcap. 8vo. 3s. 6d.

Porter (Mrs. Horace). —BISHOP WESTCOTT'S TEACHING. The Secret of a Great Influence. With a Chapter on Bishop Westcott's Commentaries by the Rev. ARTHUR WESTCOTT. Crown 8vo. 3s. net.

PRO CHRISTO ET ECCLESIA. Second Impression. Crown 8vo. Gilt top. 4s. 6d. net.

BOOKMAN.—"It is not only its anonymity which suggests comparison with *Ecce Homo.* The subject is the same in both books—the method and aim of Jesus—though treated from uite different points of view ; and the level of thought is much the same ; the easy origin. lity that cuts a new section through the life of Christ and shows us strata before unthought of; the classic severity of the style, the penetrating knowledge of human nature, the catholicity of treatment, all remind us of Professor Seeley's captivating work."

CHRISTUS FUTURUS. By the Author of "Pro Christo et Ecclesia." Crown 8vo. 5s. net.

Purchas (Rev. H. T.)—JOHANNINE PROBLEMS AND MODERN NEEDS. Crown 8vo. 3s. net.

Rauschenbusch (W.)—CHRISTIANITY AND THE SOCIAL CRISIS. Extra Crown 8vo. 6s. 6d. net.

RELIGIOUS DOUBTS OF DEMOCRACY. Papers by Various Authors. Edited by GEORGE HAW. 8vo. Sewed. 6d.

Rendall (Rev. F.)—THE THEOLOGY OF THE HEBREW CHRISTIANS. Crown 8vo. 5s.

Ridding (George, Bishop of Southwell).—THE REVEL AND THE BATTLE. Crown 8vo. 6s.

Robinson (Prebendary H. G.)—MAN IN THE IMAGE OF GOD, and other Sermons. Crown 8vo. 7s. 6d.

Robinson (Dean J. A.)—UNITY IN CHRIST AND OTHER SERMONS. Crown 8vo. 6s.

Rutherford (Rev. Dr. W. G.)—THE KEY OF KNOWLEDGE. Sermons preached to Westminster Boys in the Abbey. Cr. 8vo 6s.

Ryle (Rt. Rev. H. E., Bishop of Winchester).—ON HOLY SCRIPTURE AND CRITICISM. Crown 8vo. 4s. 6d.
ON THE CHURCH OF ENGLAND. Crown 8vo. 6s.

Schmidt (Prof. N.)—THE PROPHET OF NAZARETH. 8vo. 10s. 6d. net.

Schultz (Dr. H.)—OUTLINES OF CHRISTIAN APOLOGETICS FOR USE IN LECTURES. Ex. Cr. 8vo. 7s. 6d. net.

Seeley (Sir J. R.)—ECCE HOMO : A Survey of the Life and Work of Jesus Christ. Globe 8vo. 4s. net. Also 8vo. Sewed. 6d.
NATURAL RELIGION. Globe 8vo. 4s. net.

ATHENÆUM.—" If it be the function of a genius to interpret the age to itself, this is a work of genius. It gives articulate expression to the higher strivings of the time. It puts plainly the problem of these latter days, and so far contributes to its solution ; a positive solution it scarcely claims to supply. No such important contribution to the question of the time has been published in England since the appearance in 1866 of *Ecce Homo*. . . . The author is a teacher whose words it is well to listen to ; his words are wise but sad ; it has not been given him to fire them with faith, but only to light them with reason. His readers may at least thank him for the intellectual illumination, if they cannot owe him gratitude for any added favour. . . . A book which we assume will be read by most thinking Englishmen."

Selborne (Roundell, Earl of). — THE CATHOLIC AND APOSTOLIC CHURCH. Globe 8vo. 3s. 6d.

Service (Rev. John).—SERMONS. With Portrait. Crown 8vo. 6s.

Shepard (Rev. J. W.)—SERMONS. With a Portrait of the Author and Prefatory Memoir by the Ven. Archdeacon Bevan, Rector of Chelsea. Crown 8vo.

Slicer (T. R.)—THE WAY TO HAPPINESS. Globe 8vo. 5s. net.

Smith (A. H.)—REX CHRISTUS. An Outline Study of China. Globe 8vo. 2s. net. Sewed. 1s. 3d. net.

Stanley (Dean). — THE NATIONAL THANKSGIVING. Sermons preached in Westminster Abbey. 2nd Ed. Cr. 8vo. 2s. 6d.

Sterrett (Dr. J. M.)—THE FREEDOM OF AUTHORITY. Essays in Apologetics. Ex. Crown 8vo. 8s. 6d. net.

Stewart (Prof. Balfour) and **Tait** (Prof. P. G.)—THE UNSEEN UNIVERSE; OR, PHYSICAL SPECULATIONS ON A FUTURE STATE. 15th Edition. Crown 8vo. 6s.

Sturge (Clement Y.)—POINTS OF CHURCH LAW AND OTHER WRITINGS ILLUSTRATIVE OF THE LAW OF THE CHURCH. 8vo. 3s. 6d. net.

Talbot (Bishop).—A CHARGE DELIVERED TO THE CLERGY OF THE DIOCESE OF ROCHESTER, October 24, 25, and 26, 1899. 8vo. Sewed. 2s. net.

Talbot (Bishop)—*continued.*
THE CHURCH'S FAILURES AND THE WORK OF CHRIST.
A Charge addressed to the Clergy of his Diocese at his Second
Visitation in the Ninth Year of his Episcopate and in the Year of
Our Lord 1903. 8vo. Sewed. 1s. net.

DAILY NEWS.—"A little book that will be read with interest by all who are
concerned in the same problem here considered—the relation of Christianity as an active
inspiration of common life to such masses of toiling populations as are represented by
the millions of South London."

Temple (Archbishop)—
SERMONS PREACHED IN THE CHAPEL OF RUGBY
SCHOOL. Extra Fcap. 8vo. 4s. 6d.
SECOND SERIES. 3rd Edition. 6s.
THIRD SERIES. 4th Edition. 6s.
THE RELATIONS BETWEEN RELIGION AND SCIENCE.
Bampton Lectures, 1884. New Impression, 1903. Cr. 8vo. 6s.
CHARGE DELIVERED AT HIS FIRST VISITATION. 8vo.
Sewed. 1s. net.
(1) The Doctrine of the Eucharist ; (2) The Practice of Confession ;
(3) Uniformity in Ceremonial ; (4) The Power of the Bishops.

Templeton (J. S.).—A LAYMAN'S MIND ON CREED AND
CHURCH. Crown 8vo. 3s. 6d. net.
TO THOSE WHO SUFFER. A Heart of Compassion. Crown 8vo.
Sewed. 1s. net.

PALL MALL GAZETTE.—"We have rarely met so slim a volume more full of
suggestive and helpful thoughts. . . . A true, a beautiful book ; and we trust the modest
way it is ushered into the world will not prevent it obtaining the attention and recognition
it deserves."

Trench (Archbishop).—HULSEAN LECTURES. 8vo. 7s. 6d.

Tymms (Rev. Dr. T. V.)—THE CHRISTIAN IDEA OF
ATONEMENT. Angus Lectures. Crown 8vo. 7s. 6d.

Vaughan (Dean)—
MEMORIALS OF HARROW SUNDAYS. 5th Edition. Crown
8vo. 10s. 6d.
HEROES OF FAITH. 2nd Edition. Crown 8vo. 6s.
LIFE'S WORK AND GOD'S DISCIPLINE. 3rd Edition.
Extra Fcap. 8vo. 2s. 6d.
THE WHOLESOME WORDS OF JESUS CHRIST. 2nd
Edition. Fcap. 8vo. 3s. 6d.
FOES OF FAITH. 2nd Edition. Fcap. 8vo. 3s. 6d.
COUNSELS FOR YOUNG STUDENTS. Fcap. 8vo. 2s. 6d.
THE TWO GREAT TEMPTATIONS. 2nd Ed. Fcap. 8vo. 3s. 6d.
ADDRESSES FOR YOUNG CLERGYMEN. Extra Fcap. 8vo.
4s. 6d.
"MY SON, GIVE ME THINE HEART." Extra Fcap. 8vo. 5s.
TEMPLE SERMONS. Crown 8vo. 10s. 6d.

Vaughan (Dean)—*continued.*

AUTHORISED OR REVISED? Sermons on some of the Texts in which the Revised Version differs from the Authorised. Crown 8vo. 7s. 6d.

LESSONS OF THE CROSS AND PASSION. WORDS FROM THE CROSS. THE REIGN OF SIN. THE LORD'S PRAYER. Four Courses of Lent Lectures. Crown 8vo. 10s. 6d.

UNIVERSITY SERMONS. NEW AND OLD. Cr. 8vo. 10s. 6d.

NOTES FOR LECTURES ON CONFIRMATION. Fcap. 8vo. 1s. 6d.

DONCASTER SERMONS. Lessons of Life and Godliness, and Words from the Gospels. Cr. 8vo. 10s. 6d.

RESTFUL THOUGHTS IN RESTLESS TIMES. Cr. 8vo. 5s.

LAST WORDS IN THE TEMPLE CHURCH. Globe 8vo. 5s.

SATURDAY REVIEW.—"These discourses, in thought, in style, have so much that is permanent and fine about them that they will stand the ordeal of being read by any serious man, even though he never heard Dr. Vaughan speak."

UNIVERSITY AND OTHER SERMONS. Crown 8vo. 6s.

TIMES.—"As specimens of pure and rhythmical English prose, rising here and there to flights of sober and chastened eloquence, yet withal breathing throughout an earnest and devotional spirit, these sermons would be hard to match."

SCOTSMAN.—"All are marked by the earnestness, scholarship, and strength of thought which invariably characterised the pulpit utterances of the preacher."

Vaughan (Rev. D. J.)—THE PRESENT TRIAL OF FAITH. Crown 8vo. 5s.

QUESTIONS OF THE DAY, SOCIAL, NATIONAL, AND RELIGIOUS. Crown 8vo. 5s.

NATIONAL OBSERVER.—"In discussing *Questions of the Day* Mr. D. J. Vaughan speaks with candour, ability, and common sense."

SCOTSMAN.—"They form an altogether admirable collection of vigorous and thoughtful pronouncements on a variety of social, national, and religious topics."

GLASGOW HERALD.—"A volume such as this is the best reply to those friends of the people who are for ever complaining that the clergy waste their time preaching antiquated dogma and personal salvation, and neglect the weightier matters of the law."

MANCHESTER GUARDIAN.—"He speaks boldly as well as thoughtfully, and what he has to say is always worthy of attention."

EXPOSITORY TIMES.—"Most of them are social, and these are the most interesting. And one feature of peculiar interest is that in those sermons which were preached twenty years ago Canon Vaughan saw the questions of to-day, and suggested the remedies we are beginning to apply."

Vaughan (Canon E. T.)—SOME REASONS OF OUR CHRISTIAN HOPE. Hulsean Lectures for 1875. Crown 8vo. 6s. 6d.

Venn (Dr. John).—ON SOME CHARACTERISTICS OF BELIEF, SCIENTIFIC AND RELIGIOUS. 8vo. 6s. 6d.

Welldon (Bishop).—THE SPIRITUAL LIFE, and other Sermons. Crown 8vo. 6s.

SCOTTISH LEADER.—"In a strain of quiet, persuasive eloquence, Bishop Welldon treats impressively of various aspects of the higher life. His discourses cannot fail both to enrich the heart and stimulate the mind of the earnest reader."

GLASGOW HERALD.—"They are cultured, reverent, and thoughtful productions."

THE REVELATION OF THE HOLY SPIRIT. Crown 8vo. 6s.

"I LIVE": BEING HINTS ON THE CHRISTIAN LIFE. Crown 8vo. 1s. 6d. net.

THE CONSECRATION OF THE STATE. An Essay. Crown 8vo. 2s. net.

Westcott (Bishop)—

ON THE RELIGIOUS OFFICE OF THE UNIVERSITIES. Sermons. Crown 8vo. 4s. 6d.

GIFTS FOR MINISTRY. Addresses to Candidates for Ordination. Crown 8vo. 1s. 6d.

FROM STRENGTH TO STRENGTH. Three Sermons (In Memoriam J. B. D.) Crown 8vo. 2s.

THE REVELATION OF THE RISEN LORD. Cr. 8vo. 6s.

THE HISTORIC FAITH. 3rd Edition. Crown 8vo. 6s. Also 8vo. Sewed. 6d.

THE GOSPEL OF THE RESURRECTION. 6th Ed. Cr. 8vo. 6s.

THE REVELATION OF THE FATHER. Crown 8vo. 6s.

CHRISTUS CONSUMMATOR. 2nd Edition. Crown 8vo. 6s.

SOME THOUGHTS FROM THE ORDINAL. Cr. 8vo. 1s. 6d.

SOCIAL ASPECTS OF CHRISTIANITY. Crown 8vo. 6s.

ESSAYS IN THE HISTORY OF RELIGIOUS THOUGHT IN THE WEST. Globe 8vo. 4s. net.

THE GOSPEL OF LIFE. Crown 8vo. 6s. Also 8vo. Sewed. 6d.

THE INCARNATION AND COMMON LIFE. Crown 8vo. 9s.

TIMES.—" A collection of sermons which possess, among other merits, the rare one of actuality, reflecting, as they frequently do, the Bishop's well-known and eager interest in social problems of the day."

CHRISTIAN ASPECTS OF LIFE. Crown 8vo. 7s. 6d.

CHURCH TIMES.—" We heartily commend this volume to the notice of our readers. . . . The Church of England is not likely to lose touch with the people of this country so long as she is guided by Bishops who show such a truly large-hearted sympathy with everything human as is here manifested by the present occupier of the see of Durham."

LITERATURE.—" A sermon of the national day of rest, and some attractive personal reminiscences of school days under James Prince Lee, are among the choicest parts of the volume, if we are to single out any portions from a work of dignified and valuable utterance."

DAILY NEWS.—" Through every page . . . runs the same enlightened sympathy with the living world. One forgets the Bishop in the Man, the Ecclesiastic in the Citizen, the Churchman in the Christian."

THE OBLIGATIONS OF EMPIRE. Cr. 8vo. Sewed. 3d. net.

LESSONS FROM WORK. CHARGES AND ADDRESSES. Second Impression. Crown 8vo. 6s.

ADDRESS DELIVERED TO MINERS, July 1901. Crown 8vo. Sewed. 6d.

WORDS OF FAITH AND HOPE. Crown 8vo. 4s. 6d.

CHRISTIAN SOCIAL UNION ADDRESSES. Crown 8vo. 1s. net.

COMMON PRAYERS FOR FAMILY USE. Crown 8vo. 1s. net.

PETERBOROUGH SERMONS. Crown 8vo. 6s.

SCOTSMAN.—" They are characteristic prolocutions of an eminent Anglican divine, and will be read with interest both within and without the Church of England."

VILLAGE SERMONS. Crown 8vo. 6s.

White (A. D.)—A HISTORY OF THE WARFARE OF SCIENCE WITH THEOLOGY IN CHRISTENDOM. In Two Vols. 8vo. 21s. net.

White (A. D.)—*continued.*

TIMES.—" Is certainly one of the most comprehensive, and, in our judgment, one of the most valuable historical works that have appeared for many years. . . . He has chosen a large subject, but it is at least one which has clear and definite limits, and he has treated it very fully and comprehensively in two moderate volumes. . . . His book appears to us to be based on much original research, on an enormous amount of careful, accurate, and varied reading, and his habit of appending to each section a list of the chief books, both ancient and modern, relating to it will be very useful to serious students. He has decided opinions, but he always writes temperately, and with transparent truthfulness of intention."

DAILY CHRONICLE.—" The story of the struggle of searchers after truth with the organised forces of ignorance, bigotry, and superstition is the most inspiring chapter in the whole history of mankind. That story has never been better told than by the ex-President of Cornell University in these two volumes."

Whiton (Dr. J. M.)—MIRACLES AND SUPERNATURAL RELIGION. Fcap. 8vo. 3s. net.

Whitworth (Rev. Wm. Allen).—CHRISTIAN THOUGHT ON PRESENT-DAY QUESTIONS. Sermons on Special Occasions. With a Preface by the BISHOP OF LONDON. Cr. 8vo. 4s. 6d. net.

SPIRITUAL TRUTHS. A Volume of Sermons. Crown 8vo.

Wickham (Very Rev. Dean).—WELLINGTON COLLEGE SERMONS. Crown 8vo. 6s.

Wilkins (Prof. A. S.)—THE LIGHT OF THE WORLD : an Essay. 2nd Edition. Crown 8vo. 3s. 6d.

Wilson (Archdeacon).—SERMONS PREACHED IN CLIFTON COLLEGE CHAPEL. Second Series. 1888-90. Cr. 8vo. 6s.

ESSAYS AND ADDRESSES. Crown 8vo. 2s. 6d. net.

GUARDIAN.—" We heartily welcome a new edition of Archdeacon Wilson's *Essays and Addresses.*"

SOME CONTRIBUTIONS TO THE RELIGIOUS THOUGHT OF OUR TIME. Crown 8vo. 6s.

HOW CHRIST SAVES US, OR THE GOSPEL OF THE ATONEMENT. Being the Hulsean Lectures for 1898-99. Crown 8vo. 3s. 6d. Also 8vo. Sewed. 6d.

SPEAKER.—" This volume deserves a cordial welcome, and will reward a careful study. It is marked by a candour and courage, a sincerity and liberality of spirit, which prove very attractive."

OXFORD MAGAZINE.—" They contain a good deal of strong thought and delicate expression."

SPECTATOR.—" A notable pronouncement."

TWO SERMONS ON THE MUTUAL INFLUENCES OF THEOLOGY AND THE NATURAL SCIENCES. 8vo. Sewed. 6d. net.

SIX LECTURES ON PASTORAL THEOLOGY. With an Appendix on the Influence of Scientific Training on the Reception of Religious Truth. Crown 8vo. 3s. 6d. net.

PROBLEMS OF RELIGION AND SCIENCE. 8vo. Sewed. 6d.

Wood (C. J.)—SURVIVALS IN CHRISTIANITY. Cr. 8vo. 6s.

MANCHESTER GUARDIAN.—" Striking, stimulating and suggestive lectures. . . . The author writes with the boldness and conviction of a mystic ; he brings wide reading to bear upon every branch of his subject, and his book is impressive and interesting throughout."

Printed by R. & R. CLARK, LIMITED, *Edinburgh.*

CL. 5. 10. 07.